MIND OF THE NINJA

EXPLORING THE INNER POWER

KIRTLAND C. PETERSON
FOREWORD BY STEPHEN K. HAYES

D1557532

PRINCIPAL PHOTOGRAPHY BY PHILLIP W. SMITH, THOMAS J. KRISHER, JEAN FRENKIL, AND MARIO PRADO.

CONTEMPORARY
BOOKS, INC.
CHICAGO ▪ NEW YORK

Interior photography by Phillip W. Smith,
Thomas J. Krisher, Jean Frenkil, Mario Prado,
and Kirtland C. Peterson.

Published by Contemporary Books, Inc.
180 North Michigan Avenue, Chicago, Illinois 60601
Manufactured in the United States of America
Library of Congress Catalog Card Number:
International Standard Book Number: 0-8092-4951-0

To the memory of my mother
Mary Levering
whose strength and courage shone most fiercely
during the terrible pain and suffering
of her final days
and as she faced death

And to my son Lars
whose energy and spirit is life-giving and joyous
totally committed to experiencing the fullness of the moment
and the richness of living
even at his tender age

Contents

Foreword

MIND OF THE Ninja: *Exploring the Inner Power* is a unique work in the world of ninja publications. It is not a book of ninjutsu techniques as such but a book that examines the image of the ninja in the Western world, as well as the fascination so many people have with the shinobi warriors of ancient Japan. Furthermore, it is not a book written by an instructor of the tradition, but a book written by a psychologist who is a participant-observer of the ninjutsu phenomenon.

Nin-po is a rich tradition, certainly deep enough and wide enough to be approached and interpreted from any number of perspectives and still "survive" the translation into other fields of knowledge with many of its central tenets intact—assuming, of course, that the translater approaches his task with integrity and thoroughness. Mind of *the* Ninja is a case in point, and the reflection of nin-po in the mirror of psychology is indeed an intriguing one.

What is particularly fascinating is the significant overlap between nin-po and the psychological tradition from which Kirtland C. Peterson draws his inferences and insights. The psychological tradition from which he speaks is, like ninjutsu, all too often rejected quickly by many people who do not take the time to investigate thoroughly. Its growth-orientation, instinct-to-spirit spectrum, and transpersonal nature earn it instant dismissal because it is seen as "too mystical." Also similar to nin-po is the fact that it is a tradition that must be *experienced*—it cannot be learned from books. And those unprepared to take the leap from books to realizing this psychology in their lives not infrequently attack it in word and print with remarkable lack of understanding. The psychology to which I refer is Jung's Archetypal psychology.

The reader will be acutely aware of many fascinating parallels between what I have written about nin-po, by way of philosophy and spirituality, and what is noted in Mind of the Ninja. This should not be surprising since one of the principal factors in Jung's life was that, not unlike the yamabushi and sennin mystic-warriors of ancient Japan, he dared to make that harrowing inner journey to the depths of his soul. This followed Jung's retreat from the rigidity and authority of the psychological schools of his time, especially Freudian "doctrine," and thus separated him from the society at large, again, not unlike the ninja's separation from the rigidity and authority of the ruling samurai elite in Japan, which inspired and maintained their search for enlightenment. For many of the same reasons, both the ninja and Jung have been, *and continue to be*, widely misunderstood and viciously attacked due to their insights into the nature of reality and their creativity. It is one of those unfortunate facts of life that insight and creativity have never been welcomed by societies at large; the majority of people seem to prefer, instead, theories and lifestyles that imprison them. It is easier to live within the dictates of someone else's philosophy than live with the fear incurred through developing freedom, individuality, and personal power.

Jung was not a warrior in the sense in which I tend to use the word, but he was, using the word more generally, a warrior of the human spirit. Hence, his journey covered much common ground with the mountain mystics who were the spiritual ancestors of the ninja. And this is where we find the fascinating overlaps in orientation and perspective, especially the goal of wholeness and connection with the universe, as well as the advancement of personal power and freedom.

In addition to Jung's transpersonal psychology, the author also brings his intellectual and experiential knowledge of Tibetan Buddhism to bear on the task at hand. Also, having a good academic grounding in religion, anthropology, and East Asian studies, in addi-

tion to over more than eight years of experience living, working, and traveling in both Europe and Africa, enables Kirtland C. Peterson to bring a wide cultural perspective to the ninja phenomenon in the West. This leads to many of the fascinating insights and observations found in *Mind of the Ninja*.

The author first looks at the many images of the ninja that are "alive" in our culture, especially those found on the screen, in the martial arts world, in fiction, and through the genuine historical tradition as it has been written about and taught in the United States and elsewhere. After establishing just what it is we are seeing from these various sources he next turns to the psychology behind them, focusing on the "dark side," and the inherent wholeness and richness of the ninja image, particularly the image in its deepest and most authentic form. Finally he goes beyond psychology and examines something of nin-po mikkyo, part of the ninja's spiritual heritage. He takes us from the superficial interpretations of the ninja, through the transpersonal realm, to the spiritual, or transcendent, aspects of nin-po.

There is something else that is "magical" about this book. Mind of the Ninja represents a realization of intentions for the author. Whereas many people have the desire to reach various important goals they have set for themselves, few seem to successfully bring them to completion. Mind of the Ninja was written while the author was also engaged as a full-time doctoral candidate in clinical psychology, teaching, working regularly as a freelance writer, renovating a house, training in ninjutsu as often as possible, and raising a family.

One final point. Although he has spoken with me about Mind of the Ninja at various points in its conception and writing, and although he draws from much of what I have written, this book expresses Kirtland C. Peterson's interpretation of nin-po. Neither I, nor the other senior instructors of our lineage, nor our Shadows of Iga Society as a whole acts in an authoritative fashion to dictate what is thought of, spoken about, or written about ninjutsu as it is taught in the authentic Bujinkan system. Although he is an active training member of the Shadows of Iga Ninja Society, Kirtland C. Peterson speaks for himself, from his perspective in life, and from his current position on his own Path. He is not my spokesman and I do not wish to be his censor. Freedom of exploration is crucial to the ninja way. Consequently I do not necessarily support or agree with everything that this author has written, but then neither do I reject or oppose it. Like you, I am simply in a position to "converse" with him, to see where reading and thinking about this book leads me, to use what is usable, and to enjoy it.

Please do the same.

Stephen K. Hayes

Acknowledgments

No book is written entirely in isolation; every author is supported and aided by others. *Mind of the Ninja* is no exception.

First and foremost, had Shidoshi Stephen K. Hayes not decided to share his knowledge of ninjutsu in the way that he has, this book would never have been written; nor would I now be pursuing training in ninjutsu. My awareness of the ninja and their art would have been limited to vague impressions from *You Only Live Twice* and *Shogun*. Had it not been for Shidoshi Hayes there would have been no ninja films, books, or craze. Neither would there have been his inspirational publications, seminars, or Shadows of Iga Ninja Society.

In addition, Shidoshi Hayes quietly encouraged my various writing projects, including *Mind of the Ninja*, when I chanced to speak with him at length in Leeds, England, in the summer of 1985, and in the several long conversations I have had with him since that time. He was especially helpful when it came time to contact an editor and publisher. For his support, influence, and help, I am most grateful.

My wife, Vikkie, has been wonderfully supportive, despite her initial fears of ninjutsu as nothing more than an assassins's art. The ninja sword which is pictured in many of my photographs was a gift from her. She has also been a tireless repairer and innovator of shinobi shozoku and a wonderful photography assistant. I cannot thank her enough for reading this book, in various stages of completion, and offering her comments and advice.

In the photography sphere I must thank Phillip, Nancy, Lois, and everyone at P. W. Smith, Inc., for the fabulous studio shots and fine prints. For his tremendous patience and creative input during photographic sessions—even on days when the temperature was well below freezing—I am most grateful to my good friend Thomas Krisher. I must

also thank him for his willingness to help make those difficult choices about which photographs to include, and which not, as well as for the beautiful cover photograph. My thanks also to Jack Hoban for allowing me to use several shots of him in the various kamae. And last but not least, my thanks to Jean for magically appearing at a time of need and lending her darkroom skills to this project. The creative special effects are hers.

Many of the insights I have gained into "matters of archetypal significance" have come from my work with Betsy Halpern. In the realms of psyche and shadow her guidance and wisdom are unsurpassed; in the realm of spirit I have yet to meet a better teacher. My sense of the meaning of ninjutsu in the West has most certainly been influenced by her perceptiveness and insight. I must also thank her for allowing me to photograph her Tibetan artifacts.

My good friends Thomas and Liz were among the select few in whom I entrusted the germ-idea of this book and my interest in ninjutsu. In a world where ninjutsu is so misunderstood, their understanding was very important to me. Thanks also to my friend Harry for lending me his samurai sword.

Mario Prado, who I first met at the 1985 Shadows of Iga Ninja Festival, has been a guide through various media waters which were new to me, and a great source of inspiration and creativity. Sanmar lives! I must also thank the various editors for whom I write for allowing me to try out many of my ideas in print. A special thanks is due to David Weiss and Russell Maynard for their support, encouragement, and tremendous faith in my writing abilities.

Without the moral and financial help of my great-aunt Mary Denmead Ruffin and grandmother Henrietta Cornthwaite I could never have even begun to pursue my interests in either psychology or ninjutsu. My heartfelt thanks to both of them for their tremendously important support.

The information gathering skills employed in the research and writing of this book were learned from my friend, Dr. Maurice Prout. His thoroughness in coming to grips with any subject is unbelievable and quite inspirational. I must also thank him for making the stress of graduate school bearable, even enjoyable at times—something I could not have done without while writing this book. Genuine caring and integrity are such rare qualities today, and Maurice has been more of a friend than he knows.

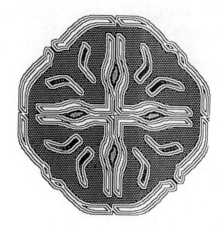

My ninjutsu training with both Stephen K. Hayes and Jack Hoban would never have been possible without the generous support of many. I am especially grateful to my wife Vikkie, Charlotte, Noel, Janie, Jena, Jane, the Kolibals, and the Myers. Thank you all for allowing me to follow my heart.

A word of thanks should not go lacking for the Apple Computer Company which invented the Macintosh. Until I saw a "Mac" I *loathed* the thought of computers (I am definitely "one of the rest of us"). Without my "Mac" and its wonderful word-processing abilities I would *never* have even entertained the thought of this book.

Finally, for keeping me firmly rooted in reality, I must thank my son Lars and his entourage of living stuffed animals: Kojiki, Tikoloshi, Leena, and Yukio Tamashii (his ferrets), as well as Sandy Pinktongue (his Siberian), and his cats, Ninja and Ashley Marie.

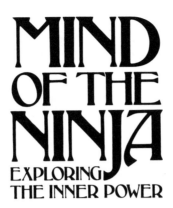

MIND OF THE NINJA
EXPLORING THE INNER POWER

Introduction

I N 1980 SHIDOSHI Stephen K. Hayes returned to the U.S. from Japan where he had been the personal student of Dr. Masaaki Hatsumi, the 34th Grandmaster at Togakure-ryu Ninjutsu, for many years. Since that time there has been a steadily growing interest in the ninja and their secret fighting art from many quarters, an interest that does not look as if it will abate any time soon. Martial arts suppliers note record sales of ninja weapons, uniforms, and books (upward of $70 million a year!); ninja films have been box office successes and ever-popular video rentals; novels with ninja characters have reached the best-seller lists; and Hayes's books are the most successful martial arts publications since Bruce Lee's books. Indeed, many commentators describe this growing interest as "ninjamania."

This book examines the current "ninja craze" in an effort to unearth what the shinobi warriors of ancient Japan mean to so many in the twentieth century. As a student of psychology I have found myself asking two basic questions, each of which corresponds to one of the two sections of this book. First, *what* is the image of the ninja and ninjutsu presented to the Western world? This image, as it is presented through the film industry, martial arts publications, fiction, and sources within the historical tradition, is examined in depth.

Second, *why* is this image meaningful? Having established what the image of the ninja is—or, more accurately, what the many images are—psychological theory is used to explain the power of the ninja phenomenon and our attraction to this centuries-old way of life.

It is my hope that readers will come to see ninjutsu not only as a devastatingly effective and comprehensive means of physical combat and survival—the ultimate warrior tradition—but also as a path leading to "wholeness" and "totality." Indeed, nin-po, the higher order of ninjutsu, is frequently described by Shidoshi Hayes as a means of facing and overcoming antagonistic forces at the physical, psychological (emotional, mental), and spiritual levels of being, as well as a means of developing one's total being. In essence, then, ninjutsu is nothing short of the warrior's way of enlightenment.

1

The Ninja of Film and Television

"I must say that there is really nothing wrong with the entertainment industry bending the lore of the ninja to fit the demands of the public. However, it is a little surprising that Japanese and American audiences would believe that the weakly researched flights of fancy of fiction writers were the true essence of *ninjutsu*."—**Dr. Masaaki Hatsumi** (1981)

"Someday there will be a producer who will want to go beyond the silly stereotyping of *ninjutsu* in the martial arts film as we know it and bring out something that shows the full potential of all the facets of the ninja warrior tradition."—**Stephen K. Hayes** (1984)

"When moving pictures were first shown to the public, they were an immediate success, which is not surprising, for they appealed to a fundamental human thirst— a thirst for the exhibition and imitation of people and things."—**Roy Huss and Norman Silverstein** (1972)

"One of the most noticeable characteristics of popular culture is the rapidity with which new forms are initiated and older, more familiar ones, revitalized."—**Peter Homans** (1972)

THERE CAN BE little doubt that the ninja have found a place in the popular imagination of America. Beginning with *You Only Live Twice*, the 1967 James Bond film, the ninja and their secret fighting art known as *ninjutsu* have fascinated moviegoers and television audiences. From *Shogun*, through the successful Cannon Films (*Enter the Ninja*, *Revenge of the Ninja*, *Ninja III: The Domination*, and *American Ninja*), to prime-time television in *The Master*, and appearances on popular programs like *Simon and Simon*, the ninja have become widely known, and are now stock characters in the Hollywood writers' minds. In short, the ninja have arrived!

But how many of us realize the importance and impact of the screen portrayal of the ninja? It is an established psychological fact that what is seen visually has a greater influence on us than either reading something or hearing about it. And for most people their awareness of the ninja first came through the visual image. What is more, many of the persons involved in local and federal legislation against the martial arts are motivated by the ninja as they are seen in films and on television—not by "reality"! Hence what the vast majority of people know about the ninja—*and consider accurate*—comes from the screen! Few stop to realize that the goal of the film industry is to entertain, not enlighten. We can *never* know the true nature of the North American Indians through Hollywood's interpretation, nor can we know in any depth what it is like to be a private investigator from shows such as *Magnum, P.I.*, *Remington Steele*, or *Crazy Like a Fox*. Most people accept this. But when it comes to the ninja our attraction to the excitement and flamboyance of the "super martial artist," and to the strongly aggressive themes, is so powerful that myth and reality blur to a dramatic extent.

If we are truly interested in the ninja, and find ourselves genuinely drawn to the *ninjutsu* lifestyle, we *must* look at how the ninja are portrayed in films and television shows and see where the inaccuracies lie. In fact, there is urgent necessity for this. It is not inconceivable, as Shidoshi Hayes, the foremost authority on *ninjutsu* in the West has said, that *ninjutsu* may become "illegal" again—this time in the U.S.A.

How Clearly Do We See the Ninja?

As we begin our tour through the many ways in which the ninja are presented to us in the West, it is vitally important that we keep one question foremost in our minds. That question is this: *Do we see the ninja and ninjutsu as they are or have we slotted them into the already available stereotyped categories within our own culture?*

If we rather rapidly come to various conclusions about the ninja and their art, chances are they have been quickly likened to something with which we are familiar and thus categorized. On the other hand, if the core of the tradition seems to elude us for some time, if we find that the ninjutsu is rather foreign and difficult to comprehend, then we are probably struggling to understand a body of knowledge from another culture fundamentally different from our own. After all, ninjutsu originated in Japan, and has interacted with and become integrated into the Japanese way of life *for more than* 900 *years.* We in the West are *only now* coming to have knowledge of the ninja.

Hence, it is crucial that we try to remember the perspective from which we look at the world, and realize that it is different from other perspectives. In particular, the perspective of nin-po, as ninjutsu is known in its highest order, *is* fundamentally different from anything with which we are familiar. Therefore we must struggle to rid ourselves of the preconceptions we bring to the ninja which do not correspond with reality. Then we must struggle to comprehend an alien worldview. But it is only through struggling with the world that we come to know it. And in so doing we may glimpse something of the ninja for who they were and are, and see a part of the magic of ninjutsu.

The Choice of Material

The films and television episodes chosen to illustrate the ninja as they are presented on the screen were selected as the most accessible examples to readers. *You Only Live Twice* may be found in most video rental stores. *Shogun* is certainly available in many. *Enter the Ninja, Revenge of the Ninja, Ninja III: The Domination,* and *American Ninja* (all from Cannon Films) are almost as common as the James Bond tapes. *The Octogon* and *Nine Deaths of the Ninja,* although not as easily found as the Cannon Film releases, are fairly available in most areas. The two episodes of *The Master* reviewed here have been marketed under the title *Ninja IV: The Master.* Many other ninja films have been excluded from analysis because of their general lack of availability to readers, and because the overall image is little different from that in the above films.

You Only Live Twice: The Ninja as Elite Commandos

You Only Live Twice was one of the first Western films to feature the ninja. The story line is familiar to most people. James Bond is in Japan to investigate a series of American and Russian spaceship disappearances before the two superpowers become convinced the other is behind the plot and declare war on one another. Bond realizes that he will need a crack commando team to take effective action, and is put in touch with a secret ninja training school. There he heightens his own ability to handle man-to-man confrontations, and subsequently hires Japan's elite fighting men for the job.

> **Synopsis:** In much the same way in which "M" leads Bond through his secret laboratories filled with marvelous inventions, the head of the ninja school guides 007 through various training exercises his students are engaged in. During this tour we are witness to hand-to-hand combat, stick and staff fighting, *kenjutsu* (swordsmanship), and *shuriken* (star-shaped weapons) training. We also learn that the ninja are already masters of many other disciplines, their specialty is stealth, and their skill with a whole host of weapons is unequaled.
>
> The attack on the enemy stronghold is dramatic. Dressed in dark fabric to blend in with the night, Bond and a team of ninja attempt to take the crater being used as a secret rocket launch pad. Each ninja carries a submachine gun and ropes for the descent into the crater, in addition to a sword and countless shuriken. The opening sequences of the battle look surprisingly like a war movie with a crack commando team. However, unlike future films where the ninja invariably win against overwhelming odds, in *You Only Live Twice* the ninja commando unit is largely obliterated by enemy machine gun fire, although 007 survives (of course!).

The Ninja Stereotyped

In a film with a stereotyped character as the lead it is perhaps not surprising to find the ninja similarly stereotyped. In essence, despite their mastery of various martial arts disciplines, they are portrayed as little more than an elite special forces team. But their ability to succeed is certainly not foremost. In fact, it is Bond, representing the Western world, who survives and wins the day while the ninja, representing the Eastern world, make little impression. Naturally this is an inevitable result of the ninja playing second fiddle to Bond!

One interesting result of this state of affairs is that many people made a mental note of who the ninja were, but because the presentation was like a war movie, or early martial arts movie, made no attempt to find out more about the ninja and their secret fighting art. Hence, in the 1980s when the ninja suddenly leapt to the forefront of popular culture, many had the odd sense of having heard of the ninja, although they could not place where they had learned about them. Chances are it was from *You Only Live Twice*.

Shogun: The Ninja as Hired Assassins

The ninja also played a minor role in the epic television miniseries *Shogun* starring Richard Chamberlain. However, here, in one of their two attacks, they are successful. The results are devastating—and Mariko, the beautiful female lead, is killed.

> **Synopsis:** Shipwrecked in feudal Japan, Blackthorne (Chamberlain) begins sharing his knowledge of the world with Lord Toranaga. Since Blackthorne is English his views threaten the Jesuits whose Black Ship takes gold bullion back to Portugal. Fearing the English pilot will be their undoing, the Jesuit priests hire a ninja assassin to gain entrance to Osaka castle and kill him.
>
> This first ninja scene is beautifully shot. It is a dark night. A man in black climbs the outer wall with great speed. He moves along the rooftops silently, making use of the shadows, and keeping out of sight of the many samurai guards. He strangles a guard in the hall outside the foreigner's room. But then the ninja is unexpectedly surprised by a group of samurai. He rushes into Blackthorne's room to carry out his assassination, but the samurai surround him. Seeing that he is outnumbered he kills himself. Lord Toranaga arrives and is relieved to find Blackthorne unhurt. But as the assassin's face is uncovered, "knowing looks" pass between the lord and his samurai—ninja!
>
> In the second scene the ninja are employed by Lord Ishido, Lord Toranaga's archrival. Ishido persuades Yabu, one of Toranaga's generals,

to betray his lord. He does so by allowing a small group of black-clad ninja into the living area of Lord Toranaga's women. During the resulting fight many of Toranaga's and Yabu's samurai are killed. The ninja are clearly expert swordsmen and make effective use of shuriken. They are also explosives experts, and it is while blowing up a door behind which Blackthorne and Lord Toranaga's women have taken refuge that Mariko is killed and Blackthorne temporarily blinded.

The Ninja as Assassin

The "ninja as assassin" is a commonly held image of the ninja, one which is stressed in *Shogun*. The idea conveyed is that, despite their tremendous skills as masters of various disciplines, the ninja are simply hired thugs, employed to do jobs that the samurai could not do, because the samurai had a code of honor (*bushido*) which the ninja lacked. Hence, the ninja are seen as cold-blooded murderers who made their money as fifteenth- and sixteenth-century hit men.

Again, this view of the ninja is heavily prejudiced by the fact that they were not central characters, and the audience only sees things from the samurai perspective. However, like *You Only Live Twice*, *Shogun* planted the image of the ninja in many people's minds. Because it was such a successful miniseries, more people saw it than would ordinarily watch a martial arts film. Therefore, to a great many people, "ninja" meant the same as "assassin"—the type of assassin who would kill a beautiful woman like Mariko. Needless to say, this is a very negative image.

Enter the Ninja: The Ninja as Super Martial Artist

It is interesting to note that in *Shogun*, a miniseries that made every attempt to be as accurate as possible about the period of Japan's history being portrayed, the ninja were not seen as dramatic martial artists, but as a group of men who "got the job done." In *Enter the Ninja*, starring Franco Nero, Susan George, and Sho Kosugi, the image of the ninja is firmly established as that of the super martial artist. The theme of the ninja as trained assassin, however, remained intact.

During the initial credits a black-clad ninja works out with a variety of weapons: *hanbo* (three-foot stick), sword, spear, *sai* (three-pronged karate weapon), *kyotsetu shoge* (flexible chain weapon with knife at one end and a thick ring at the other), bow and arrow, and blowgun. Following the intense interest in the martial arts in the 1960s and 1970s, the ninja are presented as the epitome of the martial arts warrior.

Synopsis: The opening sequence of the film does even more to establish this image. In this most dramatic opening scene, we are witness to the final test of an American ninja at the master's dojo—although we as the audience do not know this until the end of the sequence. Set against a beautiful landscape, a ninja dressed in white faces a ninja dressed in black. It is clear they are on opposing sides. The white-clad ninja is chased by the black-clad ninja and a host of maroon-clad ninja. It is a hunt, and the man in white is the prey.

Like a hunted animal, the white ninja must draw upon his every strength and ability to survive. At one point he is vigilantly moving through the forest when a maroon-clad ninja pops up behind him. The hero senses the other's presence and "kills" him. He also defends himself against two, sometimes three, sword-wielding ninja, and must rely upon acrobatic skill and his ability to disappear in order to win out against overwhelming odds.

Through exquisite countryside, over waterfalls, and past guards, the chase continues until finally the white ninja confronts the black ninja outside the training hall. The black ninja is forced to surrender. The white ninja then runs to the door of the training hall, bows to the Master standing there, and neatly cuts his head off.

It is only at this point that we realize that this has all been an elaborate means of testing the white ninja's skills. No one had died—nor has anyone been seriously wounded. The white ninja kneels down in front of the Master, and the black- and maroon-clad ninja line up on either side. The Master then instructs the white ninja to demonstrate the nine levels of power. Each *mudra*, or hand sign, is properly executed, accompanied by a brief description of the energy thus symbolized. He is then told that he has passed every test. He is given a scroll as a mark of his mastery of ninjutsu.

The essential personal conflict for the film is set as the Master and his students sit around a table following the white ninja's (Cole's) success. Hasagawa, played by Sho Kosugi, refuses to drink to his fellow student's promotion. He emotionally argues that Cole is a Westerner while he is descended from an Iga samurai family. He can therefore lay claim to being a ninja, but Cole cannot. We can already feel at this point that

Hasagawa and Cole will meet again, and this time the confrontation will be lethal.

Before Cole leaves, he spends some time walking with the Master. In many ways the purpose of this scene is to establish the Master as a man of wisdom. The Master tells him that he must always "hold onto his power," for it is easy to go wrong (like Hasagawa). He also emphasizes that Cole must be strong enough to avoid bitterness and be courageous enough to help the least fortunate.

Cole then flies to Manila and immediately becomes embroiled in a plot reminiscent of the A-Team. Frank, an old war buddy of Cole's, owns a piece of land which Venarius, a ruthless businessman, wants. Unbeknownst to Frank is that beneath his farm is a large oil reserve. In the film tradition of money-hungry sociopaths, Venarius is willing to use any means possible to force Frank to sell, and the scene is set for Cole to use his recently perfected ninja skills against a variety of thugs.

Not surprisingly Venarius meets with no success using the average "tough guy." Consequently he wants to find out more about Cole. His research leads him to the ninja. However, when told that today's ninja are teachers and lawyers in Japan, who study ninjutsu for the development of personal power, Venarius orders his men to find a ninja who believes "in the old ways"—the ways of infiltration and assassination. Predictably Hasagawa, with his untempered anger, is thus employed.

Shortly after his employment Hasagawa heads out to the ranch. He systematically kills the guards at the main house before torturing Frank with painful, but not fatal, sword cuts. In a gruesome finale to the scene, Maryanne, Frank's wife, is tied up and forced to watch the murder of her husband. First Frank is felled by a shuriken; then his throat is cut with the blade of a kyoketsu shoge. Hasagawa then runs through the workers' lodgings setting fire to the structures—laughing almost hysterically throughout.

With his good friend dead, Cole dons his white ninja suit, evokes the nine levels of power before a burning fire, arms himself heavily with ancient weapons, and goes in search of Venarius. The final scenes are set at an empty livestock auction building. In the center is a square defined by four Plexiglas walls, a door at each corner. The square is surrounded on all sides by rising seats.

In his effort to get to Venarius, Cole dramatically uses his entire arsenal of weapons—smoke and fire bombs, shuriken, sai, *tetsubishi* (caltrop), blow darts, bow and arrows, the *kusari-fundo* (short-chain), and the *ninja-ken* (sword)—in a classic ninja fight scene. Venarius meets his end as the result of an accurately thrown shuriken.

The final martial arts scene involves the confrontation between Cole and Hasagawa. Amid dramatic acrobatics and weapons use, the battle between the two opponents is the highlight of the movie. At the end Hasagawa is fatally wounded. He tells Cole that he has won with honor, and asks that he also be allowed to die with honor. With a ceremonial bow, Cole beheads him.

The New Stereotype

The image of the ninja in Enter the Ninja is probably the one most familiar to the populace at large. In a sense this is the new stereotype of the ninja. But it is interesting to note that although this is a new way of seeing the ninja, it is not a new stereotype in the West. After Bruce Lee and such exciting films as Enter the Dragon, Americans have been much drawn to the martial arts in film. The ninja have therefore become a new way of repackaging that image—although this time there are even more exotic weapons to give the actors and stuntmen.

Americans are also very familiar with the assassin, and the ninja have neatly settled into this stereotyped image, also. Our fascination with the mafia has provided many screen assassins and hit men. There is something oddly appealing about the cold, experienced killer making elaborate preparations for fulfilling his contract. Good drama is always achieved when the systematic and efficient assassin closes in on his intended target, while his opponents look like they will never catch him in time.

Where the ninja becomes refreshingly "new" is that they are a combination of these two stereotypes—the stereotype of the martial artist and the assassin. Also, because so little is known about them, and because they were so feared, they became a way of expressing our culture's aggression in a new way. We will see this theme of aggressiveness become even more central in the next two films we look at.

The Revenge of the Ninja: Good versus Evil

Although the themes of aggression and "good and evil" were certainly present in Enter the Ninja, it is only in The Revenge of the Ninja that these themes come to the forefront. In many ways this is not surprising. First of all, our culture has both an attraction to, and a difficulty dealing with, aggression. Second, our culture has its origins in Judeo-Christian thought. The whole issue of "good versus evil" is very important to us. Hence, *The Revenge of the Ninja* adds two of our greatest concerns to the stereotype of the ninja as super martial artist.

Synopsis: *The Revenge of the Ninja,* starring Sho Kosugi, Arthur Roberts, and Keith Vitali, opens in Tokyo in the grounds of a traditional Japanese house. A family is enjoying walking in the beautiful gardens, unaware that a band of hostile ninja are closing in. The tension mounts as we sense the massacre about to unfold.

There is no doubt that the opening scene is both dramatic and brutally violent. An older man rushes forward to protect the women and children, only to have four swords simultaneously stuck in his body. One ninja holds a woman while another slashes her with a sword cut, and yet another stabs her in the back. A mother hides her baby, only to return and be killed with an arrow to the chest. In the blink of an eye the entire group has been murdered.

Cho Osaki, played by Sho Kosugi, arrives with an American friend, Braden. The band of ninja instantly, and silently, hide. Cho is explaining that his father had been killed on this land, and for that reason he must stay. Then the two men see the bodies of Osaki's family strewn about the porches of the house.

Two ninja suddenly attack with ninja-ken. Another attacks from the rooftop. Cho kills all three with crisp martial arts skill. It is immediately clear that he, too, is a master. Cho finds his dead wife. Three ninja shoot arrows at Cho who expertly catches one in each hand, and one in his teeth! A ninja appears at Cho's feet and is killed with the two arrows Cho is holding.

In a dramatic finale to the opening scene, five black-clad, sword-wielding ninja attack Cho. Amid impressive choreography, sword fighting, martial arts stunts, and loud shouting, Cho eventually comes out the victor.

Braden has been trying to convince Cho to come with him to the U.S. Braden argues that Cho cannot fight the ninja forever. Cho's mother watches as Cho slowly accepts the American's arguments. Finding that her intuitions of Braden's character go unheard, she finally tells her son, in rather ominous tones, that Cho cannot escape his *karma.* Even if he were to go as far as America his *karma* will come for him.

The scene then shifts to Los Angeles, six years later. Cho's mother encourages Cho to teach Kane, his son, the "way of the ninja." But Cho has decided to give up fighting. He tells his son that his sword is sealed forever—he will no longer follow the way of the ninja. He feels that the way has killed too many. He tells Kane that they are no longer samurai, no longer ninja. They practice with their swords simply to honor their tradition.

Cho has gone into business with Braden importing handmade Japanese dolls. We learn about the ninja as Braden arrives at Cho's shop with a woman business partner who catches sight of a ninja doll. Cho explains that it is a ninja, a professional soldier. He notes that the ninja lived about four hundred years ago, and specialized in espionage and assassination. Braden notes that the ninja were the "worst bastards the world has ever known," but Cho replies that although many people think the ninja are evil, this is inaccurate. However, he does not go on to explain why this is inaccurate, only to note that the ninja's special skill was killing people ("a thousand ways of death").

We soon discover that Cho has unwittingly become involved in a drug ring when Kane accidentally knocks over a doll and breaks it. White powder spills all over the floor—heroin. Cathy, Cho's assistant and Braden's employee, tells Kane to mention the accident to no one. The next scene reveals that Braden is intending to sell the heroin to Caifano, a mafia godfather. But Caifano will not deal straightforwardly with Braden. Braden then sets out on a series of killings in which Caifano's relatives are murdered. It is revealed that Braden, too, is a ninja.

Wearing the traditional night suit, Braden also adds a silver skull mask to his attire. He carries with him an impressive arsenal of ninja weapons. One by one his victims meet their end. Caifano's brother's neck is broken, one of Caifano's contacts killed with a shuriken through the eye. Caifano's nephew is killed with a poisoned dart, and the nephew's girlfriend is drowned, held beneath the water with the sword scabbard.

We learn more about "ninja lore" as the police attempt to fathom what has happened. Calling in Dave Hatcher (Keith Vitali), the police's martial arts expert, we learn that Caifano's brother suffered dramatic injuries. His largest leg bone had been cracked like a toothpick, his sternum shattered, his ribs crushed, and his head pulverized. The coroner has already determined that no weapons were used! Dave notes that the only people capable of such precise destruction were bone-breakers from an ancient Japanese ryu. Ninja are implicated.

As Cho is included in the investigation we learn that even a professional athlete would be unable to throw a shuriken with the necessary accuracy to kill. And Caifano's contact had been killed with a shuriken thrown into his eye. What is more, the shuriken had been expertly crafted such that the length of each edge was long enough to reach through the "gate of the eye to the brain." The conclusion is clear: a ninja is afoot in twentieth-century L.A.

Although Cho hopes to avoid involvement with the murdering ninja by refusing to help the police further, he is drawn into the chain of events as Caifano decides to steal the heroin-filled dolls from the gallery. In another classic martial arts scene, Cho attempts to fight off the four men sent to rob the gallery.

Meanwhile, Braden in his ninja garb arrives at the gallery, only to find he is too late. Cho's mother sees him enter the gallery through a skylight and challenges him. Although she fights well, and has clearly been trained in the ninja way, Braden eventually kills her with his ninja-ken. As Braden takes off his mask, Kane sees him, and barely escapes with his life. Unable to catch the ninja child, Braden returns home and hypnotizes Cathy, ordering her to bring the boy to him.

While Cho and Dave are out trying to find out where Kane has gone, Cathy succeeds in kidnapping the boy. However, once she returns to Braden's the hypnotism wears off and she calls Cho to tell him what she has done, and to warn him that Braden is a ninja. She adds that Braden is going after Caifano. David offers to help Cho, but is told that only a ninja can stop another ninja, and Braden has been trained in Koga-ryu ninjutsu.

Gathering his weapons together, Cho goes to the family shrine. Raising his personal power through the ninja mudra (hand signs), Cho dramatically breaks the seal on his ninja-ken. As he pulls his mask up over his face and chants, an ominous wind begins to blow.

Braden's entry into Caifano's fortified building, and Cho's battle with Braden, are some of the most exciting ninja scenes ever shot. Braden gains entrance to Caifano's building through the use of an arrow and line. He shoots the arrow from an adjacent building. Once it penetrates the concrete in Caifano's building, Braden slides across the line and crashes through a plate glass window. Once inside Caifano's building, anyone standing in Braden's way is killed off with metsubishi, a hatchet, spikes, shuriken, and a switchblade in the end of a cane—a predictable ninja sequence in which each opponent is killed with a different exotic weapon. Caifano is summarily executed although armed with a machine gun.

Gaining entry to the building by using *shuko* (iron claws), Cho catches up with Braden just after he has killed David, his friend. The film's finale is set on the rooftop of the building, high above L.A., and epitomizes our popular image of the ninja. Despite their clear opposition to each other the final duel begins with each man bowing. This is presented as though it were a ninja ritual. There is an exchange of mudra, then the fight begins.

In addition to the usual sword fighting, smoke bombs, and acrobatics, *The Revenge of the Ninja* introduces many surprise weapons—blades in the end of staffs, knives at the base of the sword handle, hidden chains, and even a flamethrower. It becomes almost laughable. In addition, Braden is brilliant in his use of surprise and terror—an effigy of the black ninja jumps up in front of Cho at one point during the confrontation, and a mechanical hand reaches out of a Jacuzzi and grabs Cho's leg at another.

After nearly losing the fight by being thrown off the building (he catches himself with the ninja's rope and hook), Cho and Braden at last square off, both exhausted and wounded. In a classic sword fight, Cho defeats Braden, splitting his mask open with the last thrust.

The Ninja Stereotype

In *Enter the Ninja* we saw that the ninja highlighted an important stereotype in our culture: the super martial artist. In *The Revenge of the Ninja* the ninja stereotype as it has come to be known in our culture is fleshed out.

As noted earlier, it is not surprising that the theme of good against evil should become part of the ninja stereotype. Hence, there is the idea of "good ninja"—usually in the distinct minority—against "evil ninja"—almost always more powerful until the final moments. Whereas in *Enter the Ninja* the two were distinguished by the color of their ninja uniforms, in *The Revenge of the Ninja* it is their conduct that separates the two: Cho has decided forever to seal his sword, while Braden is unabashedly destructive. We also see our culture's discomfort with aggression: aggression equals evil.

However, although there is the idea of good and bad ninja, it is the evil ninja that are most remembered. The first scene in any film carries the most weight and *The Revenge of the Ninja* opens with a band of highly trained ninja attacking a defenseless family. The way the ninja are portrayed is reminiscent of the way American Indians and Nazis were once presented: even women and children are not spared. And like these other "enemies" the stereotyped image of the ninja goes beyond hatred. The ninja become synonymous with the devil and death itself.

This is most eloquently expressed in *The Revenge of the Ninja* through the mask Braden wears. Its likeness to a skull is the key. He is "the reaper," the master of a "thousand ways of death." Anyone who stands in his way—be he or she a master martial artist or gun-wielding thug, woman or child—is tortured and killed. Only another ninja stands a chance of stopping him.

The power of the ninja is also emphasized more in *The Revenge of the Ninja*. Dave likens the blows that killed Caifano's brother to a truck. The police note that the bones were broken as if by a machine, at precise ninety-degree angles. This power is cultivated from childhood with very special training, a training that includes espionage and assassination skills. And the extent of this power is underlined by the ability of the stereotyped ninja to accurately throw a shuriken into a man's eye from a distance.

We now have a whole stock of characteristics that are associated with the ninja of the screen. Among these are the ninja's use of supernatural powers, the ninja's ritual bowing and mudra before a fight, the hidden weapons, the ever-ready rope and hook, the dramatic ability to disappear in a puff of smoke, ninja hypnotism, and, of course, the ninja's brilliant gymnastic abilities.

A final point, one which will be expanded upon in *Ninja III: The Domination*, is the theme of misogyny, or hatred of women. The drowning of Caifano's nephew's girlfriend is a good example of this. Also, left out of the short synopsis above, *The Revenge of the Ninja* includes a scene in which Cathy is almost raped by Braden's Oriental servant. The film also includes lengthy torture sequences in which Cathy is tied in a Jacuzzi and kept precariously close to drowning by having her head only just above the water level, intermittently forced to struggle for life by another of Braden's sociopathic henchmen. But we will have more to say about this after the next section. For now it is sufficient simply to note this theme.

Ninja III: The Domination: Ninja Mysticism

In both *Enter the Ninja* and *The Revenge of the Ninja* there is an obvious stretching of reality. In *Ninja III: The Domination*, however, the bonds of reality are broken altogether. We find that the screen ninja goes far beyond the possible, and enters into the superhuman, nonhuman, and supernatural realms. Nevertheless, despite the clear preponderance of fantasy in the film, we are still attracted to the ninja, and the film has certainly furthered the cultural stereotype of the ninja in the West.

Synopsis: As in the two previous ninja films, the opening sequences are stunningly dramatic. In Ninja III a Japanese man is walking alone in a desert landscape. He enters a secret underground cave and opens his arms cache. We see the ninja-ken and shuriken, and immediately know that he is a ninja. Tension mounts as the man picks up his sword and reverently gazes at it. He dresses slowly, as if this were an established ninja ritual.

As the man leaves the cache we are witness to beautiful silhouettes of the ninja against the dawn sky. He makes his way across the landscape, moving like a stereotypic ninja: crouching, with quick moves, and frequent glances left and right. He makes his way to a golf course and stealthily approaches a man playing golf, surrounded by his personal bodyguards.

When the golfer—the ninja's assassination target—accidentally lands a ball in the bushes, the ninja is waiting. First, unsettling a bodyguard by crushing the golf ball and demonstrating his superhuman strength, he goes on to kill all five of the man's bodyguards. They are killed with accurately thrown shuriken, and—unbelievably—one guard's gun explodes as a ninja dart enters the barrel just as the bullet is leaving.

The "target" and his girlfriend try to escape in a golf cart, but the ninja runs after them with great speed, and—again, unbelievably—lifts the back wheels off the ground! He gives a disturbingly evil laugh, and then slays the man and woman in a particularly ruthless way.

The golf security guards arrive at the scene and see the bodies of the man, woman, and the bodyguards lying on the ground. They call for help and the local police arrive in force. The ninja assassin is spotted. He is chased down an open road, running as fast as the police cars! We know here that drama is the name of the game since the ninja does not slip into the vegetation at the side of the road and "disappear."

The ninja jumps on top of one of the police cars. One of the officers below shoots through the roof with a shotgun, but misses. The ninja replies with a sword thrust downward, killing the man. Driving his fist through the roof, the ninja kills the second officer.

The many police on motorcycles become target practice for the ninja and his shuriken. Never missing, each throwing star finds its target in an eye or the side of a head, killing the policeman instantly. At one point the ninja uses his rope and hook to swing around a tree and knock a policeman off his motorcycle.

The suspenseful fantasy increases with the arrival of a police helicopter. The ninja uses his belt to climb into a palm tree, but rather than staying hidden to avoid capture, he emerges at the top of the tree and grabs hold of the helicopter's landing gear. One man is thrown out of the chopper. The pilot meets his end with a shuriken propelled by the ninja's foot! And the last man falls with the ninja into the lake they are hovering over just before the helicopter crashes.

Waiting to see when the ninja will surface, a policeman notices a tube moving in the water. As he approaches, the tube slants toward him and a poisoned dart kills him. Again, however, rather than staying hidden and avoiding capture the ninja runs off, and there is another dramatic chase with shuriken flying everywhere.

It seems the long battle is over when the ninja assassin takes countless rounds of gunfire. However, as the police approach he jumps up and resumes killing. The police reply with another barrage of gunfire, and when the smoke clears there appears to be about twenty dead officers and the dead ninja. However, yet again the ninja jumps up, taking automatic fire in addition to pistol fire, and this time disappears after throwing a smoke bomb—despite the fact that he is surrounded. As the police fan out to search for him we see that he has dug himself into the ground—an impressive feat in a scarce five seconds.

The scene shifts to Christi, a telephone repair woman, who from her vantage point atop a telephone pole, notices the ninja stumbling through the undergrowth. She goes to help him, but can only find a piece of his uniform—whereupon a "mystic wind" blows. Suddenly the ninja attacks the woman and attempts to kill her. Somehow Christi manages to escape and begins to run off.

But the ninja calls her back with a commanding voice, and she obeys. He hands her his ninja-ken, covered in blood, and a light appears on her forehead, as well as his. She begins to "see" through his eyes, and "sees" the fight with the police. The ninja then dies. A "mystic wind" blows again, and again Christi reexperiences the fight with the police. There is little doubt that she has been possessed. And as the camera pulls back we see that the sword is suddenly, and quite magically, spotless and shining.

What then begins is a systematic killing of the police who survived the battle with the ninja. Surrounded by flashing lights and bizarre poltergeist phenomena Christi time and again dons the ninja's uniform and takes up his sword. She then wreaks revenge upon the police survivors.

Christi notices that something is wrong, but a consultation with a

psychiatrist produces no meaningful results. Her boyfriend, a policeman, and also one of the men who finished off the ninja, takes her to a
Japanese spiritualist. Tied up in case the spirit gets angry, the spiritualist invokes the spirit. The "mystic wind" blows, candles flare up,
lightning flashes, and thunder roars. In a scene all-too reminiscent of
The Exorcist, the spirit of the ninja speaks. There are horrible, evil laughs,
growling, and the baring of teeth.

Christi's boyfriend asks what a ninja is. The spiritualist replies that it
is best that he does not know. Under pressure he finally reveals that
Christi is possessed by a Black Ninja. He says the only thing that will
help is to take Christi to Iga Mountain in Japan. It seems only one power
can destroy a ninja: another ninja!

At this point in the film, Yamada (Sho Kosugi), a one-eyed Japanese
man, enters the picture. He stealthily enters the morgue where the
body of the ninja is kept. Several guards and two doctors are knocked
out or killed by impressive spinning back kicks and the use of shuriken.
It is clear that Yamada, too, is a ninja. In the morgue Yamada experiences a flashback. A gang of evil ninja kill his father. Then one of them
throws a shuriken in his eye, laughing horribly. It is the Black Ninja.
Returning to the present, Yamada takes the body of the dead ninja to
a Japanese temple perched on a hill.

After the next assassination, Yamada is waiting for Christi/Black
Ninja. As the police race around looking for the assassin, Yamada and
Christi/Black Ninja battle it out in an abandoned house. But when
Yamada sees that he is fighting a possessed woman, he helps her
escape, allowing himself to be arrested in her place.

Before taking Yamada to the police station, however, Christi's boyfriend wants to talk with him. Yamada tells him that he has come from
Japan for revenge, and instructs the man to bring Christi to the temple
on the hill. Then, as the car drives off, Yamada sets about freeing
himself. He kills two of the officers with poison-tipped darts, and then
knocks out the driver.

Although Christi's boyfriend is unable to force her/the spirit to
submit, Christi/Black Ninja goes to the temple anyway. Yamada explains that he and she must fight it out. *Only a ninja can kill a ninja*. If the
spirit does not leave her body, then she will die. In the ensuing martial
arts sequence Yamada quickly wins, and the spirit returns to the dead
ninja. And suddenly the Black Ninja is alive again!

At first, the Balck Ninja possesses the many attendants at the temple
who are also martial artists. After defeating these men, Yamada chases

the Black Ninja. An impressive fight follows with much use of gymnastic escapades and smoke bombs. Yamada finally kills the Black Ninja with his own sword. The assassin evokes the gods with mystic hand signals, and disappears into the earth.

An earthquake follows which Yamada survives as the result of using the ninja rope and hook. And the Black Ninja is back in action yet again. However, in the final martial arts fighting scene Yamada stabs the Black Ninja in the head with a knife; he is dead at last. He tells Christi that it is finally over, and walks off. The body of the Black Ninja evaporates, leaving only his knife and sword.

The Dark Side of the Ninja Stereotype

The central characters in *Enter the Ninja* and *The Revenge of the Ninja* were both "good." Not so in *Ninja III: The Domination*. Here the central "character" is the Black Ninja. Hence, what we are glimpsing is the dark side of the ninja as they are presented to us by the filmmakers in Hollywood.

Hasagawa only killed one person, and Braden only killed mafia. The Black Ninja killed a businessman, his girlfriend, the bodyguards, and countless policemen, all in addition to possessing Christi and the attendants at the temple for the sole purpose of more killing. What is more, in the murders of the policemen we find the ninja destroying that which symbolically protects our society.

The image of the ninja portrayed in *Ninja III* goes beyond that of the assassin. In effect the Black Ninja is so possessed by evil that he cannot use the many real and stereotyped ninja means of escape in order to survive, but instead purposefully draws more persons to him such that he might kill them. In short, he has become a wanton murderer. What is more, the Black Ninja is also imbued with superhuman martial arts skills and supernatural powers.

It is clear that there has been an evolution of the ninja character through the three films discussed so far. Hasagawa was filled with hatred, but it was personal, and he retained his honor. Braden had less honor, but restricted his killings to his enemies. The Black Ninja represents Evil itself, bent upon revenge over those who were simply fulfilling their roles in life. Almost in confirmation of this we see that the battle of good and evil takes place within Christi, whose name, interestingly, has its origins in "Christ."

The other aspect of the dark side of the ninja which evolves is the misogynist element—the hatred of women. Hasagawa tied up Frank's wife and forced her to watch the death of her husband, and Cathy was tortured by Braden's sociopathic thug, but Ninja III carries an even stronger undercurrent of misogynism. First, the businessman's girl-friend is cruelly *killed* with a sword, helpless to defend herself. Then, soon after her possession, Christi is attacked by four men, and in one of her possessed states *kills* two women who were with a policeman the Black Ninja wished to kill.

The most obvious example of misogynism is the scene with the spiritualist: Christi is tied up with ropes and chains—the allusion to sadomasochistic practices being all too obvious. Hence, we find that our own culture's deeply rooted misogynism is added to the ninja stereotype—as part of the stereotyped ninja's dark side.

What is most surprising is that Yamada, supposedly the "good ninja," is not of the same ilk as either Cole or Cho Osaki. Rather than using subtle methods to escape arrest by the police Yamada kills innocent men against whom he carries no grudge. Hence, we see that the interest in the dark side of the ninja image spills over into the depiction of the presumably good ninja. The result is that the stereotype takes on a decidedly more negative flavor. Regardless of whether they are "good" or "bad," the ninja are *first and foremost killers*.

This is underlined by the idea that the ninja can survive past the grave for the sole purpose of killing those whom they desire to see dead. Put otherwise, their lust for murder is so strong it even *defies death itself*. Clearly this is a figment of Hollywood's imagination. It is designed to entertain. The disturbing thing, though, is that the feeling tone attached to the ninja persists in the minds of many who are unable to separate myth from reality. Consequently the ninja are frequently known exclusively as assassins and ruthless murderers, cowards and scum.

Even the clear level of fantasy in Ninja III adds to the idea that the ninja are little more than killing machines. Most ninja enthusiasts are aware that shuriken were used as "delaying weapons." They were not designed to kill, but to hold up anyone pursuing the ninja, much as the metsubishi were. But in many films—and this one in particular—the shuriken become "deadly." They do not slow down pursuers, but stop them dead in their tracks. Thus we find that even the fantasy element in the film underscores the theme of ninja violence and murder.

To summarize, then, Ninja III: *The Domination* paints a decidedly more negative picture of the ninja. "Ninja mysticism" takes the form of possession, and the dark side of the ninja is fleshed out in terms of misogynism and endless killings. Even the "good ninja" kills unnecessarily. In short, the stereotype of the ninja is given a particularly sinister side. At a deeper level what has happened is that the stereotype of the ninja has become fused with the stereotype of the

American Ninja: The Schizoid Ninja

From the sociopathic image of the ninja in Ninja III: *The Domination*, we move to the schizoid ninja of *American Ninja*. It would seem Hollywood, having latched onto the negativity of the ninja image it created, was determined to explore its dark side.

Synopsis: *American Ninja*, starring Michael Dudikoff and Steve James, begins with a convoy about to leave an army barracks. One man, Joe, sticks out; he is a loner who seems not to want to interact with anyone. He is distant, detached. But when the convoy is attacked by a band of black-clad ninja, this soldier comes alive with brilliant martial arts work. Several men are killed. Although he does not succeed in preventing the takeover of the convoy, he does manage to facilitate the escape of the commander's daughter. Together they take off into the jungle. As the ninja fan out to find them he proves himself to be adept at evading capture. The leader of the attacking ninja, the Black Star Ninja (Tadashi Yamashita), recognizes Joe's skills as ninjutsu.

Back at the camp Joe is accused of getting the servicemen killed through his heroics. As the camp gathers around to watch him fight Jackson, a seasoned fighter, we see that he has tremendous martial arts abilities—including a sense perception of things he cannot see. But after the "fight," when Jackson decides to befriend him and discover where he has received his training, Joe claims to be unable to remember. An explosion at an early age had brought about amnesia, although in dreams he sometimes remembers things. From the filmgoer's perspective it is clear he was once trained by a ninja.

Meanwhile we are taken inside an organized crime figure's compound and there witness the training of his private army of ninja. Their purpose: to guard and protect his operations and to make sure that buyers receive their shipments intact and unhassled. The Black Star Ninja is the chief instructor, and his cruelty and disregard for life is immediately apparent. While a potential client is touring the facility the

Black Star Ninja is asked to give a demonstration. To drive the point home that the ninja are reliable and effective killers, one of the master's students is ruthlessly murdered. The Black Star Ninja is completely unaffected.

Concerned over the appearance of an "American ninja," the organized crime leader orders Joe killed. He is set up when he is ordered to deliver a truck to a warehouse. Countless ninja attack him, but all are defeated. Once again his ability to see without his eyes permits him to stay alive. When one of the goons sees what is happening he drives off with the truck. The American ninja manages to board the truck, and is thus driven into the organized crime leader's estate. While he is running from the guards he comes face to face with the ninja teacher in his dreams, a man working as a gardener on the property. The master helps him to escape, but notes that karma will bring them together again.

The American ninja is accused of losing the truck and thrown in the brig. The Black Star Ninja is sent in to assassinate him, but despite being weaponless and trapped in a confined area, the American ninja manages to defeat the master ninja. Despite his survival, however, the dead and wounded guards, which in reality the Black Star Ninja took out, are blamed on him. And with his short, but recent, history of criminal involvement, his story is not believed. His attempts to convince the Colonel fail, ultimately, because the Colonel has sold out to organized crime himself.

In the end, with the help of Jackson, the American ninja infiltrates the drug king's estate. While there the ninja master finds him, and reveals to him his heritage. Donning a black shinobi shozoku, Joe, the American ninja, together with his master, takes on the Black Star Ninja's army. With backup finally arriving from the U.S. Army base, the organized crime operations are smashed. The final confrontation between the American ninja and the Black Star Ninja is all drama.

The Detached, Schizoid Ninja

In terms of the movie image of the ninja there are two major contributions made by American Ninja. The first obviously relates to the allegiances of the ninja. As employees of organized crime, it is clear that money speaks louder than morals. The ninja are not in control of themselves, they are the servants of a corrupt organization. The Black Star Ninja is obviously uninterested in the lives of others—taking one of his own students' lives without batting an eyelid. Viewed psychologically, he is a sociopath.

Here, then, there is not the image of the ninja as hired assassin who works alone, but the ninja as "private army." Ironically this sworn obedience to a boss was more becoming of the samurai who were fiercely loyal to the warlords of feudal Japan, regardless of the level of integrity the daiymo had.

With respect to the American ninja, he is clearly a disturbed individual. In fact, he meets the diagnostic criteria for a schizoid personality disorder. He demonstrates a marked defect in his capacity to form social relationships. In particular he lacks warm feelings for others and is indifferent to praise or criticism. He is vague about his goals, self-absorbed, absentminded, and generally detached. His difficulty in relating to women is readily apparent in his encounters with the Colonel's daughter.

On the whole the ninja are usually represented as highly aggressive in the Hollywood screenplay. Here, the central character, the American ninja, is represented as psychiatrically disturbed, although probably not intentionally. If he seems like a caricature of the "cool, macho guy," that is because many of the tough, dark-glasses-wearing, detached men in our culture are themselves schizoid personalities. Hence, the ninja in this film has been associated with one of the character disorders most commonly found in psychologically disturbed men.

In sum, *American Ninja* perpetrates the image of the ninja as inherently negative. The Black Star Ninja is clearly sociopathic, the American ninja schizoid. It seems that filmmakers, in their desire to portray the ninja in a negative light, leave no stones unturned.

The Octagon: The Ninja-Terrorist Connection

In *American Ninja* we find the oft-portrayed connection between the ninja and the "criminal underworld." In *The Octagon* the ninja are portrayed as running a clandestine training camp for terrorists. The connection forged in this film is of the ninja and the brutal world of international terrorism.

Synopsis: *The Octagon*, starring Chuck Norris, Karen Carlson, and Lee van Cleef, opens with a truckload of recruits arriving at the Octagon, the secret ninja training camp for terrorists. As the recruits get out of the truck, ninja descend from the trees and lead them to the training area. When they enter the compound they are met by three evil-looking men—the ninja masters.

From our introduction to the ninja camp, the scene jumps to a brutal assassination of an obviously wealthy man. No reason is immediately forthcoming for the attack. The terrorists use machine guns, and in a matter of seconds the target and his driver are left dead and bloody. A flashback to the camp shows Seikura (Tadashi Yamashita) ordering the murder of an entire family.

Meanwhile Scott James (Chuck Norris) meets a beautiful performer, Aura (Carol Bagdasarian), who integrates the martial arts with her performances. When he takes her to her residence, he is aware, through his "sixth sense," that there is someone in the house. Suddenly a band of ninja attack. Scott James is able to defeat them with deft karate moves, but when he turns on the light he sees that the family which lived in the house has been murdered by Seikura's ninja. Scott is unable to believe that the ninja still exist.

At the camp the trainees are taught to "expect the unexpected." They are told that they are now bound by certain codes. Among these is the preference for death over capture. At no point will the trainees *ever* reveal the nature of their training. Should they breach this order their families will be killed. No exceptions.

Scott James realizes that if the ninja are still in existence then Seikura is behind it. Seikura, it turns out, is Scott James's "brother." He seeks out a friend, McCarn (Lee van Cleef) to bounce his ideas off, but he is told that he is "seeing ghosts." The ninja have been outlawed for more than 300 years.

In a rather complex set of interactions, Justine (Karen Carlson) attempts to hire Scott James to find Seikura. It turns out that she is the one surviving member of the family assassinated in the earlier scene. But Scott is uninterested in helping her. He is following a path of nonaction and resents her interference in his life.

Flashbacks to the camp show black-robed ninja training the recruits in the use of sai and nunchaku. One of the ninja wears an armored face mask and chest plate. There is a scene in which Seikura and his instructors rush in upon the sleeping recruits in a simulation of a surprise attack. Those who did not react fast enough and who would have been killed in a real raid are beaten up. The trainees are told that though the body rests the mind must remain always alert. At another point a recruit, tired of the brutal treatment, attempts to leave. His life is ended with a shuriken accurately thrown into the base of his skull. A glimpse of outside maneuvers has the recruits rushing up to what appears to be a dead body, only to have ninja attack from beneath the ground. The way of life for the ninja, they are told, is illusion; trickery is one of the ninja's foremost weapons.

As Scott James is thinking about the events that have transpired, he has a memory of his childhood. He and Seikura are training. There is a final test set by the father for the two boys—a race over a difficult obstacle course requiring nerve, skill, and balance. The boy who wins receives the father's sword. Scott wins, but Seikura grabs the sword claiming that Scott cheated. Having broken "the discipline," the father rejects him. Scott is told never to make amends with his brother; Seikura is now his enemy.

Back at the camp the recruits finish their training. They are told that for the rest of their lives their actions and affiliations will be known to the ninja. Again they are told that any violations of the "code" will be punishable by death.

Scott James eventually decides to go in search of Seikura. He signs up for overseas mercenary work, but when he asks for special training with Seikura, he is thrown out—but not before he "shows his stuff." He goes to another man who he knows finances the mercenaries, but that man claims to know nothing of the whereabouts of the camp. Meanwhile Justine has hired A.J., Scott's friend (Art Hindle), as a bodyguard.

When Scott James returns to his room, Aura is there. She holds him at bay with a machine gun, and explains that she needs his help. She had "defected" and soon Seikura's men will be after her to punish her for violating "the code." Justine arrives and announces that A.J. has gone in search of Seikura. As Justine leaves, a ninja assassin, armed with a blowgun, kills her with a poisoned dart.

That night ninja climb the building in which Scott James and Aura are staying. As one is about to kill Scott, he awakens automatically. He kills the two ninja who attack him, and manages to free Aura from the third black-clad assassin. The third ninja is shot by McCarn when he tries to rappel down the outside of the building.

Scott and Aura arrive in Central America. Unknown to them, A.J. has also arrived and is a few steps ahead of them in locating the Octagon. A.J., however, is soon captured. Caught in a net while observing the training, he is taken to Seikura. Soon afterward Scott and Aura arrive. Scott is dressed in black. As he slips a throwing blade into his glove he wonders whether he can kill his own brother.

Scott approaches the Octagon. A ninja in a tree begins to slip a knife out of his tabi in preparation of using it against the intruder, only to have Scott sense his presence and kill him first. Once in the training compound, ninja appear from every direction. Wresting a sword away from one of his attackers Scott uses it to finish off the remaining attackers. Eventually Scott is outnumbered by black-clad ninja and taken to Seikura.

Holding A.J. hostage, Seikura makes Scott James "walk the path," an obstacle course not unlike the one the brothers mastered in the early years of their training. Only this time Scott must defeat numerous ninjutsu-trained attackers. When Scott kills all of Seikura's ninja, the black-robed ninja appears. Although Scott wins, he does not kill the ninja, and the downed ninja throws a knife into Scott's shoulder. When Scott kills the defeated ninja, Seikura has A.J. killed.

Seikura calls upon more of his henchmen for help in the brothers' final confrontation. In a strange turn of events, the trainees at the camp who are watching the duel accuse Seikura of being a coward. While Scott and Seikura settle their personal score with one another, the recruits destroy the Octagon. Aura arrives with grenades and a truck full of gasoline to be used as a car bomb.

As the Octagon explodes and burns, Scott and Seikura clash in a spectacular martial arts finale. The two men are well matched, and when Seikura does not meet with an early victory he "vanishes." Against a backdrop of the rising sun, Seikura creeps up on Scott from behind. But as he attacks he impales himself on Scott's sword.

The Image of the Ninja-Terrorist

There can be little doubt that The Octagon paints a highly negative picture of the ninja. They exist as a training body for international terrorists as well as an independent force meting out their own savage judgment on those they feel have broken the code or threaten their operations. Again we meet the familiar "good" versus "evil" theme as Scott James has given up fighting while his brother trains terrorists.

But the "evilness" of the ninja builds as the film progresses. Despite the fact that the recruits are themselves terrorists, they are treated brutally, even killed. It is as if the ninja are far worse than the worst of the world's murdering fanatics. Certainly the assassinations committed by the ninja are pure violence. Interestingly, one of Seikura's chief instructors is dressed in black robes, and with his armored face mask, chest plate, and pained breathing is clearly a clone of Darth Vader, the Jedi knight of Star Wars fame who followed the "dark path." In the end the depths of the ninja's evil is seen by the terrorist trainees who accuse Seikura of being a coward, and then rebel against their instructors.

The image of the ninja as ruthless assassins, terrorists, and murderers is underlined in *The Octagon*. Scott James, the "good" brother, together with a woman who has "seen the light," attacks and destroys the ninja camp. Good defeats evil. The "good" karatedo-trained samurai, Western and blonde-haired, single-handedly wins out over the "evil," and more powerful, Oriental ninja.

If *The Octagon* achieves anything, it is firmly establishing in our minds the evil nature of ninjutsu. Needless to say, this image of the ninja is a stereotyped fantasy of Hollywood, very inaccurate and one-sided. Again, if we are to see through to the real essence of the ninja symbol we must recognize the distorted images put forth in the media, and resist the temptation to take at face value the visual image.

Nine Deaths of the Ninja: No Compassion

Nine Deaths of the Ninja, starring Sho Kosugi, Brent Huff, and Emilia Lesniak, furthers the highly negative image of the ninja.

Compassion, perhaps the most human of emotions, is regarded by the ninja master in this film as an emotion a ninja must not have. Since Spike had "too much" of it he had to be denied further training. Hence there emerges the image of the ninja as lacking all feeling, particularly all warm feelings for other living beings. To underline this point, the ninja appear in the film as the "defenders" of the terrorists who are clearly sociopathic and drug-psychotic megalomaniacs.

Of all the films mentioned, this one is perhaps the most poorly made. It is not worth going into detail about this movie; the timeworn Hollywood plot, minimal direction, complete lack of character development, ubiquitous poor acting, and absence of any creativity tarnishes the image of the ninja. In essence, the shinobi warriors of ancient Japan become reduced to seedy comic book dimensions without even the entertainment value of the other films. To any genuine practitioner of the art this type of presentation is an insult.

Ninja IV: The Master

A discussion of the ninja as they are portrayed on the screen would not be complete without a brief mention of *The Master*, the prime-time television program about a ninja Master and his student. Currently two of the episodes, "High Rollers" and "The Good, the Bad, and the Priceless" are distributed by Transworld Entertainment in a videocassette entitled *Ninja IV: The Master*. More are apparently scheduled for release in the future. Although *The Master* did not do particularly well in the Nielsen ratings and was canceled after only one season, its influence was felt in the shaping of the stereotyped image of the ninja from Hollywood.

In a recent interview, Sho Kosugi noted that one of the reasons *The Master* failed to satisfy the public, despite the current ninja craze, was that the stories were "corny" (Gort, 1985). Unlike the excellent **Kung-Fu** series (which lives on in syndication), *The Master*, Kosugi felt, failed to stir up a sense of mystery. The writers refused to focus on what it meant to be a ninja, the practitioner of a little-known martial art, and instead repackaged typical and timeworn Hollywood stories, but with a touch of ninjutsu thrown in. Consequently, the image of the ninja was largely unaltered by *The Master*. A little-watched program, it quickly slipped from the public's awareness when canceled.

In some ways this was a pity, for *The Master* certainly offered the most human, and most plausible, portrayal of a ninja master. The writers' intent was to paint a picture of a man whose goal was to enlighten his student, rather than turn him into a super martial artist. Emotional maturity and control were far more important than brilliant feats. The producers, however, concentrated on the brilliant feats and left credibility, it seems, on the cutting room floor.

At the same time, rather than being sociopathic, the Master and his student were the sworn opponents of sociopathy. They evoked the well-known stereotype of the misunderstood vigilante. What is more, although decidedly paternalistic, *The Master* was certainly not misogynist. In short, then, the image was considerably more human and less negative than many of the images created on the wide screen.

As with many criticisms made of the ninja films, it is unwillingness to portray anything of the reality that brought about the downfall of *The Master*. It seems inevitable that Hollywood only rarely makes an attempt to reflect reality, preferring to create its own interpretations of various traditions. This is ironic, though, since Hollywood has been in existence but for a fraction of the time that the ninjutsu tradition has. And yet it is Hollywood that so arrogantly seeks to manipulate "what is."

In Conclusion

In conclusion, we see that the screen image of the ninja is by and large superficial. Ninja tradition is laid aside, and peculiar mixtures of martial arts lore are passed off as ninjutsu's secrets. Genuine ninjutsu also makes no appearance in ninja films; instead, the hard martial arts take center stage. After all, the ninja have come to epitomize harshness and strength on the screen, and the portrayal of a relaxed martial art would threaten this.

Martial arts movies have by and large never been profound. They have existed simply as entertaining displays of physical brilliance. And it is this tradition into which the ninja have fallen. Perhaps one day a director will take up the challenge of representing the unique aspects of ninjutsu on the screen and, with integrity, attempt to give the audience a more truthful glimpse of the 900-year heritage of ninjutsu. It is unlikely, but hopefully not impossible.

2

Ninjutsu in the Martial Arts Arena

"The thing I cannot understand is why students are willing to believe in, and pay money to, a teacher who has no credentials, no evidence of any connection with a recognized master teacher of the art, and who is a living contradiction to everything that has ever been written about the authentic art and its legitimate teachers."— **—Stephen K. Hayes** (1984a)

"Recent trends in the Western world have . . . attempted to portray the ninja as mere technicians of violence who feel justified in supporting any cause for the right amount of money or power."—**Dr. Masaaki Hatsumi** (1981)

"Without the proper frame of mind, continuous exposure to fighting techniques can lead to ruin instead of self-development."—**Toshitsugu Takamatsu**

As WE SAW in Chapter 1, the images of the ninja in current films tend to be amalgams of various stereotypes quite familiar to us in the West. Consequently we get a variety of images of the ninja and ninjutsu: "good" and "bad" ninjas, the super martial artist, ninja ritual, the fantasy representation of mysticism or the supernatural in ninjutsu, as well as many others.

However, within the martial arts arena the image of the ninja is fairly uniform. In essence the ninja represents "aggression and violence," and there is very little emphasis on other aspects of ninjutsu. In fact, so uniform is this portrayal that this chapter will be short, since there is no richness or diversity in the image. Clearly this entirely one-dimensional interpretation of what the ninja really are is very appealing to a great many people. However, as we shall see in Chapter 4 when we consider the image of the ninja as depicted in the historical sources, neither Dr. Masaaki Hatsumi, the 34th Grandmaster of Togakure-ryu Ninjutsu, nor Shidoshi Stephen K. Hayes, the foremost authority on ninjutsu in the West, consider ninjutsu to be a "tradition of violence" or "path of aggression." Indeed, as we shall soon discover, the ninja as the "embodiment of aggression" is not only a greatly oversimplified image, but a grossly distorted one as well.

Violence, Aggression, and the Path

There is little doubt that the image of the ninja as quintessential violence is inaccurate. However, we must be careful that the aggressive side of the image is not discarded and ignored. At the Fifth Annual Shadows of Iga Ninja Festival, held in May 1985, Jack Hoban asked for a show of hands in response to his question as to how many of the participants had initially been attracted to the ninja because they were "assassins" and "super martial artists." Many hands went up, *even though most people had since learned that ninjutsu was infinitely more than ritualized aggression, and the real essence of ninjutsu was something else altogether.* The point is this: were many of the participants not attracted to this aspect of the image, further exploration of the ninja tradition may have never gotten off the ground.

This was an important observation. So often "aggression" is viewed in a highly negative light and expelled from our lives. It is rarely explored, and rarely followed to see where it might lead us. However, as those involved in the martial arts are very aware, highly aggressive people can learn to "tame" this side of themselves through diligent training. By allowing this side of themselves to exist, and finding ways to express it, their aggression is transcended. It can lead to inner discipline, to increased self-esteem, even to the spiritual search. We shall have more to say about this in Chapter 5 when we consider the Shadow, the "dark side" of our personalities.

Although "ninja = aggression" is a highly problematical pairing on any number of levels, it is a factor in the image of the ninja as it is presented in the West. If this is what attracts us to ninjutsu then it is crucial we realize that this is not altogether bad. Provided we follow through with this aspect of ourselves, explore it, and work with it, then there is the possibility of glimpsing what is deeper and more meaningful in the image. At the same time, we must also understand that the aggressiveness we are attracted to is *something in us*, something in our culture, something we have "put into" the image of the ninja. When we can realize this to be the reality of the ninja, their secret fighting art becomes infinitely more accessible.

Hence "aggression" and "violence" are often "doorways to the Path"—the path to deeper knowledge of ourselves and higher states of awareness. "Aggression" and "violence" may not be the prettiest of doorways, but they may be the only doorways some people have. Therefore this chapter seeks to look at the "aggressive ninja image" not to condemn it, but to explore it. At the same time we indulge in this perceived attraction to aggression, we will also make clear where this image can lead us astray. Hence, we shall always look toward the most accurate image of the ninja, that which is painted by historical sources (see Chapter 4). Put otherwise, we shall always be looking through or beyond aggression and violence to the Path.

Of Aggression, Violence, and the Ninja in the West

Before we look deeper into the image of the ninja as it is presented in the martial arts world there is another important question that needs to be dealt with. Why is it that ninjutsu has remained associated with violence and aggression for so many years, whereas traditions such as karate-do and kung-fu seem to have freed themselves from this negative label, and may even be regarded as traditions that "promote discipline"?

The answer would seem to lie in the limited opportunity for

authentic ninjutsu training in the West. To explain further, most of the other martial arts were regarded as violent when they were first introduced to the Western world. Since we did not have any martial traditions of this sort, many people had difficulty understanding why someone would want to learn how to be a "fighter." But as training in karate-do, judo, kung-fu, aikido, and other traditions became increasingly popular and available, most people began to see that there was more to these combat systems than the promotion of violence and aggression. Indeed, the discipline required to master these arts usually meant that either an aggressive person was transformed, and became less "aggressive," or that aggressive people wanted nothing to do with the difficult training.

But this has not happened with ninjutsu. If you are interested in studying genuine ninjutsu you must be prepared to travel hundreds, even thousands, of miles to receive the training. Most people are not prepared to do this. The result is that ninjutsu is never seen by the vast majority of martial artists, nor by the public, as a tradition that has any discipline, or any transformative power. When someone sees a film about the ninja, or hears about someone throwing shuriken and practicing with "chains," they immediately think the worst. And the problem is, unlike other martial arts, there is usually no one there to explain what is genuine ninjutsu, or to explain the philosophy behind weapons training.

The misunderstanding about the use of weapons, in particular, is one factor that maintains the "ninja aggression" equation. The fact that many so-called ninja weapons are readily available to people, coupled with the general lack of genuine ninjutsu teachers in the U.S., leads to a situation wherein the true spirit of weapons training is lost. Consequently, few realize that weapons training is a very powerful way of working with, and overcoming, fear—essential if you are to survive an attack on the streets. And few see the awareness of the physical movements of the body and the "extension of the body" as an awareness with any value.

And the result is obvious. Not only do many people regard ninjutsu as nothing more than a violent tradition, but many unqualified and bogus "ninja masters" have appeared on the scene to reap the financial rewards from the current interest in the ninja. But one way people can protect themselves from this is to understand deeply what image of the ninja is being sold in the martial arts arena, a task to which we will now turn.

Weapons, So-Called Ninja Weapons, and More Weapons

Open any martial arts magazine today and you will see scores of advertisements for ninja weapons. Most popular are, not surprisingly, throwing stars, or shuriken as they are traditionally referred to. Ninja swords are also very popular. Then follow "ninja blowguns," "ninja tantos," "ninja black wood nunchakus," "ninja kamas," "ninja fighting chains," "ninja walking sticks" (with hidden blades), "ninja hook knives," "ninja blinding powders," "ninja throwing spikes," "ninja caltrops," "ninja smoke bombs," "ninja blade butterfly knives," "ninja hidden katanas," and many more. There are even "ninja key chains" on the market! So enthused are a great many people that all a martial arts equipment distributor need do is preface a weapon with "ninja" and it sells.

It goes without saying that the American public has been captivated by some of the exotic weapons attributed to the ninja. So much so, in fact, that many of the leading martial arts magazines are currently supported largely through mail-order companies specializing in "ninja

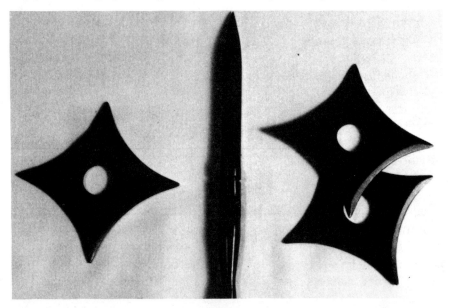

gear." Indeed, the "ninja weapons industry" currently grosses some $70 *million* each year! What is more, there is now a demand for specialists to "design (new) ninja weapons"!

Accompanying this tremendous availability of weapons are numerous "instruction manuals." Again, not surprisingly, throwing star manuals are by far the most prevalent. "Official ninja throwing star manuals," claiming to demonstrate the authentic "ninja grips" and "ninja stances," and usually accompanied by illustrations of a "genuine ninja star," fill many columns in today's martial arts magazines.

If we needed confirmation that the "ninja aggression" image is a popular one, this is it. What is particularly interesting is that it is so popular that people are willing to buy poorly made equipment, fake equipment, and fantasy instructional manuals rather than explore the

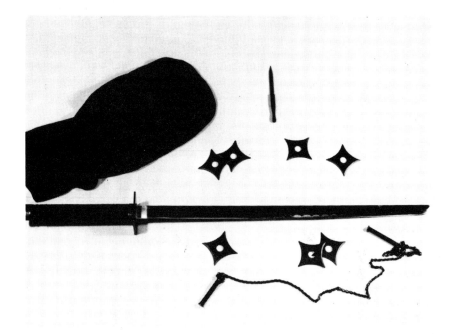

ninja deeper and discover what is real and what is fake. It is almost as if the ninja are simply a way to indulge in aggression, there being no genuine interest in the ninja apart from the "aggression connection" which has been created in the West.

Ninjutsu as "Weapon-Wielding Violence"

It is hard to imagine a ninja without a small arsenal of weapons hidden about his body. Ninja are *always* armed with deadly weapons, blades sharpened to a razor's edge, ever ready to attack, brandishing a throwing star, knife, or concealed sword.

Where does this image come from? It comes from the way many people in the martial arts community have chosen to represent the ninja—especially the training equipment companies. Why? *Because it sells.* As we noted earlier, many people are attracted to the ninja because they associate the shinobi warriors of ancient Japan with aggression and violence. Ninja weapons sales in the West are simply the commercial reflection of this side of the image. The end result is an image that is constantly reinforced—that of the ninja and their weapons. Indeed, if anyone coming to the martial arts world afresh were to glance through several martial arts magazines it would not take long for even the most critically thinking person to give way to the bombardment of advertisements painting the ninja as weapons addicts. It is not surprising, therefore, that many less critical people simply accept this image as "factual." Hence: ninja = violence.

What is remarkable is that many accept this image without any regard for its authenticity. Although it might be possible for a group of families to survive for over 900 years simply by brute force, it seems highly unlikely. But there is so much "indulgence" in the violence attributed to the ninja that little thinking goes on about who they really were. Part of the reason so many may latch onto this association may derive from the lack of parallel traditions in the West. Those who carry weapons are, often, violent. Certainly the military's image was permanently scarred after Viet Nam. Police misuse of weapons and authority, although hardly epidemic, is overpublicized whenever it occurs. And with the current rise in international terrorism flashed on our television screens almost daily the link is forged between "those who carry weapons" and "violence." But if we are truly interested in the ninja we must fight back the tendency to oversimplify, the tendency to simply slip the ninja into one of our categories for seeing the world.

Perhaps, also, if the U.S. had a greater sense of history this unfortunate association would be less pervasive and tenacious. Without it the ninja do not get placed against an historical context. Most people do not see them as living day in and day out in a political structure. They do not see them in an environment. Instead, the image of the ninja floats free of grounded reality. Whereas a ninja in feudal Japan would have to be careful about the way he was seen, what weapons he might have, etc., our image of the ninja is able to wear

black night-suits at all times, carry small arsenals of weapons, and act, usually violently, at will. Hence, it seems for any number of reasons, we are destined to endure a badly distorted and poorly understood ninja in the West—at least for the time being.

The "Deadly" Ninja

If we recall from our discussion of the image of the ninja as represented in the movies, the visual image is perhaps the most powerful one. What is seen in the advertisements tends to "carry more weight" than what may be heard or read about. Another way in which the "ninja = violence" image is perpetuated is in the way ninja articles are presented in various magazines.

Following on from the weapons advertisements, it is only logical that many of the most popular articles written about the ninja focus on the weapons. And here something very interesting happens. Almost always an article about an authentic, or so-called, ninja weapon will be prefaced by "deadly," or another similar word. We find "The *Deadly* Shuriken," "The *Deadly* (or *Lethal*) Art of Knife Throwing," "The Chain of *Death*," "Darts of *Death*," "*Deadly* Blades," and "The *Deadly* and Exotic Weapons of the Ninja."

What is even more interesting, as numerous editors of martial arts magazines have told me, is that although a magazine does not necessarily ascribe to this image of the ninja, and although the principal ninjutsu writers may not be advocating this view, it is necessary to title articles in this way to sell the magazine. Put otherwise, people have an image of the ninja which is *fixed*. They *want* to see the ninja as deadly assassins and masters of lethal bladed weapons. They are *not* interested in images that challenge this ideal. Again we come back to the idea that many people are attracted to aggression and violence—and by equating the ninja with these two human attributes this attraction is somehow satisfied.

This leads us to a rather puzzling paradox. As mentioned earlier, ninjutsu can remain "violent" in many people's fantasies because there are not enough practitioners around who can accurately present and teach the discipline and reality of the art. In other words, there are not enough "genuine ninja martial artists" around. The result, ironically, is that martial arts magazines are caught in perpetuating an image that has not been brought down to reality by "martial arts training!"

Here, then, is yet another area in which the image of the ninja can float free from reality. Anyone who has trained in karate-do, kung-fu, aikido, judo, or other reasonably available martial arts soon discovers that what is seen on the screen in Bruce Lee or Chuck Norris films is highly dramatized. Actually training in these traditions is a very

different matter involving dedication, perseverance, frustration, and ultimately transformation. Certainly there are many people who still have highly fantasized images of the martial arts in general, but a significant proportion of people have tied those images to the reality of the dojo training hall.

But the ninja with their secret combat art are, in image form, untempered by the hard knocks and grounding realizations of the dojo and the time it takes to gain proficiency in the system. In a sense, the "image" is unexperienced. And certainly by being ungrounded the image cannot "mature" in any sense of the word. The ninja as weapon-wielding masters of death seems destined, therefore, to live on for some time in this immature, and, quite frankly, childish way.

The Terrorist Ninja

Perhaps the most disturbing image of the ninja perpetuated in the martial arts world is that of the "terrorist ninja." By and large the ninja of Hollywood wear the "traditional" mask which leaves a strip open for the eyes. As we shall see in the next two chapters, the image of the ninja in fiction and from the historical tradition, tend to deemphasize the use of the mask. (Indeed, as Hayes has pointed out, the idea that the ninja wore black masks derives from the *Kabaki* plays of Tokugawa, Japan, not from reality.) But some unqualified ninjutsu writers have chosen to portray the ninja as wearing a "terrorist hood"—the black ski mask with two holes for eyes so well known to us from the many hostage situations of recent years. Not only does this distort the history of ninjutsu, but it also paints the ninja in a decidedly negative light—as terrorists.

Immediately scenes of Munich, Beirut, and Libya flash before our eyes. Brutal murders of passengers waiting to board airplanes, the smoldering remains of buildings that have been car-bombed, and political assassinations and executions also come to mind. Only a few sociopathic individuals find anything positive in these scenes. The vast majority of people are appalled and sickened by such blatant disregard for life. And it is this image to which some writers have wedded the ninja.

Again we must bear in mind the power of the visual image. Regardless of what is said in a book or article on the ninja it is the visual image which has the most powerful impact and which is remembered the longest. What is more, any person who picks up a ninja book, flips through it, sees the ninja portrayed as terrorists, and never looks into the ninja tradition in any greater depth *can only be left with* the idea that the ninja wear black ski masks.

Some writers even connect the ninja tradition directly with terrorism. "Ninjutsu," in some broad use of the term, is painted as currently involving skyjacking, hideous punji pits, deadly booby traps, the famous Molotov cocktails, letter bombs, car and truck bombs, terrorism in general, etc. It is astounding that this relationship is forged so strongly by various authors and teachers, particularly since the reality is altogether different. It seems some are almost fanatic in their desire to downtrod the image of the ninja.

Violence: Ninja Style

Not surprisingly, those who choose to paint the ninja in black ski masks fill their articles and books with numerous ways to cause pain and death to your opponent. There are instructions for how to bring unconsciousness to a guard by blocking the air in the windpipe, for how to break your enemy's neck, and for how to hide a body. There are also lists of "assassination options" to be considered when using a knife—with suitably violent names such as "slitting the throat," "kidney thrust," "subclavian artery thrust," "jugular thrust," and "the heart thrust." Each is naturally accompanied by detailed instructions and photographs. Specific times are also given for how long it would take to bring unconsciousness or death to an enemy with varieties of the "Japanese strangle."

So-called secret ninja lore also creeps into such publications. Readers are taught the "laws of the death touch" whereby death might even be caused with no physical contact with the enemy! The "*Nien Jih Ssu Ch'u Chueh*" is supposedly a highly specialized method of killing with origins in China. It is translated by one author as "Ninja Death Touch" and it is claimed that three aspects of it must be mastered ("the three ways"): Dim *Ching* (attacking nerves of the body), Dim *Hsueh* (striking blood vessels), and Dim *Mak* (using acupuncture alarm points on the body). The actual application of the "death touch" is executed by the "hidden hand system" with nine forms—each with yet another *Chinese* name: *Ch'ien Ch'uan* (forefist), *Tsai Ch'uan* (backfist), *Ch'ui Ch'uan* (hammer fist), *Chang Ken* (palm heel), *Pien Chang* (side palm), *Hsi Chang* (sucking palm), *Tao Shou* (sword hand), *Mao Shou* (spear hand), and *Chen Chih* (needle finger). In keeping with the nine hand positions are nine

"fatal blows"—"The Nine Fatal Blows of the *Dim Mak* Way": *Hsin Chuan* (heart punch), *Fei Chuan* (lung punch), *Shen Chuan* (kidney punch), *Hsueh K'u Chuan* (spleen punch), *P'ang Kuang Chuan* (bladder punch), *Kan Chuan* (liver punch), *Te Ch'ang Chuan* (small intestine punch), *Ta Ch'ang Chuan* (large intestine punch), and *We Chuan* (stomach punch). Readers are also given exercises to test their knowledge of the "death touch," although they are warned not to try it until they have studied ninjutsu for ten years or more! Hence the reader is empowered with "the power of life and death."

The tremendous potential for activating the violent aspect of weapons is also exploited in this type of material. Consider descriptions of using "the hook knife" as a means of "slashing the enemy to ribbons" or "slashing the cartoid artery," using the "*Shinobi Zue* Lead Weight" to "beat the enemy senseless" or clubbing the enemy into submission, and using "*tonki*" (edged throwing weapons) which "dig into the enemy's neck" or "drive into the base of the enemy's skull."

The "Chan Sheng" or "Rope of War" is, in this type of presentation, an excellent tool for stopping the flow of blood to the brain.

Finally the ninja themselves are described in blatantly aggressive terms. Ninjutsu is portrayed as the "most savage and terrifying martial art known to man" and an "unholy science." The ninja are therefore seen as characteristically "ruthless." Their "kata dan'te" or "dance of the deadly hands" results in eyes being slashed, lips and cheeks being "ripped" off the face, even the whole face being removed from the skull. Snapping the neck is thrown in, as is encouragement to gouge out an opponent's eyes with your fingertips! And in case the enemy is still struggling, methods for "crushing" the sternum, "crushing" the medulla at the base of the skull, "severing" the spinal cord, "crushing" the chest, and "cracking" the forehead open are all described in

detail. All of this violent destructiveness is also meant to occur in a scant four or five seconds!

To look through the catalogs of certain mail-order publishers is an eye-opening experience. The titles and descriptions of these books are shocking, leaving one to wonder if it is even legal to write such books, let alone sell them. But these publishers are cashing in on a certain market that wants to read about how to kill and maim.

Although much of this seems blatantly absurd, there is no doubt that this way of depicting the ninja has added to the overall impression that the ninja are nothing but terrorists, scum, and villains. As we shall see shortly, this means of presenting the ninja is not only negative, but also grossly inaccurate and very far from the true essence of ninjutsu. However, to repeat again, this image of the ninja is a popular one, and one many people want to see. People are, in fact, so enthralled with this image that they make bestsellers out of this type of material, thereby encouraging more of it to be written, published, and distributed. It is, as will be very clear in Chapter 4, *extraordinarily misleading*.

Bogus Ninjutsu

Certainly the martial arts world is flooded with "sources" that consider the ninja as nothing more than thugs with a rather flamboyant means of destroying people, a means known as ninjutsu. But there is another very distorted image of the ninja on the "martial arts market." It is the image of the art as portrayed not by genuine practitioners, but by practitioners of other traditions who don a shinobi shozoku, hoping to make a fast buck as ninjamania sweeps the country. Sadly there are all too many of these bogus ninja instructors. As Stephen K. Hayes once noted, not only do these con artists take advantage of young people's genuine interest in ninjutsu to operate their schemes, but they are often teaching ineffective defensive techniques that could result in serious injury or death if ever a student were to attempt to use them.

Anyone can pose as a "ninja master." And there will be no one to refute the claim. What is more, editors of martial arts magazines are placed in the same position as the public—who is, and who is not, a ninja? Not only are bogus ninja selling ninjutsu throughout the U.S., but these charlatans are also passing themselves off as certified instructors and masters through the media.

Obviously the easiest thing for a person wishing to pose as a ninja to do is to use whatever system he has been trained in, but perform it in a black gi. Instant ninja! In articles that appear in the martial arts media all that is required is to throw in some drama and that person is a ninja instructor. It is as simple as that, and a disturbingly large number of people have risen (or sunk) to the occasion.

What does this do to the image of the ninja? First and foremost it trivializes it and strips it from its genuine historical and traditional

roots. In fact, since many people are taken in by the rather large number of inauthentic ninja teachers, it subtly, sometimes perma- nently, warps people's impressions of the art. One of the easiest ways to determine whether it is genuine ninjutsu you are witnessing, or fake ninjutsu, is to see whether the practitioners are tense or relaxed, "hard" or "soft." It comes as a bitter disappointment to many to learn that ninjutsu is not "karate-plus." It is not an even harder martial art than the hardest traditions currently practiced. Rather, it is a system that emphasizes relaxation and subtlety. Dramatic spinning kicks and cocked arms look impressive on the screen and in the media, they epitomize what we have come to identify with the master martial artist, but they are not always as effective as they look, and they are not *ipso facto* ninjutsu.

Worse, though, than the obfuscation of the genuine form is the fact that it is usually inexperienced and lower-level practitioners of other traditions who pass themselves off as genuine ninjutsu instructors. The terrible result is that persons who would be very poor representatives of judo, karate-do, tae kwon do, or aikido are able to be sensational representatives of (bogus) ninjutsu. A true practitioner, say of karate, who had honestly integrated the samurai values of such an art, would *never dishonestly claim to be something that he was not*. Were a karateka wishing to learn ninjutsu, he would approach it with *integrity*, and begin at the beginning.

Such a person would, in actuality, have to unlearn a tremendous amount before he could begin to practice ninjutsu correctly, let alone teach it. Hence, we see what a distorted image of the ninja certain persons are creating, and what *type of people* are propagating such images. It is no wonder that the ninja are so misunderstood and that there is so much confusion in the martial arts field.

The "Unimpressive" Ninja

Some writers have taken a different tack to becoming authorities on ninjutsu. Here the strategy is to discredit something that is appropriately attributed to the ninja, note that others have developed the "same thing," and then go on to authoritatively write about whatever it is they want to write about by stripping the ninja of their legitimate claim to it. Inevitably there is a subtle bending of logic to achieve this.

A good example is a discussion of ninja stealth techniques by one writer. The author begins by noting that the origins of ninjutsu are vague "at best." He mentions a few possible beginning points but does not go on to discuss or review the many genuine sources of information available to us now (e.g., Hatsumi, 1981; Hayes, 1980, 1981a, etc.). He leaves the reader with the impression that since "no one" knows of the origins of ninjutsu *his view is as legitimate as any other*.

What is rather disturbing is that many people accept this! Again we see that a general lack of appreciation of history can stand in the way of understanding ninjutsu. The idea of the ninja "shrouded in the mists of time" is attractive. But it is nonsense. There is an accessible authority on the subject: Dr. Masaaki Hatsumi, the *only surviving*

Grandmaster of ninjutsu. To those unfamiliar with how these things are proven, each Grandmaster passed his scroll onto his successor. Those who could find no successor either gave their scrolls to another living Grandmaster, or destroyed them. Dr. *Hatsumi is the only possessor of such scrolls.*

It is, therefore, with a tremendous disregard for the historical traditions, as well as integrity, that certain writers proceed to establish their authority in ninjutsu. Their disrespect for Dr. Hatsumi and his various ranking personal students in the West, such as Shidoshi Stephen K. Hayes, Jack Hoban, and Bud Malmstrom, should in itself discredit their authority. Unfortunately, in our culture where image is more important than substance, this does not always occur.

This particular author next claims that saying that the ninja invented stealth is similar to saying brand name sports shoe companies invented running. He supports this by noting that many animals are "stealthy" and that many people have used camouflage. His crowning argument is that Mother Nature is the only one that can be credited with such skill!

Whatever "logic" there may be to such arguments fortunately fades in the face of the simple intuitive sense that there is something wrong with this approach to understanding anything. American Indians may never be credited, whatever that means, with skills in tracking and archery because animals have tracked for many thousands of years before man or because other peoples have developed the bow and arrow, also. But the Indians will *always* be associated with these skills, *because they developed them to such high levels of proficiency.* The Swiss may never be credited with inventing watches, but they are regarded as perhaps the finest watchmakers in the world.

And so it is with the ninja. The ninja families survived for as long as they did *because the skills they developed were so advanced and so highly perfected that they ensured the art's survival and success.* It will always be true that "there is nothing new under the sun" and that "everyone has said everything"—but certain people and certain groups take "something ordinary" and plumb its depths, while others explore and fully develop particular ideas.

To say that the ninja cannot be credited with "the skill of stealth" is to split hairs. The truth of the matter is that "the skill of stealth" *is* "credited" to them because they perfected it. *No other group of people has made such a precise science out of it, nor has any other group developed a reputation for such skill.*

Again we need to bear in mind that such writers make these types of arguments not for the sake of clarifying our understanding of the ninja, but to confuse it. Their goal is to confuse it to such a degree that they can pass themselves off as authorities on the subject and, most important, *make money doing so.* Logic supported by this type of intention can only buckle under close scrutiny. This is one of the reasons we are scrutinizing it here.

When we realize all of this, it becomes clear that if there are "real ninja," and they are the possessors of such knowledge, then we *must* find genuine ninjutsu instructors if we are to develop such skills. We must be exceedingly careful who it is we entrust ourselves to in order to learn ninjutsu. Genuine instructors do exist, but as we have said all along, they are few and far between. For the interested reader, training information is available at the end of the book.

The "Outdated" Ninja

There is another tactic that some writers take to discredit the genuine ninjutsu tradition and credit themselves. This tactic involves arguing that "ninjutsu is outdated." Again, as we shall see, twists of logic, and avoiding any in-depth discussion, are the methods employed for accomplishing this end. Fortunately these arguments also crumble under close scrutiny.

One author deplores the large numbers of books and articles about ninjutsu which advocate many techniques and stances that are mismatched with the realities of the twentieth century. He notes that a sideways handspring may be an appropriate and effective escape technique from an armor-clad samurai, but ineffective as a means of escaping from a speeding car. This writer then uses an example of evolution in the animal kingdom as a parallel to 'how things become outdated and ineffectual.

Ironically, and rather humorously, too, the example he uses does not apply to the point he is trying to make! The animals in question, his example of animals without effective camouflage and appropriate feeding habits, *have not died out!*

Although the example of the handspring is a direct reference to Hayes (see Hayes, 1981, pp. 54–57) it is only successful if one has not worked within the genuine system of ninjutsu. The truth is that if one has trained well in handsprings, and can react with a handspring instantaneously, then it is an effective means of escape, even from a speeding car.

The motive of this writer should be clear. He is making the argument that ninjutsu is so wedded to the past that it is useless today unless it is "updated." He discredits genuine practitioners and teachers of the art, such as Shidoshi Stephen K. Hayes, through associating them with the "anachronistic art of ninjutsu." He then attempts to call upon scientific rationalism to back up his arguments. Again, when a writer sees it necessary to attack authentic teachers and students of the art it opens to question his own legitimacy.

Other writers *directly* put down authentic practitioners and instructors of ninjutsu as a means of establishing their credentials in the profitable world of ninjamania. One author writes about Dr. Masaaki Hatsumi's view of ninjutsu as simply "a pastime." He describes the 34th Grandmaster of Togakure-ryu Ninjutsu as an aging man who now practices ninjutsu with no speed, no power, no focus, no feeling, and no effort. Since he is in his fifties, everyone practices as if they were in their fifties. Rather than being "geared toward reality" and teaching a system aimed at survival, Dr. Hatsumi is portrayed as teaching a subtle, artistic, "Japanese version" (!) of ninjutsu. The Grandmaster is misquoted as saying that ninjutsu is just a martial art now, presumably like any other martial art.

In contrast to the Grandmaster who is involved in an "art" and a "pastime," the writer portrays himself as someone who trains police and military people ("real men") who do not want aesthetics but something that *works*, something that will help them *win in a confrontation*. His training is therefore more advanced and more realistic. It is Americanized and pragmatic. It is very different from the "Japanese version."

The aim of these approaches is only too clear. First, paint the Japanese version of ninjutsu as outdated and ineffective. The Japanese version? Obviously the author's intent is not only to discredit Dr. Hatsumi, but also to reject over 900 *years of ninja history and tradition!* Second, paint current American versions, primarily his own, of course, of ninjutsu as realistic, pragmatic, and aimed at survival. Realism, pragmatism, and survival have a long history of appeal for us in the U.S. and are well chosen adjectives to get his point across. And the conclusion is left for the reader to draw: the Japanese version is tied to a long-gone past and developing into a pleasant pastime involving no real effort, strength, or stamina, while (his) American version is rooted in the *present reality* and evolving into the *only means of surviving real-life confrontations.*

The "Japanese" vs. "American" Image of Ninjutsu

There is no disputing that when writers criticize ninjutsu as "unimpressive" or "outdated" yet another aspect of the image of the ninja is created. Here we have the development of "Japanese ninjutsu" and "American ninjutsu." One cannot help but note the almost schizophrenic nature of this division.

It is interesting to note that this somewhat intellectual division of the ninja tradition (for obvious purposes) really hides a familiar image we have already considered. If we look carefully we see that so-called American ninjutsu is, in fact, "*aggressive ninjutsu*," although it is hidden beneath other adjectives. "Pragmatism," "realism," and "more advanced" appeal to us in the West—*regardless of the accuracy of the statements*—but ultimately they appeal to our desire to see the ninja as violent practitioners of an esoteric form of ritualized aggression.

What is new to our collection of "ninja images" is "Japanese ninjutsu," as if there could really be anything *but* Japanese ninjutsu after 900-odd years of the tradition! Japanese ninjutsu, portrayed as a spineless pastime for aging men, is indeed a new formulation of the art of stealth. When viewed in this light it should be clear how ludicrous this image is.

What is vitally important for the person truly interested in ninjutsu to realize, however, is that this image is *created by certain persons for certain reasons*. And in commercial America there can be little doubt that money is behind it. Fortunately this image, quite simply, does not stand up to the acid test. Ninjutsu would never have been effective for the length of time it was were it nothing more than a pastime. What is more, authentic historical sources contradict such observations. Perhaps the simplest way of putting this into perspective is to ask: "Why even call these American forms of combat survival ninjutsu at all, if ninjutsu is in fact nothing but an outdated tradition?" We do not even need to answer this question.

Everyone's a Ninja

There is also a current fascination with recognizing every elite commando and paramilitary group as "ninja." Some writers, for example, present the "Wildcats," an elite Green Beret group, as ninja. Others present the followers of the Thugee religion in India ("Thugs") as ninja equivalents, as well as certain "guerrilla groups" during the

American Revolution! One author devotes an entire book to linking the Lin Kuei clan from China to the ninja of Japan. However, all of these pairings are misleading, and only further the already confusing picture of what is, and what is not, a ninja. And again we see the desire to attach the "ninja label" to traditions or groups with only superficial similarities in order to sell books.

There is a world of difference between the various groups that are now considered "hinja" and the genuine ninja families of Japan. This will become abundantly clear in Chapter 4 when we consider the historical sources. However, one point needs to be made. Just because there are similarities between traditions (and these similarities are almost always superficial) *does not mean that the two groups are identical.* True, a Volkswagen Beetle is a car, and so is a Mercedes Benz. Both are of German design. But anyone can quickly appreciate the difference between the two, despite their similarities. To confuse the two is to make a serious error of judgment and logic. More than likely when this same degree of objectivity has developed with regard to ninjutsu the differentiation between what is genuine ninjutsu and what is bogus ninjutsu can be as easily made.

Emphasis on Technique

As we will see in Chapter 4, ninjutsu, or nin-po as it is known in its higher order, is more than a combat method. At the risk of oversimplifying, it is a *way of life* that encompasses philosophy, spirituality, medicine, health, etc. However, the martial arts world is focused primarily upon techniques. Hence, when articles are published about ninjutsu, they tend to emphasize the technical aspect of the system. What is more, those who have not been trained in genuine ninjutsu know almost nothing about its deeper aspects and higher levels of awareness.

The result is that ninjutsu is reduced to one aspect of its totality, one which itself is distorted by bogus instructors. What this does to the image of the ninja is to reduce it to its most fundamental physical facet and then emphasize this aspect, which, though important, is probably not the cornerstone of genuine ninjutsu. Technique is technique. It is lifeless, and ultimately useless, when employed by a person without a proper attitude toward the tradition.

Kunoichi: Female Ninja

Another fascinating focus of the martial arts world is the *kunoichi*, the woman ninja. Although the image of the ninja in the martial arts arena is primarily that of the "aggressive ninja," discussions of kunoichi do allow the fusing of sex and aggression we saw very clearly in the screen image of the ninja. There is frequent talk of how the kunoichi were able to go unsuspected where their male counterparts could not. Inevitably there is mention of sexual relations with the enemy as a means of securing vital intelligence information, or as a means of assassination.

What is different about this image is that rather than the male ninja attacking women, we now see women ninja killing men. But the root fascination is the same: violence and sex are mixed together. This is a preoccupation of our culture, and a problematical one at that. What is important for us to realize is that this is a Western concern that is projected onto the Eastern tradition of ninjutsu. Just because we associate it with the ninja does not mean that it is inherently a part of the ninja way of life. It is not "reality" but "image."

Signs of Change

It was inevitable that ninjutsu would enter Western culture through the vehicle of the martial arts. In this chapter we have seen many of the problems that have been created during this passage. However, the situation is not as hopeless as it might sound for the person genuinely interested in discovering more about ninjutsu. In fact there seem to be important chances occurring to correct some of the misrepresentation and distortion that has gone on.

In addition to the fact that the historical sources are widely sold in martial arts stores, and advertised in martial arts magazines, several high-ranking, fully licensed ninjutsu practitioners are now writing regularly in a number of magazines. Foremost among them is Shidoshi Stephen K. Hayes who, in addition to running regular articles, often answers readers' questions about the ninja. Two of Shidoshi Hayes's most advanced students, Bud Malmstrom and Jack Hoban, have also begun writing regularly. It goes without saying that as more people become involved in the study of genuine ninjutsu, there will be more and more writers who are qualified to write accurately about the tradition.

So the person curious about the ninja who is getting his information within the martial arts arena is not at a loss. Good, accurate, and genuine information is available. Of course, the next step for the ninja enthusiast is to follow through with that interest and move beyond the image of the ninja as it is portrayed in the martial arts world and discover the reality of the ninja through actual involvement in the tradition. This type of person is referred to the Afterword at the end of the book, which outlines training opportunities.

3

Fictional Accounts of the Ninja

"[Art] and ideas come out of the passion and torment of experience; it is impossible to have a real relationship to the first if one's aim is to be protected from the second."—**James Baldwin** (1972)

"There is no such thing as a moral or immoral book. Books are well written, or badly written."—**Oscar Wilde**

"The creative mind plays with the object it loves."—**C. G. Jung** (1976)

Having looked at the image of the ninja as it is created and expressed through the film medium and in the martial arts arena, we now turn to the ninja as they are represented in fiction. Here we find a wide variety of images, depending upon the sophistication of the writer. There is "adolescent fiction" which reads something like a comic book, in which the image is essentially that which we encountered on the screen. Not surprisingly, the image here is very superficial, poorly researched, and aimed at nondiscriminating readers. There is also "ninja thriller fiction" which tends to recreate the aggressive ninja that we encountered in the martial arts arena. Finally, there is well-written fiction which adds something to our growing pantheon of ninja images. Here the ninja and their secret fighting art are placed against the historical and cultural backdrop of Japan. Here, too, the ninja become "personal," not just stereotypes.

Adolescent Fiction

With the ninja capturing the imagination of our culture, it is not surprising that there should be ninja fiction that is geared toward adolescents. Since they tend not to think in sophisticated terms, the images in these books are one-dimensional and predictable. Given this is a rather uninteresting portrayal of the ninja, this type of fiction will be looked at but briefly. We shall spend the most time on those works that are well written and that contribute something new.

In the U.S. the books that most represent this type of fiction are those by Katsumi Toda (1982, 1984a, 1984b). *Shadow of the Ninja* and *Revenge of the Shogun's Ninja* are simplistic yarns about ninja and samurai. They are as much picture books as they are storybooks, with profuse illustrations of weapons and shadowy ninja. Most curious is the fact that the ninja are not "good," but "evil"! At the end of the first book the ninja master falls off a rope bridge into an abyss, defeated by a samurai; the second book ends with the ninja master's death and with the rest of the ninja "fleeing for their lives."

In England this type of fiction is represented by "role-playing adventure games." "You are Avenger, a Ninja warrior trained in the Way of the Tiger, and outstanding master of the martial arts." *Avenger!*, *Assassin!*, and *Ursurper!* by Smith and Thompson (1985a, 1985b, forthcoming) are among these. Also profusely illustrated, this form of interactive fiction places the ninja in the same category as *Dungeons and Dragons*: interesting fantasy figures.

It goes without saying that these books are poorly researched and exist solely as entertainment. However, it should be noted that for many adolescents these books often lay down their first impressions of the ninja and first impressions are very difficult to change.

Fictional Masters of Aggression

In *Dragon Rising* the reader is invited to "enter a world of vengeance and gathering violence." The Ninja Master is a Western ninja who is going insane, and who, in his search for psychological well-being, leaves countless corpses behind him as the plot takes the reader into the steamy jungles of El Salvador. *Lion's Fire* takes the Ninja Master to the Middle East where the tension of this part of the world lends itself as a backdrop to continuing violence. The forthcoming *Serpent's Eye* and *Phoenix Sword* will complete "The Year of the Ninja Master" series.

These books by Barker (1985a, 1985b) are an odd mixture of pop-culture ninjutsu, martial arts, violent fantasy, and profoundly Western views. The ninja of these novels mirror, and bring to life, the image of the ninja as introduced in the martial arts arena. They are merely highly aggressive fiction that uses the ninja as a means to sell what is currently popular.

You Only Live Twice: Ninja-Trained 007

Moving now to better-written and more substantial fiction that includes the ninja, we turn to Ian Fleming's (1964) *You Only Live Twice*, the James Bond classic, and James Clavell's (1976) *Shogun*, both of which were made into films. Although the ninja are not central characters in either film, ninjutsu is placed against the backdrop of Japanese culture and history. Even more interesting is that both preceded the ninjamania of the 1980s.

In Fleming's (1964) novel, James Bond is given some training in ninjutsu to aid him in taking out his archenemy, Blofeld. The plot is different from the film, and it is ninjutsu that is meant to give Bond an edge in a highly dangerous situation that he faces alone. It is Tiger Tanaka, head of Japan's secret service, who introduces 007 to the ways of the ninja.

> **Synopsis:** Tiger reveals to the British agent that his "Central Mountaineering School" is, in reality, a ninja training camp. Ninjutsu, he says, is "the art of stealth or invisibility." His men have already graduated from

ten of the eighteen arts of bushido. They are now learning to be ninja, or "stealers-in." He notes that this has been an aspect of the basic training of spies, assassins, and saboteurs for centuries. Tiger dispels all of the myths about the ninja, except for their superhuman strength. However, he does add that the secrets of the ninja are still closely guarded. These secrets belong to two main ryu, which Fleming identifies as the Iga and (interestingly) Togakure schools, and it is from these traditions that he draws his instructors.

Bond is taken to the castle training camp. There he sees men dressed from head to foot in black. They "ski" across a moat with the use of interesting flotation devices and then, using climbing equipment, seem to run up the walls of the castle "like fast black spiders." When one man dies in the ascent, 007 is told that it is of no account. At the top of the wall there is a confrontation involving bojutsu staff fighting, every bit as fierce as if it were real.

Inside the castle Bond is led to a ninja museum. There he sees "spiked steel wheels," "chains with spiked steel weights at each end," hollow bamboo for breathing under water, brass knuckles, and "gloves whose palms were studded with very sharp, slightly hooked nails for 'walking' up walls and across ceilings." Bond considers these armaments as "primitive," and in comparison to Russian inventions, thinks that Tiger's ninjutsu is simply not in the same league. In response to Tiger's pride for his men Bond replies with appropriate grunts of approval.

After his training, Bond is given ninja clothing in preparation for his attack on Blofeld: a black suit for night, and a camouflage one for the day, both of which will give him "complete protection." Bond is also given a ninja chain. When he notes the absence of a good gun with a silencer, Tiger tells him to use ninjutsu. The art of stealth is the "only way."

Once Bond penetrates Blofeld's establishment he becomes a "shadow" in his "ghostly black uniform"; he is "black in the blackness." He quickly discovers that shinobi shozoku has many concealed pockets, and he likens it to a magician's tailcoat. Eventually he is caught by Blofeld's guards, caught in an ancient castle trap. His apparel is quickly identified as a ninja night suit. After informing Blofeld that ninjutsu is "the art of moving by stealth, of being invisible, of killing without weapons," one of the guards concludes that Bond has doubtlessly been sent to assassinate Blofeld. Regardless of his capture, Bond, predictably, succeeds in his mission.

1960s Ninja

Since Fleming was writing many years before the current ninja craze, it is interesting to note the impression he creates. On the one hand the ninja are assassins and saboteurs; on the other hand they are "primitive" and "not in the same league" as Russian and European practices. At the same time, there is clearly a fascination with this "ancient art of stealth and invisibility," so much so that Bond is "trained" in ninjutsu to aid in the accomplishment of his mission.

Fleming certainly focuses on many of the outer paraphernalia of the ninja that have so fascinated the West in the 1980s. Although he does not use the proper Japanese names for the various weapons and tools, it is clear he is describing shuriken, shuko, kusari-fundo, and others. He is also intrigued by the shinobi shozoku ninja outfit, and emphasizes the "shadow" quality of the ninja. Fleming also draws the all-too-familiar parallel between "ninja" and "assassin."

The image of the ninja as created by Fleming is interesting historically; it foretells much of what has happened in our own time. At the same time that there is a focus on the "negative" aspects, such as assassination, there is a "romantic hero" flavor to the black-clad ninja. And certainly, by having Bond "become a ninja," all of the fantasies about "secret agents" are carried over to their Japanese counterparts, the elite ninja. Hence, we may conclude that the image thus created is of Japanese 007s!

Shogun: The Ninja as Seventeenth-Century Assassins

As in the miniseries, there are two scenes involving ninja in Clavell's Shogun (1976). The first is a classic description of ninja infiltration and stealth technique. The second scene involves an armed assault on Toranaga's quarters in Ishido's castle. While the book supplies greater detail to these ninja depictions, the miniseries was quite faithful to the book. Therefore, no synopsis is necessary.

1970s Ninja

There can be little doubt that Shogun casts the ninja as hated and feared assassins, as deadly as they are silent. Indeed, the first ninja to appear in the novel is introduced simply as "the assassin." They are clearly as talented at bringing death as a surgeon is at preserving life, and their intelligence information is so good that one of them can gain easy access to Blackthorne. The ninja are referred to as "devils." Violent death for pay was the sole *raison d'etre* for these semilegendary mercenaries. When wounded they fought on like "rabid animals." Again their combat superiority has "appalling" effect.

   Shogun is clearly a "samurai" novel, so it is not surprising to find the ninja so negatively cast. At the very least, amid a detailed and lengthy story that reveals much of Japanese culture, the reader sees clearly how the ninja were viewed by their samurai counterparts in seventeenth-century Japan. Certainly our allegiances are not with the ninja,

as they make an attempt on the male protagonist's life, and succeed, albeit accidentally, in killing the female protagonist of the novel.

What is interesting to note is what the ninja are "not" in *Shogun*. They are not martial arts superstars, nor are they mystical wizards. Instead they are a deadly group of close-knit families who seek to accomplish their goals with as little notice as possible. Although, as we have already noted, the ninja are seen from the perspective of the powers-that-be, that image is accurate. Most definitely the fantasy element has not begun to interact with the ninja image at this point. We know now that changes were wrought in the 1980s.

It is important to note, also, that *Shogun* was a massively popular novel and its success allowed James Clavell to have full control over the miniseries that came later. Tens of millions of Americans watched that program and our cultural understanding of the Japanese changed over the course of that week.

The Ninja: The Ninja as Central Character

In turning now to the bestseller by Eric van Lustbader, the image of the ninja takes on a decidedly different flavor. *The Ninja* is better researched than the books looked at so far. In addition, Lustbader has placed ninjutsu within Japan's historical and cultural context, making great efforts to draw out the differences between Western and Eastern thinking. Consequently the novel has a sense of realism beneath the complex story line, in addition to well-developed characters:

Again, however, it is necessary to point out that this is a work of fiction, and if we keep this in mind while reading Lustbader's thrillers, we are then in a better position to distinguish between the ninjutsu of fantasy and the ninjutsu of "reality." Put otherwise, when Lustbader was researching the ninja for his first book in the late 1970s, little was known about the ninja, and almost no *bona fide* historical sources were available. Consequently, the author had to draw largely upon other martial arts, such as *kenjutsu* (swordsmanship), to give the book an air of authenticity, and use his fertile imagination to weave an image of the ninja and their art.

1980s Assassin

The purpose of this book is to examine the image of the ninja as it has come to be in the West. Therefore, we will focus our synopsis on this image rather than retell the whole complex story. The Ninja is readily available in most bookstores, where the reader can look for the entertaining tale. Compared to The Miko, Lustbader's 1984 sequel, The Ninja embodies considerably more "factual" information about the ninja and ninjutsu.

Synopsis: The Ninja opens with a black-clad assassin killing a man and then disappearing into the night. To accomplish his ends he makes use of a poisoned shuriken. The victim never knows what really happened and dies thinking he had a heart attack. The authorities are stumped for a while, until Nicholas, the central character, arrives on the scene.

We learn that the man had been killed by a shaken ("wheel-like shuriken"). It had been dipped in doku, a powerful poison made from the pistils of the chrysanthemum. The secret technique required to make this poison is almost unheard of outside Japan, and even there few know of it. The drama for the novel is set as we learn that only one kind of man could have used this: a ninja.

Historically, according to Nicholas, the ninja first made their appearance in the sixth century when Prince Regent Shotoku successfully used them as spies. Because of this success their numbers increased rapidly during the Heian and Kamakura periods. At this time their actions tended to be focused in the south of Japan, near Kyoto. Apparently they were last heard of in 1637 when they crushed a Christian rebellion on the island of Kyushu during the Shimabara war, although they were known to be employed by the Tokugawa shoguns.

Nicholas explains that their skills covered many areas, and that the samurai learned a great deal from them. These skills included woodsmanship, disguise, camouflage, codes and silent signaling, and the preparation of firebombs and smoke screens. In short, the ninja were "military Houdinis."

The ninja were divided into schools, each specializing in a different form of combat or espionage. Nicholas notes that through examining the method by which a person had been assassinated, the school responsible could be discerned. He then gives a number of examples. The Fodo-ryu worked with small, concealed blades; the Gyokko-ryu specialized in attacking nerve centers in one-on-one combat; the Kotto-ryu perfected means of bone breaking, and the Niten-ryu taught one of the most difficult swordsmanship styles. Finally, there was the dreaded Kuji-Kiri-ryu, the most feared of all the ninja ryu. "Kuji-Kiri," according to Lustbader, is the Chinese word for "nine hands cutting," apparently a reference to nine ninja mudra (hand signs). These hand signs are considered by some to be the last vestiges of magic in this world.

Nicholas notes that the art of ninjutsu is so old that no one knows its origins. Speculation places those origins in China. He then reveals that there is an element of magic and superstition about the ninja, stating that various acts performed by the ninja could not have been executed without the intervention of some kind of "magic."

In describing the shaken Nicholas explains that the shaken is part of the ninja's arsenal of shuriken—small, easily concealed, short-bladed weapons. Poisoning shaken was a favorite method of the ninja. A quick-drying syrup was made, and the shaken coated with it. So powerful were the ninja poisons that the shaken need not even hit a vital spot to kill the target.

Finally, Nicholas claims that the ninja are still in existence today, stating that there are traditions so powerful that neither time nor opponents can stop them from continuing. He goes on to say that in a ninja you cannot find a "more deadly or clever foe." Extreme caution would have to be taken by the police in apprehending this assassin. Ominously, he states that even the wide variety of modern weapons—guns, grenades, tear gas, etc.—are useless in stopping him.

In a conversation shortly after the one with the police described above, Nicholas stresses that the ninja assassin is not the equivalent of our "hit man." The ninja are not interested in ego-gratifying fame; they make themselves known only to an elite few possible customers.

The Initial Image

As many psychologists have noted from a variety of disciplines, the first image we have of something tends to be the strongest and most difficult to change. Even the introduction of valid information at a later point in time that is at odds with our first image may not be sufficient to change this image. Consequently, when comparing the image of the ninja created in this first section to the image as it evolves in the novel, the former is most often the strongest. However, if we are to penetrate to the core of the ninja symbol, we must not only remember this, but go beneath the surface to the "reality" of the ninja, as best as we are able to see it.

The presentation of the ninja here is clearly that of an assassin and little else. The book opens with a murder, and the first explanatory passages about the ninja are focused upon this aspect. Hence, one of the most prominent associations to the ninja emphasized here is that of killer. And this fits in well with our apparent fascination with the C.I.A., K.G.B., assassins, mobsters, and mercenaries, as reflected in films, television shows, and fiction.

But the ninja are not simply "hit men" or common criminals. They are highly trained assassins with history behind them, a stunning variety of methods, fascinating weaponry, and a hint of magic. What this information does is cloud over the facts as they have been presented. In other words, the man in black who murdered someone for no apparent reason—other than that he was highly paid to do it—is romanticized as a magician and super martial artist. And this somehow justifies it, in an odd way.

What is more, the ninja is not just a killer, he is a devastatingly effective killer immune to any attempts to stop him. And poisons appear to be his favorite way of completing his task, poisons manufactured from little-known sources and by exotic means.

Less dramatic, but still associated with this central image, are a number of other features. Among these is the fact that ninjutsu is a secret lore, little understood outside of the families that practice it. What is more, it is "jealously guarded," inspiring fantasies of swift executions for anyone betraying the family secrets.

The question of why we are attracted to the ninja will be taken up in the second section of the book. What is of interest at this point, however, is that there seems to be little else needed to attract our attention than the ingredients presented so far.

A Second Murder: A "black-clad" figure kills a second victim, this time with a sword. Again we do not know why this killing has occurred. The victim is attacked by what seems to be a "tornado." He lashes back, but does not connect with a target. He then feels two sensations at once, both of which were more painful than anything he had experienced before. Later we learn that the body had been cut, from the shoulder clear through to the hip, *with one cut of the ninja's sword.*

At a later point Nicholas is analyzing the sword cuts used to kill this second man. He notes that Miyamoto Musashi, the legendary Japanese swordsman, founded the Niten ("Two Heaven") ryu of kenjutsu. This school taught the practitioner to wield two swords at once. Apparently Musashi also used bokken, or wooden swords, in combat since he felt they were even more effective. Nicholas then claims that the man was killed not by one strike, but by two. At the same time he held a wooden bokken, and used this to crush the victim's collar bone at the same moment the katana cut him from shoulder to hip.

A Ritual Warning: The initial image of the ninja is furthered by the use of a dead animal, covered in blood, thrown onto Nicholas's girlfriend's kitchen floor. The animal used was apparently the kind ninja utilized for "ritual warnings." Ordinarily ninja strike without warning, Nicholas explains, unless there is a blood feud or the ninja wishes to boast of invincibility. However, the use of this animal is also the "calling card" of the dreaded Kuji-Kiri-ryu, and is designed to create terror. Terror, it is noted, is one of the ninja's most powerful weapons.

Two More Murders: The ninja, at one point in the book, arrives at a martial arts studio to work out. The studio is owned by a friend of Nicholas, Terry, a kenjutsu master. During his sparring with the ninja

Terry sees in his opponent's martial philosophy "a lack of regard for human life." The man is described as a "killing machine," lacking in compassion and possessing "the eyes of the dead." He is equated with the corrupt samurai who worked for Ieyasu Tokugawa, the first shogun, who had abandoned the code of bushido. Terry "had been appalled at the man's strength and agility."

Not long after this workout the ninja breaks into Terry's apartment. Eileen, his girlfriend, is in the apartment alone. The ninja, wearing matte black fabric, enters silently. His eyes are "dead as stones." When Eileen is attacked she has the impression she was being grabbed by "something elemental." The sheer power of the attack is so strong that it seemed impossible that a human being could contain, let alone possess it. The ninja strips her naked, pulverizes her bones, and uses her own hair to strangle her. She is stripped of her humanity by his inhumanity. The ninja is described as being "beyond the living." The ninja is death.

When Terry arrives home the ninja is waiting. The two men face off with katana versus bokken. Throughout the exchange the ninja is using classic Musashi swordsman's techniques. Whenever the two connect the ninja seems to "explode" with power. Terry is killed with "the classic body strike" from the *Go Rin No Sho* (Book of Five Rings)—repeated strikes with the left shoulder until the enemy is dead. With his opponent viciously defeated, the ninja calmly packs up his bag, and, without emotion, leaves.

When Nicholas reflects upon his friend's death, he notes that the ninja was able to attack and kill a kenjutsu, aikido, and karate sensei. He notes further that the key to the ninja's success was not physical strength, but inner strength. He describes the murders as "spiritual killings."

The Ninja as "Death"

Although *The Ninja* is often likened to natural phenomena, like a tornado, and attributed "elemental" power, it is the negative side of nature that he represents—the side of nature that destroys. The ninja inflicts pain, creates terror, and kills mercilessly, all without the faintest glimmer of emotion. And if it is emotions that assure us that we are alive, their lack surely signifies death itself.

And this is the strong image of the ninja thus created: *ninja = death*. Like the Reaper, but ever so much more viciously, the ninja takes the life of whomever he pleases, however he pleases. Worse still, he has a complete disregard for life. He is an "inanimate object" bent on reducing living forms to his lifeless state. He is ninja.

Haragei

If the image of the ninja created so far seems little more than incarnate destructiveness, this is offset by the allusion to extrasensory abilities. Both Nicholas and Terry are described as haragei adepts—as is the ninja too. The concept derives from *hara*, which Lustbader defines as "centralization and integration," and *ki*, "an extended form of energy." More than a sixth sense, haragei is in fact a "true way of perceiving reality."

If one were a haragei adept, it would be as if one had eyes in the back of one's head and extraordinarily perceptive hearing. However, haragei did not work just one way. If one were an "ultrasensitive receiver" one was also an excellent "transmitter." If one haragei adept was within a certain range of another, he would be aware of the other's presence—without ever having to make visual contact with him, or hear him move. Terry knew the man who had entered his dojo was a haragei adept from the moment he walked in. Also from time to time in the novel, while walking along the New York streets, Nicholas is aware that he is being followed, because he can sense the presence of another haragei adept in the vicinity. Haragei results from bujutsu martial arts training.

Kansatsu sensei: As *The Ninja* moves forward and back in time, we are witness to several conversations between Nicholas and his kenjutsu sensei, Kansatsu. In these conversations a great deal of "historical" data is produced about the ninja, data which not only brings depth to the plot at hand, but which also adds a sense of authenticity to this complex image of the ninja.

The first comments that Nicholas's sensei makes about the ninja involve bushido. In stressing the importance of this code of honor he notes that without bushido they would be "nothing more than ninja." He then likens the ninja to criminals, the type of criminals who make their money in the lowest of ways.

Later on Kansatsu speaks more about the ninja. He stresses that they are from a "caste" of society that the Japanese regard as the lowest of the low, a caste for which no person could have any pride. By this he is referring to the ninja deriving from the hunin ("not human") class, rather than from the bushi (samurai) class.

Kansatsu explains that the reason the ninja were so successful is because the bushi employed them. He authoritatively states that their rise was rapid and that as their wealth increased so did their sophistication and diversity of techniques. He notes that the samurai eventually began coming to the ninja to learn, but bemoans the fact that this brought about the perversion of bushido. Apparently there were many ninjutsu ryu—more than anyone could count, and the variety of disciplines that were taught was "limitless."

Curiously, despite his former comments, the kenjutsu 'master suggests that Nicholas train in ninjutsu himself. Unbeknownst to Nicholas, Saigo, a former student of the master's, has trained in ninjutsu and will, in the future, square off against him. It is for this reason that Kansatsu sends Nicholas to be trained as a "ninja"—although we shall soon enough see that the school to which he was sent is not a ninja ryu at all, but a samurai ryu dedicated to defeating ninja. Kansatsu explains that the art of ninjutsu could be equated with the darkness, but Nicholas must explore the darkness as well as the light—explore it so as to be able to defeat it.

The Honorless Ninja

Bushido, the samurai's Way, has always been viewed positively in the West. It is a tradition of honor, of loyalty, and of courage. It embodies much of what is "good" in the Japanese culture. It is the mark of those with deep integrity and honesty, coupled with the fearsome skills of the warrior.

But the ninja are "not bound by the Way"—they lack bushido. Not only are they derived from the lowest of low classes, but they are common street criminals. Worse still, as they became increasingly influential they "perverted" bushido. They are the embodiment of darkness.

It goes without saying that this image of the ninja, presented to us from a "martial arts authority"—a kenjutsu sensei—is decidedly negative. It paints a picture of honorless criminals who have perverted one of Japan's dearest traditions. Since they are not bound to the Way, they are free to commit the worst of atrocities, actions which only "not humans" could perform. We are left with the impression that the ninja are dangerous scum.

With the history of the ninja so authoritatively presented, it is crucial that we understand that The Ninja is fiction. As we shall see clearly in Chapter 4, the historical evidence presents a very different picture. And again, as we shall see further on in our analysis of The Ninja, the point of view we are seeing the ninja from is a samurai point of view. The fact that we need mention this here is both a caution to our own formulations of what the ninja "really are," and also a credit to Lustbader's ability to create realism within his fiction. But as with any good storyteller who lulls us into believing that fantasy is reality, we must never forget which is which, especially when our task is to penetrate through to as accurate an image of the ninja as possible.

Ninja Torture: Dr. Deerforth, the medical examiner in *The Ninja*, has also had experiences with the ninja, during World War II. He prefaces his encounter with comments such as "they're devious bastards" and "they're not human." It is clear that the image that he will create is also negative.

He tells a story from the Pacific Theater of the war. At night the camp he was in was infiltrated silently, with lethal results. A doubling of the guard produced no noticeable reduction in the infiltration. In fact the guards started shooting at noises in the dark, never hit anything, and were subsequently killed themselves. He states, in a quietly bitter way, that they were used to fighting flesh and blood humans, not shadows that were insubstantial and seemed to vanish into the night.

One night Doc came face to face with a ninja. The ninja's face was coal black, dull so that no light would shine off it. His eyes "had an odd light about them," which Doc attributes to the fact that the ninja was not focused on our universe, but on another one. He describes the man as "beyond morality"—as no longer human, as having reverted to his animal ancestry. Indeed, there was no "intelligence" in his eyes, only a frightening cunning. Drawing somewhat mystical images, he describes the ninja as not living "in time," but outside it. Worse, though, was the ferocious energy of chaos he felt to be the essence of the man.

This ninja blindfolded the doctor and placed him across his shoulders. As he ran there was no sound, and staying always in the shadows, they were invisible. Doc was convinced beyond any doubt that the ninja was a "magician." He claims no one but a magician could have gotten in and out of the camp. As they entered the jungle the ninja's speed increased, despite the vegetation. His endurance was exceptional.

Doctor Deerforth was taken to a Japanese camp. Many of the men were wounded. The only operational men were in black, and they were not the usual fighting men. Since the Japanese soldiers' problems were primarily that of malnourishment there was nothing the doctor could do for them. His status therefore changed from that of M.D. to P.O.W.

The doctor was subsequently tortured. But he was tortured in a highly sophisticated way—only the ends of four fingers were manipulated—and in the end not a mark was left on his body. Doc claims his tormentor was truly a magician. Working not just on the major nerve centers, but also the nerve chains themselves, he was able to inflict the most painful torture on his subject.

Lustbader describes the torture in detail. In short, pain was taken to the limit. But before the doctor passed out the ninja would back off. Once "recovered," the ninja would begin creating pain again. In this way the doctor was never allowed to "rest" in unconsciousness. Not only did the ninja manipulate his subject's body, but he also manipulated his mind. After a while the doctor felt "guilty" about keeping silent about certain secrets. Doc felt as though he had been reduced to a primitive psychological state, like that of infancy. What this did, he reports, was to bring about feelings of dependency within him toward his torturer.

In the end a crippled Japanese soldier allows the doctor to escape. No mention is made as to why this soldier should want Doc to leave, particularly since the ninja had presumably gone in search of medical aid for the wounded Japanese soldiers. Before leaving he asks the soldier who the men in black are. The soldier replies that he does not want to know. But the doctor presses for an answer. "Ninja."

Later in the novel the doctor is killed with the saw-toothed edge of a kyoketsu-shoge, but only after he has been tortured by having all his fingers broken. This time the torture does not end in eventual release—this time the torture is but a prelude to death.

Magicians and Torturers

We are accustomed to the idea that the ninja were masters of infiltration. Indeed, Nicholas reaffirms this by noting that this is one of the ninja's hallmarks. But the images of magician and torturer are less common. Again, they are also very negative as presented here.

Furthering the idea that the ninja are not human, the Doc notes that they are "beyond morality." Indeed, they are the embodiment of chaos, men who had reverted back to their animal ancestry. They did not possess "intelligence," only "cunning."

His amazing infiltration skills convinced the doctor that the ninja were magicians. But he also learned that they were ruthless torturers who attacked the body and the mind at once. We are even left with the impression that the crippled Japanese soldier was as frightened of the ninja as the doctor was.

Hence the image of the ninja expands to include the idea of the "black magician" and the "torturer." And as if to confirm this impression of the ninja, the doctor is murdered by what seems to be "the devil himself."

Nicholas vs. Saigo: Saigo is the ninja who has as his goal the assassination of Tomkin, the tycoon father of Nicholas's girlfriend. He is also the bitter enemy of Nicholas. The many persons who are murdered in the novel are killed simply to bring pain and suffering, to terrorize Nicholas.

Saigo had been sent to the most fearful of all ninjutsu ryu by his father, a powerful man involved in underworld politics. In the end Nicholas's father had Saigo's father killed. When Saigo discovered this he put to use the basic elements of kan-aku na ninjutsu which were at his disposal at that time and killed Nicholas's father with slow-acting poison. Saigo's desire to kill Nicholas also began here. And because of this, Kansatsu sent Nicholas to be trained as a ninja—such that he might be prepared to defend himself against Saigo. And so it came about that Nicholas trained in the Tenshin Shoden Katori ryu of ninjutsu under Master Fukashigi.

With Saigo now seeking revenge, Nicholas returns to Fukashigi "to renew the old vows." Aka i ninjutsu is described as the only way of defeating the forces of kan-aku na ninjutsu which were set in motion by the arrival of Saigo. Fukashigi refers to aka i ninjutsu as a serious calling, "quite as serious, quite as mysterious as the calling to serve Amida Buddha—to that one is born and bred" (p. 450). And he regards Nicholas as one of his finest students.

With regard to Saigo, Fukashigi notes that Saigo had gone "beyond" the Kuji-kiri teachings. He had sought out teachers whose teachings could never be allowed into any ninjutsu ryu. These teachers were steeped in the ancient lore of esoteric, hidden China. He warns Nicholas that the magic that Saigo has learned now possesses him.

Not only has Saigo taken up magic, he has also begun using hallucinogenic drugs to augment his senses. In fact he had been forced to leave the Kuji-kiri ryu when he had done it in training. Even the Kuji-kiri masters regarded the use of such drugs dangerous—they reduced consciousness, creating a "narrow-beam awareness" while giving the impression of just the opposite.

And so the stage is set for the final confrontation between Saigo and Nicholas—ninja against ninja. Aka i ninjutsu against kan-aku na ninjutsu. Nicholas would need "all the fearful shades of steel to be victorious this one last time."

Good vs. Evil

The Ninja certainly brings to light a great deal of Japanese culture and martial arts tradition. However, it is a Western novel, and so it is not surprising to find, true to our Judeo-Christian cultural heritage, the battle between good and evil again. Here we have Nicholas, the "good" ninja (or samurai as it will turn out), squaring off against Saigo, the "evil" ninja.

Lustbader translates aka i ninjutsu as "red ninjutsu" which is "used for good." Kan-aku na ninjutsu is translated as "black ninjutsu." Invariably this form of ninjutsu is "used for evil." Its most virulent form is the subdiscipline known as Kuji-kiri. Hence the battle of good and evil is set amid Lustbader's characterization of various ninjutsu ryu.

There is another interesting polarization that occurs between the two opponents. Aka i ninjutsu is likened to the calling of Amida Buddha. It is, therefore, equated with the compassion and cultural achievements of Buddhism. The proponent of kan-aku na ninjutsu in The Ninja is the opposite, and his name is the key. Saigo may be a Japanese name, but it is also—phonetically—closely allied with "psycho." Therefore the battle between "good and evil" is also the battle of deep compassion and true civilization against the sociopathic psychopathology evidenced in Saigo.

If "reality" is brought to bear on the confrontation between Nicholas and Saigo we find, perhaps surprisingly, another good-evil polarity. The Tenshin Shoden Katori Shinto ryu, which in The Ninja is referred to as a ninjutsu ryu, is actually a very formal and traditional school of the samurai fighting arts in Japan. As Shidoshi Hayes has noted, the teachers of the Tenshin Shoden Katori Shinto ryu may indeed refer to ninjutsu when they instruct, but it is not because they are teaching students how to become a ninja, but rather *how to defeat one*. It seems that students of this ryu would be "insulted" and "offended" to be regarded as "ninja." The age-old samurai-ninja polarity continues, and comes alive in the pages of The Ninja.

Hence, the confrontation between Nicholas and Saigo is, looked at from this angle, a confrontation between an "evil ninja" and a "good samurai," a samurai highly trained in ways of *defeating ninja*. And this takes us back to a variety of stereotypical ways of seeing the ninja, "ninja = evil" being foremost among them. It also sets in concrete the negative aspects of Saigo as truly representative of the ninja, and the positive aspects of Nicholas as essentially "anti-ninja" or samurai.

The Final Confrontation: Saigo at last makes his move to assassinate Tomkin, a move that will bring him face to face with his archenemy Nicholas, Tomkin's bodyguard. The office tower where Tomkin has taken refuge is surrounded by police, but Saigo uses an explosion as a distraction, and penetrates the perimeter. Using an aluminum bow, and arrows with highly crafted layered steel, he kills a sniper.

He moves like "an animated shadow" making no more sound than the warm night wind. A razor-sharp set of claws runs down one of his hands. With this steel extension of his body he kills a patroling policeman. Saigo is confronted by a policeman wielding a submachine gun, but he uses "his eyes" to prevent the man from pulling the trigger. Saigo then produces a "ninja weapon"—a blunt black stick. Housed therein is a four-inch steel spike that is shot through the policeman's mouth and into his brain.

Saigo uses *haragei* to negate the effect of snipers, and a variety of acrobatic and gymnastic techniques to effect his infiltration. At one point he is hurt, but "compartmentalizes" the pain, "trivializing" the nerve shock. He finally gets into position to ascend the office building. Using a long nylon cord with a triangular hook at the end and four pads, one for each hand and foot, Saigo climbs the outer structure. We are told that this means of infiltration was one of the most fundamental ninjutsu techniques, used in the past for entering an enemy's castle. No structure, no matter how seemingly impossible to climb, could prevent a ninja from scaling it. Lustbader describes Saigo as moving upward "with appalling rapidity."

As Nicholas feels the ninja approaching he prepares for their confrontation. He utilizes the element earth, *Dai-en-kyo-chi*, as it was referred to and taught in the aka i ninjutsu. Translated as "Great-round-mirror-wisdom," this is apparently the energy Nicholas needs to consolidate within him to bring him to final preparedness, an energy he evokes through the use of mantra. He wears a lightweight black silk shirt and cotton trousers. He stands in a Musashi swordsman posture, katana in hand.

Nicholas's sixth sense tells him of Saigo's arrival. A soft click on the floor alerts him to the explosive Saigo has tossed at him, and he rolls out of the way. The hand-to-hand combat between Nicholas and Saigo is fierce and intense. Suddenly Saigo realizes Nicholas is also a "ninja," or, more accurately, trained to defeat ninja. Sensing time running out, Saigo throws an explosive toward Tomkin. Nicholas abandons his grappling with the kan-aku na ninja to get Tomkin's body out of the way. The blast destroys just about everything in the office.

The police who storm the upper floor just after the explosion notice that a window pane has been shattered. Looking out they see a crumpled body many floors below, and conclude that Saigo had jumped immediately prior to launching his last attack on Tomkin. To those confused by Saigo's suicidal leap, Nicholas notes simply that Saigo was a warrior, and that to die in battle was a warrior's highest honor.

Nicholas and Tomkin leave the area in a limousine. The limo has been moving but a few minutes when there is an alarming crash through the front window and the driver is impaled. Saigo appears reincarnated, fully vital, and still fixed upon fulfilling his goal: the assassination of Tomkin.

The body thrown to the ground had not been Saigo's, but that of a decoy. The black ninja had found a drunk earlier who was similar in build, destroyed his face, and then positioned him well in advance of his attack on Tomkin as a back-up diversion to any difficulties he might encounter. As the limo had pulled out, Saigo had nimbly and silently jumped onto its roof.

The fight between Nicholas and Saigo in the confined space of the limo is vicious. Both men use *hsing-i*, "the so-called imaginary mental fist." The two eventually roll through the shattered windshield, and the confrontation continues in the open. Both men attack and respond, aided not only by their heightened sense perception and knowledge, but also with haragei. It is Nicholas's body awareness that allows him to move out of the way of two shaken expertly, and invisibly, thrown at him by Saigo. Then it is katana against katana.

In the midst of their duel Saigo begins to evoke the Kobudera, a form of evil magic. Drawing from his years of training in Musashi's philosophy of swordsmanship, Nicholas finds the strength to break its effects and immobilizes Saigo. The fight ends as Saigo is decapitated.

The Fight After the Fight: In addition to the decoy body that Saigo made sure was in position in case of failure, he had also made another move to ensure that he had a chance to kill Nicholas. Using *saiminjutsu*, the "art of ninja hypnotism," he placed his will within the mind of Nicholas's girlfriend. Saigo's will: it becomes the very ground she walks on, the universe itself. Lustbader notes that ordinary hypnosis is to the Kobudera as the bow and arrow is to the atom bomb. Beyond Kuji-kiri, Kobudera was magic that even Saigo's kan-aku na ninjutsu sensei feared.

As Nicholas meditates one morning, his girlfriend, becoming Saigo's will, silently approaches with every ninja skill at her command, katana unsheathed. She is clearly possessed by Saigo. Directly behind Nicholas the katana is raised and brought down with ferocious intensity. At the last instant, Nicholas, warned by haragei, slips to the side of the descending blade. A fight ensues. Only advanced fighting techniques for confronting a sword unarmed allow Nicholas to bring an end to the ordeal.

It takes Nicholas four hours to undo what Saigo accomplished in fifteen minutes. Also an adept of *saiminjutsu*, Nicholas works to "exorcise the demon" Saigo had placed in her soul. With much effort, and three days of recovery for his girlfriend, the exorcism is successful. Saigo's will, as well as his body, has been defeated. Nicholas is victorious.

The Physical, Mental, and Spiritual Victory

In these final scenes of *The Ninja* we see the classic, stereotyped image of the ninja. Saigo successfully infiltrates a heavily guarded installation using a variety of predictable ninjutsu skills, coming close to fulfilling his goal of assassinating Tomkin. Most entertaining, and most appealing to our fantasy images of the ninja, is Saigo's cleverness— particularly his faked death.

These concluding impressions of the ninja reaffirm our sense that the battle before us is one of "good" against "evil." Saigo is described by one policeman as killing in the same way others would eat breakfast. Tomkin, upon catching a glimpse of the kan-aku na ninja, feels he has seen Lucifer. And for the reader there can be little doubt that Saigo is a powerful, conscienceless, antilife power.

But Saigo's evil influence extends beyond his physical and mental actions. It extends into the spiritual realm. He has trod where even kan-aku na ninjutsu sensei would fear to tread, into the dark depths of the Kobudera. He attempts to influence the outcome of the duel between himself and Nicholas by calling forth his demonic powers and "possesses" Nicholas's girlfriend's soul. Hence, he is "evil" on all three dimensions: the physical, the mental, and the spiritual.

It follows, then, that Nicholas, the Tenshin Shoden Katori Shinto ryu ninja—or more correctly, samurai—has seen to it that "good" defeats "evil," the evil of the Kuji-kiri, the evil of the ninja. He has upheld the beliefs and teachings of the great samurai swordsman, Miyamoto Musashi, whose spiritual influence he calls up when facing the Kobudera. The sword saint's "Body of a Rock" shatters the influence of the magic all about Nicholas. Musashi finally has his revenge upon the ninja who, armed with only a fan, defeated him so many centuries ago.

Tulku: A Tale of Modern Ninja

So far we have been examining the image of the ninja as it has been explored by those who are not participating members in the authentic ninja tradition. True, these images are not without value, but it should be clear that these images *can only be* shallow reflections of the reality of ninjutsu. For an accurate image of the ninja it is necessary to "go to the source." In the U.S. that is Stephen K. Hayes, a personal student of Dr. Hatsumi's for over a decade, and a *shidoshi* ("teacher of the warrior ways of enlightenment"). Despite the fact that *Tulku: A Tale of Modern Ninja* is a work of fiction, it does a great deal in terms of presenting an accurate, flesh-and-blood glimpse of the shinobi warriors.

Tulku: A Tale of Modern Ninja is a unique book in the "martial arts fiction" category. As we have already noted its writer is not only a practitioner of the art in question, but a high-ranking teacher of the tradition. Hence we are treated to a sense of ninjutsu as it is actually

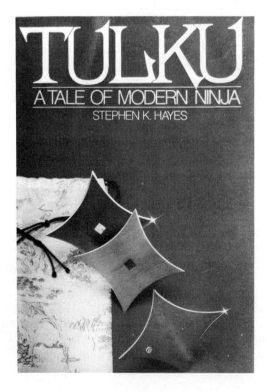

experienced through the life of the author not only when there is an
"action" scene that calls for accurate labels and descriptions of various
techniques, but also when there is simple description, reflection, or
character development. Hayes's book has also been superbly researched and carries with it a powerful ring of authenticity, as it
should. Literary references (e.g., Musashi's *The Sound of Waves*), contemporary events (e.g., the assassination attempt on the pope and the
Union Carbide disaster in India), and, of course, genuine historical
information about the ninja and the Dalai Lama's escape from Tibet
(following the Chinese takeover in 1959) are creatively woven into the
fabric of the story. What is more, the book is very well written. All in all,
Tulku provides the reader with an exciting story, but also many insights
into ninjutsu that would be unavailable in any other delivery—even in
Hayes's technical books.

Tulku provides the perfect bridge between the image of the ninja in
fiction and the image of the ninja as it is revealed through the
historical sources (Chapter 4). We must therefore pay close attention
to its message.

> **Of Subtlety and Shadows:** *Tulku* opens with Taichi Nakamura, a ninja
> operative, infiltrating the well-guarded Jaejun International warehouse.
> Patiently the "sinewy Japanese" scales the building, blending his
> breathing and muscular efforts. He uses a tsubogiri boring tool and a
> kunai leverage tool to effect his climb and entrance. As the guards are
> momentarily lured away from their station by a subtle alteration to the
> warehouse's computerized security system, the ninja makes his way
> into the ventilation shaft. Once inside the building Nakamura moved
> like "a formless shadow." Unbeknownst to the operative, except
> through vague, unverbalized body sensations, a Korean assassin is
> watching, preparing to kill him.

First Impressions

The opening scenes in ninja movies, and the opening paragraphs in
ninja novels, tend to be highly predictable: dramatic action, usually
with an assassination or violent confrontation. This is the image of the
ninja we are familiar with. But Hayes chooses to set the tone of *Tulku*
differently. Rather than create tension with overt, flashy drama, he
chooses to introduce us to the subtle, shadowy side of ninjutsu.

Hayes chooses as his opening symbol the ninja skill of infiltration.
Even in modern surroundings the operative manages to slip into a

well-protected warehouse and take pictures of a crate. No one is killed. Indeed, no one even knows he is there—except a Korean assassin. Hence from the very beginning we see the ninja as working quietly in the gaps of perception. The ninja are not presented as assassins; instead, the assassins are working against the ninja. Clearly a balance is being brought to the usual portrayal of ninja performing loud, ostentatious displays of martial arts brilliance and callous, sociopathic cruelty.

The Matsutani Ninja: Shortly after the opening scene we learn something of the Matsutani family. A ninja family for over eight and a half centuries, the Matsutanis had their roots in Iga. The Matsutani ninja *ryu* was founded by an outcast samurai named Masakado Tokuoka. Originally from the Matsutani district of Japan's northern Joshinetsu Plateau, the founding member of the ryu had been forced into the desolate regions of Iga by a turn of political events against a family with which he was allied.

"Stripped of honor, title, and family, Masakado became a political refugee and had to wander in despair throughout the pine-covered peaks and lowland marshes of haunted Iga, far from those who would hunt him down for martial vengeance" (Hayes, 1985b, p. 15). However, in Iga the young Masakado encounters the hermit wizard Yugen Doshi, a wilderness ascetic who possesses mystical knowledge. Becoming an apprentice to the doshi, Masakado explores the mysterious realms which lay beyond the physical body and the occult arts of "accomplishing that which is willed by means of invisible action."

In time Masakado became "an enlightened holy warrior." He took the name of Kaisen Matsutani to celebrate his origins and his spiritual transformation. And it was his descendants who went on to establish the Matsutani ryu of ninjutsu. The use of subtlety and illusion has allowed the Matsutani family to survive throughout the centuries.

"Fictory"

Hayes's presentation of the Matsutani ninja ryu's origins mirrors, as we shall see, the history of Togakure ryu ninjutsu. Hence, *Tulku* is, in some ways, a work of "fictory"—a blending of *fiction* and his*tory*. This is what gives Hayes's story the background feeling of authenticity. We shall see more of this later on, especially as he introduces Tibetan Buddhist elements to the story.

Ninja Intelligence Gathering and Interpretation: Through a well-placed female spy, intelligence agent Ozawa, Director of Field Projects

Operations, Matsutani clandestine operations group, has learned of a plot that would affect the company's project in the Himalayas, and that, if successful, would not only threaten the very continuation of the corporation, but many thousands of innocent lives as well.

Ozawa muses about the differences between American intelligence operations and the use of intelligence within the ninja tradition. "The key to effective use of intelligence gathering lies in the ability to successfully analyze the data procured, Ozawa often emphasized to his subordinates who carried out the fieldwork under his direction. That was a weak poiht in many of the world's major intelligence organizations. No one could top the American CIA in terms of ability to get information. What the Americans lacked, Ozawa felt, was the ability to use the information to predict accurately the likely future in order to initiate appropriate actions" (p. 28). Interestingly, the son of the company's chairman of the board looks down upon the family's intelligence gathering as an anachronism of the past, and regards the ninja operations as little better than the activities of the Japanese yakuza crime families.

Eventually we learn that whatever plot is brewing, it involves deadly nerve gas to be used for "the complete eradication of the population of an entire stretch of the Himalaya Mountains."

Intelligent Intelligence

Again we find the image of the ninja undergoing an interesting change. So often the image we have of the ninja is "clever" or "instinctual." But it is rarely human. In other words, the ninja are seen as brilliant martial artists, but not necessarily as intelligent. Indeed, the chronic lack of intelligence among the ninja of Hollywood attests to the image of ninja as dangerous but somewhat subhuman.

Hayes introduces the reader to a fundamental aspect of the ninja families' survival: the "intelligent use of intelligence." To add weight to this he draws the differences between ninja information gathering and CIA operations. Clearly the ability of Matsutani Shoji Ltd. to secure information vital to its well-being is highly sophisticated—as sophisticated, if not more so, as the CIA. But what gives the ninja family the edge is not what they know, but how they process what they know and turn that knowledge into appropriate action. And here the CIA, as was demonstrated in Iran, falls terribly short.

Hayes has another point to make. "Intelligence information" is not necessarily a self-serving thing—although, like the chairman's son, there is the tendency to think so. Here what the phantom warrior agents have turned up will affect thousands of people who have never even heard of Matsutani Shogi Ltd. Knowledge of the world permits those who have it to take action on the behalf of those who do not have it. (It is worthwhile noting that a story which Hayes tells in the introduction to Ninjutsu: The Art of the Invisible Warrior is very similar in this regard. Here farmers threatened by a greedy warlord turn to the ninja for assistance—and it is the ninja's sophisticated intelligence that allows them to work their way to the benefit of others.)

This is a very different image of the ninja. Not infrequently the ninja of fantasy are hired to fulfill or protect the ruthless plots of others, or to assassinate for personal gain. But through Hayes we gain an image of the ninja that carries concern for others. As Hayes (1984c) states elsewhere in the writing of an imaginative ninja scroll,

> Yours is the legacy of service to those in need
> protection to those in distress
> and strength to those who are overpowered.

Contemporary Ninja Training: Kenichi Odate, one of two principal characters in the book, is introduced during a ninja training exercise in Indiana—although the reader does not know this in the beginning. Ken, regarded by his captors as a "wimp," is led to an outhouse, machine gun pushed in his back. Ken enters the outhouse, but then fails to come out. The guard, anxious about the amount of time the prisoner is taking, and worried lest he take his own life, opens the door, only to find the prisoner gone.

Suddenly Ken is upon the guard with powerful blows and thumb drives. The ninja agent disarms the guard, and "cuts" his throat with his own boot knife. "Within minutes, he had vanished into the underbrush and barked columns of beech, maples, and hawthornes that had, over the centuries, sheltered the warrior braves of the Miami, Shawnee, Chippewa, and Iroquois tribes from their armed pursuers" (p. 40).

The young ninja then grinds his clothes into the black earth to make them camouflaged. Walking in a style used in ninjutsu, he takes off. "As he moved through the woods, the agent mentally projected an energy and awareness probe ahead of himself, so that by the time he reached a position that would have been blocked by a tree, his body was already aligned to brush past without being hindered in the slightest" (p. 41).

As Ken's personal history is described we learn more about the Matsutani family. After the war, despite the general level of peace in the world, Keikichi Matsutani and his son Hitoshi continue to train an active force of clandestine agents "financed between the entries in the corporate accounting ledgers." Candidates for the Field Project Operations group were recruited from descendants of past generations' family agents.

Ken, half Scottish and half Japanese, was trained from the age of seven. By the early teen years it was clear he was destined to be a "warrior." He learned the skills of *shinobi iri* (silent invisible movement), *taijutsu* (unarmed combat), *koppojutsu* (bone-breaking), *koshijutsu* (muscle and organ destruction), *tantojutsu* (blade fighting), and *hojutsu* (firearms work). Ken eventually became a candidate for the very rare third-level classification, and so became the personal student of the instructor-in-chief for the Matsutani ninjutsu ryu. This also meant grooming for the elite Hasatsutai, "the force that never fails."

Abruptly the training exercise comes to an end as Ken is informed of the emergency brewing halfway around the world. Hauled up into a waiting helicopter, Ken is quickly on his way to Hong Kong.

The Image of Ninjutsu as a Martial Art

Not infrequently people looking at Stephen K. Hayes's technical books consider ninjutsu to be an ineffective, made-up martial art. This impression is given weight, unfortunately, by all-too-many bogus ninja masters who do "invent" ninjutsu. But the image of ninjutsu as ineffective and inappropriate to real combat conditions is false. Indeed, after 900 years of battlefield trials and subsequent "revisions," ninjutsu is by far the most tested "martial art" known to man.

Ken's real-life training episode does much to correct this impression. Not only does the training exercise encompass realistic situations, it also requires realistic solutions. What is more, Hayes draws a parallel between the ninja's struggle for survival against overwhelming military and political powers in feudal Japan, and the fight the North American Indians fought against armed aggressors. Each was involved in life-and-death warfare, not dojo martial arts training.

In addition to the "ninja style of walking/running" which uses the muscles running along the upper surface of the thighs, Ken projected an "energy and awareness probe ahead of himself." To many this sounds rather absurd and may be regarded as entirely fictional on Hayes's part, or the conventions of the "ninja mystique" we have sampled earlier. However, within Tibetan tantric practice there is *lung-gom*, or "trance walking," which embodies a similar type of "energy and awareness probe," for want of a better description for an indescribable perceptive ability.

As Lama Govinda (1966) notes, Gom (sgom) can be translated as meditation, contemplation, or concentration of mind and soul upon a certain subject. It also encompasses the gradual emptying from the mind all subject-object relationships, until "a complete identification

of subject and object has taken place." Lung (rlun) means "air," or the "vital energy" or "psychic force"—*prana* in Sandskrit. The lung-gom-pa trance walker is one who has learned to control his psychic force through the yoga practice of pranayama. This practice begins with breathing, and gradually takes this ordinary activity as the basis for realizing higher levels of awareness and insight. There is a *transformation* of the mind, body, and personality of the practitioner through this practice. Among the results of this practice is the ability to move at amazing speeds over very rough ground—*without harm*.

The point is this: although Ken's movement through the Indiana woods is not identical to the Lung-gom of Tibetan tantra, there is enough similarity to lend credence to his unusual perceptive abilities. Curiously, Lama Govinda notes that the trance-walk was not just a spiritual practice, but a *necessity* in certain parts of Tibet were a monk caught out in the elements. Ken is also running for his life.

We also get a glimpse of the arsenal of skills that Ken has been taught. Each is a science unto itself, although each rests upon *taijutsu* natural body movement. Ken makes use of *hensojutsu*, the ninja's art of disguise, to protect himself from his captors during the training exercise. Passing himself off as something of a pathetic individual, he gradually lulls the guards into relaxing their watch over him—just enough to allow him to take effective and decisive action. Ken's turning of the tables also encompasses the ninja art of invisibility (*shinobi iri*). Hence we see "standard" ninja associations brought to life in a realistic way, for once.

And this is doubly satisfying. On the one hand Hayes confirms some of the lore of the ninja; on the other, he relates these skills to the authentic core of ninjutsu training. Hensojutsu, taijutsu, and shinobi iri therefore become enlivened, rather than trivialized.

The Dying Rimpoche: As potential disaster hangs over Matsutani Shogi Ltd., a Tibetan R*impoche* (literally "precious one") arrives at the Matsutani Cancer Research Clinic of the Kumamoto University Medical School. He is dying of cancer and there is no chance he will recover. The Tibetan holy man is looking for a way to continue teaching for as long as possible, to pass on his accumulated wisdom to his followers.

Gyelsop Rimpoche is a *tulku*, a reincarnated Buddhist saint whose rebirth had been predicted by his dying predecessor. As a three-year-old child he had been discovered by monks and tested strenuously. Only after he had successfully identified all manner of personal objects which belonged to the eleventh Gyelsop Lama was he declared the twelfth reincarnation.

In his hospital bed the high Lama delivers his teachings. He speaks of all of existence as suffering, of letting go of the need for labeling and qualification. Discussing the concept of "good" and "evil," he makes extensive reference to the Chinese invasion of Tibet, and the escape of many thousands of refugees. He notes that this event, though seemingly "bad" in some respects, had resulted in the Tibetan teachings becoming known in the West. Therefore, was the Chinese action "good" or "bad"?

The Tibetan Connection

Hayes's presentation of Tibetan Buddhism is well-researched and accurate. The description he gives of the testing of the young Gyelsop Rimpoche parallels descriptions Lama Govinda (1966) gives of the discovery and testing of Saraha Tulku, and descriptions Chogyam Trungpa (1966) recounts of his own discovery and examination. The teachings the dying holy man gives are standard Tibetan teachings that can be found in books by the Dalai Lama (1975, 1984), Ketsun Sangpo Rinbochay (1982), and others. Also accurate is the attitude the high Lama shows about the Chinese invasion of Tibet. Those who have been fortunate enough to hear the Dalai Lama speak will recognize this natural disinterest in classifying it as "evil." Instead it is seen against a much deeper backdrop, the backdrop of karma.

The question naturally arises—why introduce Tibetan Buddhism into a thriller about ninjutsu? Is it there to simply make the book more varied and rich, or is there some other purpose?

The answer is hinted at in the fictional history of the Matsutani ninjutsu ryu and overtly addressed, as we shall see in Chapter 4, in the historical documentation of the ninja. The origins of ninjutsu were not military or combative, but spiritual. The forerunners of the ninja were mountain ascetics and warrior sages, not guerrillas.

This does not fit in well with most people's conceptions of the ninja. The image of the ninja in the West may include some mystical hocus-pocus, but when all is said and done, what it all comes down to is martial arts supremacy. In a jam, the ninja could *fight* their way out of anything—no need for "oneness" or mystical insights.

And it is this image of the ninja to which Hayes addresses himself. The introduction of Tibetan Buddhism into the story brings with it the heritage of perhaps the most spiritually advanced religious tradition in the world. Hence, at least at this point in the story, we have the warriors of the physical world represented by the Matsutani ninja, and the warriors of the Void represented by the holy men of Tibetan Buddhism. A balance is therefore struck between two poles—the

physical and spiritual. However, this is our Western division. As we shall see, what Hayes does is to educate our image of the ninja through the education of the ninja in the novel. In this way, the physical and spiritual poles of ninjutsu are reconciled and the stereotype is transcended.

Thangme: "The Lama Who Arrived Late": We are soon introduced to Thangme, interpreter to the dying Gyelsop Rimpoche. It appears, however, that he is more than he seems. He, too, is a *tulku*, the eighth

Khundor Lama. He has concealed his true identity to evade detection by vengeful Chinese assassins.

Thangme's history is interesting. He arrived in Llasa, the capital city of Tibet, in 1948. In 1950, while the Dalai Lama was escaping the Chinese, Thangme chanced to overhear a plot against him, and acted to save the Tibetan god-king. He then joined the escape, and through the intervention of the commander-in-chief of the Tibetan army was introduced to the Gyelsop Lama. While in exile in India, Thangme and the Gyelsop Lama became close friends.

Upon returning to Tibet in 1951, Thangme studied Tibetan, and was initiated into the "extremely well-guarded secrets of *trulkor*, the sacred warrior tradition of Tibet." Eventually it was discovered that Thangme was the prophesized Khundor Tulku. Since he had been discovered many years after the search had ended, he became known as the "lama who arrived late."

In 1959 during the Dalai Lama's escape from the invading Chinese, Thangme lagged behind the entourage to throw off the pursuing Chinese units. "The *tulku* surrendered to the necessity of breaking his vows of total reverence for life if he were to accomplish his purpose of assisting the revered god-king in his flight to freedom. . . . By means of carefully engineered rock slides and well-timed flash floods, night raids on temporary encampments, and a chilling barrage of psychological warfare tactics gleaned from the arcane teachings of Tibet's *trulkor* warrior tradition, the Khundor Tulku time and again derailed the Chinese pursuit" (p. 81).

Kozo Matsutani: It soon becomes evident that Thangme, the Khundor Tulku, is, in actuality, Kozo Matsutani, brother of the current head of Matsutani Shogi Ltd. Against his family's wishes, Kozo joined the army of *Dai Nippon*'s Showa Emperor in 1942, and after training as an infantryman was channeled into officer training school. From there he was trained in the Japanese army intelligence school, where "subtlety replaced boldness. Versatility replaced commanding presence" (p. 101). With his Matsutani ninjutsu ryu background this is where he felt most at home.

After extensive intelligence training Kozo Matsutani was stationed in Burma. There, "no scouting mission was too dangerous for agent Matsutani" (p. 103). However, he learned that his previous convictions about the war were not entirely in accordance with the facts. It was not an honorable cause.

At the conclusion of the war, Kozo disguised himself as a Burmese monk and vanished, for his shame prevented him from returning to his family. He wandered for years, eventually arriving in Tibet where, after being rescued from certain death by nomads, he assumed the name of Thangme.

The Essence of Ninjutsu

We noted earlier that the image of the ninja in the West was largely devoid of genuine spirituality. In keeping with this Hayes created a fictional ninjutsu ryu that is, essentially, the best of what our Western ideas of the ninja could be. The Matsutani ryu ninja are subtle, intelligent, and highly trained; however, there was nothing particularly spiritual about them.

With the introduction of Kozo/Thangme, the ninja/tulku, all of this changes. He unites in one person the centuries-old ninja tradition, as well as the even older tradition of Tibetan Buddhism, particularly the trulkor warrior tradition. He integrates "positive" ninjutsu with perhaps the deepest and most powerful spiritual heritage known to man. The highest forms of matter and spirit are united in Kozo/Thangme. (Tibetan Buddhism and Nin-po Mikkyo share a tantric philosophy, something we shall look at more closely in Chapter 8.) Hayes is *recasting our image of the ninja to include the spiritual aspects of true ninjutsu tradition*. He is saying, too, that the spiritual legacy of the ninja is very powerful, and very deep, similar in fact to the spiritual legacy of the Tibetans.

> **The Invisible Trulkor Warrior:** The Matsutani ninja enter a warehouse owned by the Tri-Seas Security Co. Since there was no way to effect a security breach as had been orchestrated for the infiltration in Seoul, the ninja were forced to use their methods of disguise. Hence they infiltrate the warehouse as two inspectors and a flustered guard (Ken).
>
> As the *hisatsutai* agents are looking for the canisters of nerve gas, Kozo appears. Ken is stunned, and demands to know how the holy man got in. Kozo replies, "I created a feeling of not needing to be seen. Therefore, no one bothered to see me" (p. 128). Still suspicious, Ken questions him further, only to discover that the tulku has actually made himself invisible.
>
> Despite his ninjutsu training, and despite the fact that he had heard of the "nine powers of the *kuji*," Ken had dismissed the ninja's invisibility, future reading, water walking, and clairvoyant sight as "the stuff of Japanese children's novels." He felt "the legends were creations of fiction, used by the family ancestors to give themselves a needed

psychological edge over their forbidding adversaries hundreds of years ago" (p. 129).

In response Kozo notes that, like the others, Ken has "fallen into the trap of technicality thinking." He goes on to warn him of the dangers of this. "The more you rely on technology to do the work for you, the farther you get from the essence of the creative power of your own channeled intentions. Be aware that technology can blind you to perceptions of broader realities as well" (p. 129). Kozo offers to teach Ken "the nine powers" when he is ready; he need only ask. On his part Ken was interested.

Although the canisters of deadly nerve gas are discovered and photographed in detail—in the hopes that an identical set of harmless replicas can be put in their place—the ninja agents are discovered and held by the Albanian and Bulgarian assassins. Kozo, however, is nowhere to be seen.

Utilizing ninjutsu disarm tactics, sokuyaku heel stomp kicks, and both senban and bo shuriken, the ninja attack their captors and attempt their escape. Running toward an open door a man appears and levels a machine gun at them. But before he can fire, he is thrown backward, and Kozo stood in his place. From all quarters men attacked the tulku. "A club would descend, seemingly smashing right through the monk's shoulder, only to continue on its swing unslowed by any target. Kicks drove in and looped around, appearing to land with deadly force right on their target, only to wag in the air impotently as Kozo drifted right along with them in the direction of their power" (p. 152).

The ninja effect their escape with the aid of Kozo, while Kwon, the Korean assassin, is viciously torturing, drugging, and cruelly raping the *kunoichi* agent assigned to monitor the infiltration by radio. After subjecting her to lethal doses of medication, the Korean learns that he is up against Japan's legendary phantom warriors.

The Power of Intentions

In Hayes's telling of the entrance into, and escape from, the warehouse, our hypothesis that Kozo represents the epitome of ninjutsu appears to be confirmed. Even Ken is unaware of "real invisibility"— an example of the realization of intentions in the world. Kozo himself says that invisibility training is not unique to the trulkor tradition but is inherent in the ninja's kuji, but Ken dismisses all of this as fantasy.

Further confirmation comes from Kozo's emphasis upon creativity and the channeling of personal power, rather than relying upon technology. As we shall see in both Chapters 4 and 8 these factors are central to genuine ninjutsu as Hayes presents it. It is the scriptwriters, the bogus ninja masters, and other authors who give us our images of the ninja who think too technically. Also, Hayes's description of Kozo's "combat method" matches descriptions that he, Jack Hoban, and Bud Malmstrom give of ninjutsu at its highest level of development, ninjutsu as it is practiced by Dr. Masaaki Hatsumi and his shihan.

At the same time Hayes educates us to the reality of ninjutsu as he sees it, he also makes an important distinction—the differentiation of the ninja from assassins and rapists. We have already discussed the prevalence of the "ninja = assassin" equation. Also, in *The Ninja* it was Saigo, a ninja, who demonstrated perverted sexuality. In *Tulku* we find it is the ninja's antagonists who are assassins and rapists. Assassination for its own sake and barbarous sexual acts are anathema to the freedom and creativity that ninjutsu creates for its practitioners. And at last this point has been made.

The Tulku's Teachings: In the aftermath of their failure at the warehouse and the death of a fellow ninja and family member, Kozo shares some of his insights. He notes that there is a wide gap between what most people regard as "religion" and "the active pursuit of transcendent all-piercing enlightenment." He notes that, provided the surface level is penetrated, the ancient teachings are "tools for the personal cultivation of freedom through spiritual power."

The first step Kozo notes is ridding oneself of preconceived ideas. Concepts that seem timeworn and empty of meaning need to be seen anew, as if radically different. He then goes on to emphasize the importance of focusing on the present moment. This leads to true invincibility. "From that state of consciousness, any attacker who faces you represents only the quality of energy that exists between you for that minute fraction of a second. You do not have any fears of what he could do to you if he gets hold of you in the next moment. You have no recollection of your own success or failure the moment before. You place no value on the outcome of the clash. There is no significance to the clash whatsoever" (p. 165). This is the perspective from the *kongokai,* or cosmic realm of realities.

Kozo goes on. "When I talk about focusing on the present moment in combat . . . I mean being clear enough in your own mind to know who it is you are facing. Demons left over from the pains of childhood work right alongside your adversary. These demons are ghosts left over from another time. They have nothing to do with the present moment. If you have already cleared out all the demons, then you have only the external adversary left to overcome" (p. 171).

Kozo continues his instruction to Ken when their operation moves to the Himalayas. Drawn to a Tibetan temple, Ken suddenly finds himself face to face with Kozo. When he tries to explain away their meeting as coincidence Kozo replies that he has, in actuality, been waiting for Ken. "There is no such thing as 'mere coincidence.' Do not fall into the trap of belittling your own powers" (p. 190).

Ken also continues to spurn what he sees as Kozo's "religious" talk. But the holy man's response dispels this. "I am not talking about religious practice. I am referring to warrior invincibility. The melding of the body and spirit in the flame of fearlessness . . . [The] place to begin with a search for the completed powers of the enlightened warrior is the bone and muscles and juices of the body we were born in" (p. 190).

The Final Confrontation: A terrifying Himalayan storm blows in as Kozo and Ken move to prevent the Korean assassin from letting the nerve gas flood the area. When Ken gets within range of the Korean and the canisters he finds himself unable to move. Hearkening back to Kozo's teaching [not covered in this synopsis] Ken realizes that his body has sensed a sniper nearby.

When Ken takes out a sentry the Korean turns a spotlight on Kozo. Two shots and the monk flies back at the sudden impact of the bullets. Thrown by the sight of the *tulku* going down, and surrounded by demons suddenly emerging from his own unconscious, Ken takes on the Korean. As Kozo had predicted, "there is great danger in confronting a warrior who possesses more power than you" (p. 192).

The confrontation between Ken and Kwon is vicious. As Ken's semiconscious body lies crumpled over the bumper of a truck, suddenly the killer hears "an unholy wail." As it crescendos, he realizes that it is human. Then Kozo appears "somehow back from the dead," having already eerily buried the sniper beneath a rock slide.

The Korean advances upon Kozo, hating everything he stands for. But vivid childhood memories suddenly begin crashing into his conscious awareness—and he begins crying. But bringing himself back to the present, the "reptilian killer" points his gun at Kozo's forehead and squeezes the trigger.

While the Korean had been recalling his childhood, a light had begun to glow about Kozo. This light energy had swelled to the point where it touched the Korean, but the assassin was dominated by darkness.

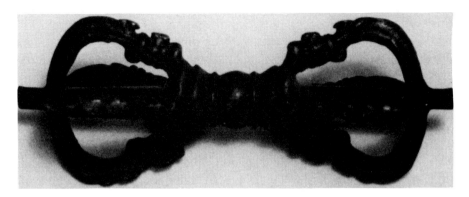

Drawing a vajra thunderbolt from a silk bag that Gyelsop Rimpoche had given him, Kozo stood before his opponent. A bolt of lightning then struck the killer—just as he had been about to shoot—and he suffered a most ghastly death.

Looking at Kozo, Ken sees "a wreath of ghostly flames danced around the hideous visage, and a garland of skulls was draped around its neck. The fearsome thing roared and the earth shook and Ken slipped back into unconsciousness" (p. 219).

Mahakala Incarnated

Earlier we noted that the confrontation in *Tulku* was not so much one of "good vs. evil" but of the meeting of energies that would lead us to transcendence versus energies that would drag us downward to subhuman realms. This is clearly symbolized in the final duel between Kozo and Kwon. The conscienceless, "reptilian" Korean who loathes Tibetans, especially monks, squares off against one who has transcended the human realm and sees with the "mind and eyes of God."

Even more symbolic, however, is the specter Ken sees. Those familiar with Tibetan Buddhism will recognize the fearful image of *Mahakala*, one of the most gruesome of the Tibetan deities. "Deities," it should be noted, though regarded as gods by most people, are, in actuality, symbolic representations of various types of psychic energy. Mahakala, despite his psychotic looking eyes, garland or crown of skulls, killing limbs, and cloak of brilliant flames, is regarded as a "protective divinity" (Trungpa, 1973). To those who would threaten the sacred, as the Korean had, this energy appears as horrifying, to keep such spiritually destructive energy away. As it is noted in *The Tibetan Book of the Dead*, if you do not realize the oneness of existence, all of the peaceful deities (or psychic energies) will take the terrifying form of

Mahakala, and all the wrathful deities will take on the shape of the Lord of Death. The result will be wandering in samsara (suffering) with your projections assuming the form of demons (Guru Rimpoche, in Fremantle and Trugpa, 1975, p. 68). Hence the assassin encounters *Mahakala* in such a wrathful form. Since he despises "oneness," since he despises the goal toward which his psychic energy might lead him, his psychic energy and projections turn into the demonic form of *Mahakala*.

The appearance of this terrifying energy is, surprisingly, quite in accordance with Kozo's "blessing" of the Korean before the lightning bolt. At the same time Mahakala protects the sacred from those who would destroy it. Within Tibetan Buddhism the flames surrounding Mahakala represent tremendous energy, but energy devoid of hatred. The energy is, in essence, the energy of *compassion*. The garland of skulls symbolizes emotions that have not been destroyed, abandoned, or condemned for being "bad" (Trungpa, 1976).

Curiously enough, at the same time Mahakala "protects" through his horrific form, he also aids the spiritual adept. To maintain an awakened quality of mind, the mind sometimes requires sudden shocks. Hence, the shocking image of *Mahakala*, whose energy destroys hesitation and all obstacles on the path. So the same form that terrified and brought about the destruction of the "spirit-killing" Korean was a "spirit waking" for Ken. As Trungpa (1973) has noted, the *Mahakala* leads one to openness, the *Mahakala* represents the "leap into penetrating awareness."

Kozo appears not only to the Korean assassin, but also to Ken. Clearly to Kwon, Kozo is but the demonic projection of his own evil. But for Ken, the terrifying form of Mahakala is an assault on his technical way of thinking, providing the seasoned ninja an opportunity to penetrate through to oneness, to take that leap into penetrating awareness.

In the president's office at Matsutani Shoji Ltd. there hangs a scroll, its calligraphy by Kozo Matsutani: "After the ten thousandth triumph, yet a beginner." With all of Kozo's spiritual triumphs he returns to the Himalayas, saying "Onward to what has ever eluded me" (p. 225), yet a beginner in finding that which has eluded him. Ken, the highly trained ninja operative, also realizes that despite all of his triumphs, new universes have been opened for him—universes in which he would be but a "beginner."

In essence, then, the concluding sense of *Tulku* is that although each step forward in knowledge or personality development represents the

triumph of getting to where one is now, there is always the next step to be taken. Knowledge is not a thing, it is a process, a path. This is something of the heart of ninjutsu that Stephen K. Hayes clearly wishes to communicate.

In Conclusion

The image of the ninja in fiction spans the spectrum from utter superficiality to spiritual depth. Although the adolescent tales, thrillers, and even well-written novels are entertaining, they still pale in comparison to the true power of the ninja, the image as it is cast by those who are living representatives of the tradition. With the insights into the ninja gained from Stephen K. Hayes's *Tulku: A Tale of Modern Ninja*, we are now in a position to examine the historical image of the ninja. Although we may find this image a little dry, a little lacking in the flesh and blood of personalities and adventure, if we can take the feeling tone generated from Hayes's book with us we will arrive at perhaps the most complete and accurate image of the ninja that we can without extensive training in the art.

4

Historical Images of the Ninja

"Ninjutsu developed as a highly illegal counter culture to the rulling samurai elite, and for this reason alone, the origins of the art were shrouded by centuries of mystery, concealment, and deliberate confusion of history."—**Dr. Masaaki Hatsumi** (1981)

"[In a sentence, the purpose of ninjutsu training is] the joy of freedom and lightness of the spirit, as attained through an intimate understanding of the natural laws of physical reality."—**Stephen K. Hayes** (1984a)

"The great events of world history are, at bottom, profoundly unimportant. In the last analysis, the essential thing is the life of the individual."—**C. G. Jung** (1970)

THE LAST SOURCE of information that generates an image of the ninja is that which is derived from writings within the historical tradition. Here we must turn to the books of Dr. Masaaki Hatsumi, 34th Grandmaster of Togakure Ryu Ninjutsu, and Shidoshi Stephen K. Hayes, the only American ever granted teaching credentials in ninjutsu. Surprisingly, writers in the previous three domains—screenwriters, martial arts authors, and the majority of novelists—have drawn very little from these historical sources. In part, this is due to the complexity, richness, and depth of the image presented. As such it is too unwieldly and multifaceted an image for most to produce readily identifiable characters for films and books, and it is so much more than simply an image of a martial artist.

At the same time, however, the image of the ninja that emerges from Hatsumi's and Hayes's writings is *the most accurate image we have in the West.* If we are to penetrate to the heart of the matter, we must grapple with the seeming incongruities, inconsistencies, and difficulties of the image produced. In short, the reality of the ninja does not fit into nice, precise, pre-made categories that we can readily understand. However, if we are willing to look deeply we are rewarded by the true power and beauty of *ninjutsu.*

Mythic Origins of the Ninja

Like many cultural institutions ninjutsu does not have a precise place or date of origin. It did not appear fully developed, but rather, evolved slowly over time and in a number of different locations. In fact the early ninja did not even refer to themselves as such; they simply saw themselves as cultural opposites of the ruling powers and samurai ethic. It should be noted, however, that we are referring to a period of history well over 900 years ago. Ninjutsu does have a clear point of origin if we do not go as far back in time. This point needs to be clear since so many illegitimate ninja teachers and writers use this "obscure origin issue" to bolster their authenticity as knowledgeable authorities.

Since the "precise origins" of ninjutsu are not known, it is not surprising to find that myths have emerged to take the place of missing facts. It is said that the ninja were descended from *tengu*, monstrous half-man, half-crow demons with long noses and the ability to change nature's laws (Hayes, 1981a). This legend is interesting in that it embodies the ambivalent feelings the Japanese had toward the ninja. On the one hand they were seen as less than human (i.e., half crow), and yet, on the other hand, they possessed supernatural abilities far beyond the capacities of ordinary human beings (i.e. altering the laws of nature). Since they were seen as descending from "demons" we may surmise that the ninja were cast in a negative light from the very beginning.

Facts on the Origins of the Ninja

According to Hatsumi (1964), ninjutsu has its origins in a number of separate, and quite different, cultural currents. These combined to produce what has come to be known as the way of the ninja. Among these currents are Japanese shinto (animistic beliefs), *kiaijutsu* (a means of living in harmony with the universe), *rekigaku* (an early form of Japanese astrology), *jojutsu* (cane and staff fighting), and Chinese military philosophy.

Hatsumi notes that from these original sources grew *shugendo* (power cultivation), *bujutsu* (the "sciences" of individual combat), *heiho* (strategy for military operations), and *yamabushi heiho* (what we would refer to as "commando warfare"). The next stage in development was the integration of these traditions into ninjutsu.

The early history of the ninja, as noted in one of the scrolls Hatsumi inherited from Toshitsugu Takamatsu (33rd Grandmaster of Togakure Ryu Ninjutsu), embellishes our knowledge of the origins of ninjutsu. Important persons in the early development of ninjutsu were certain Chinese warriors, scholars, and monks who fled China circa A.D. 900 Among them were Cho Gyokko, Ikai, and Cho Busho, generals from T'ang China, who, together with Chinese scholars, brought military strategies, religious philosophies, folklore, cultural concepts, and medical practices to the isolated wilderness of Ise and Kii in feudal Japan. In essence, these men brought with them the wisdom from China, Tibet, Eastern Europe, and South East Asia (Hatsumi, 1981).

Also included in this early group of Chinese expatriots were Gamon Doshi, Kain Doshi, Kasumikage Doshi, Garyu, and Unryu, Taoist sages who appeared on the Kii Peninsula circa A.D. 1024. These men held to philosophical positions that sought to enhance "integrated mind-body awareness." This way of life rested upon a *personal understanding* of the nature of the universe. The teachings of these sages were taken up by the mountain warrior-priests and the warrior-ascetics of the wilderness (Hayes, 1981a). These beliefs had their origins in the tantric lore of Tibetan Buddhism as well as Indian and Chinese Buddhist tantric traditions (Hayes, 1980, 1981b).

The Search for Enlightenment

The goal of the early forerunners of the ninja was *enlightenment* (Hayes, 1980). Within Japanese cultural history these forerunners were trained in the ways of Togakure Mountain shugendo. Shugendo was a practice of "warrior asceticism and power development." Within this practice the shugenja learned not only how to attune himself with the natural forces within the universe, but also how to channel these forces (Hayes, 1983). Inherent in the shugendo practice was an approach to enlightenment in which the practitioner repeatedly exposed himself or herself to danger, possibly even death, in the remote mountain wilderness of Japan (Hayes, 1984b). The idea behind this, an idea which the Togakure shugenja practitioners actually experienced, was that by walking the fine line dividing life and death, personal power and spiritual knowledge arose.

It was during the reign of Tenmu Tennu, circa A.D. 637, that the mountain dojo of the Togakure shugenda practitioners was establishing by En no Gyoja (Hayes, 1983). And it was these practitioners, known as yamabushi, who were attracted to, and who integrated, the tantric lore brought to Japan by the Chinese sages. Whereas in India and Tibet the tantric teachings became stylized in the form of a pantheon of gods and goddesses, these teachings were incorporated and transmitted by the Japanese warrior-ascetics in such a way that *the power inherent in every individual was stressed* (Hayes, 1981b).

Hence, the close association between ninjutsu and the esoteric, tantric Buddhist sect known as mikkyo. Although nin-po mikkyo will be explored further and in greater depth in Chapter 8, it is worth noting here that this spiritual worldview stresses the interrelatedness of all things. There is no such thing as coincidence, no accidents in this world. As Shidoshi Stephen K. Hayes has written, it is through the transcendence of, and differentiation from, the material world, a

position gained through the practice of mystic exercises, that it is possible to go directly to the experience of the universal law itself. When this is achieved the practitioner is said to have attained the state of shin-shin shin-gan, or "the mind and eyes of God." He is then able to view the world from a spiritually refined and enlightened perspective (Hayes, 1981b).

At this point in time the ancestors of the ninja "lived their lives as naturalists and mystics" (Hatsumi, 1981). However, changes within Japanese culture were in the direction of increasing structure (e.g., ranking and stylization) and greater "governmental" control. And it is with these movements within Japanese cultural history, with the disruptive effects these had upon the early ninja, that ninjutsu appears to take a form more recognizable to us today.

The Sennin Taoist Immortals

The yamabushi and the shugenja practices are written about extensively in Hayes's and Hatsumi's books. Many other so-called ninjutsu experts have also mentioned these forerunners to the ninja, some of them erring widely—often humorously—off the mark. What has been given little attention is the sennin roots of ninjutsu. Fortunately, quite recently in fact, Stephen K. Hayes (1985d) has revealed something of the taoist mountain hermits known as sennin, also known to be forerunners of the ninja families of Japan.

Although there is no doubt a connection between the Japanese sennin and their Chinese mountain hermit counterparts, Hayes (1985d) notes that "Japan's *sennin* 'mountain recluse' lore has been part of Japanese culture for over a thousand years." Myth had it that these "immortals" inhabited the clouds and possessed powerful supernatural powers. They were said to be able to "control the laws of nature," to predict the future, and call upon earthly and cosmic forces to aid them. "Perhaps closer to historical reality is the explanation that the hermit sennin were religious recluses who dwelled in remote, lofty, cloud-ringed peaks and engaged in a form of taoist meditation and yogic practice that led them to extremely refined and heightened sensitivities" (p. 2).

The goal of the mountain sennin was an intimate understanding of the workings of the natural laws. Although intellectual approaches were rejected in favor of direct interaction with the environment, the sennin did draw upon the ancient yin and yang view of the cosmos,

mystic lore, shamanism, folk witchcraft, and the arts of divination. As with many North American Indian medicine men, many of these sennin mystics were closely associated with the animal spirits which guided, aided, and taught them. As with the mythology of the Indians, the involvement of animals in the lives of such mystics was frequently regarded as a matter of fact, rather than a matter of symbolism.

The sennin apparently drew upon taoist dokyo practice that combined meditation with physical conditioning. "Complementary practices involving meditation, visualization, projection of consciousness, and extrasensory experience concentrated on the development of the spiritual factor" (Hayes, 1985d, p. 3). To develop and effect transformation of the physical body, yoga, breathing exercises, diet, and the channeling of sexual energies were employed. The goal was to blend the spirit with the body, *yin* with *yang*, earth with heaven.

In essence, the sennin sought to realize tao in their lives. As Hayes presents it, tao, or the "way," refers to "what is." To fight "what is" was reckless stupidity, for one's personal energies are minute indeed when compared with the forces at work in the universe. Far better to bring one's own life and energies into accord with "what is."

Clearly there are parallels in lifestyle and philosophy between the sennin and yamabushi shugenja practitioners. In all likelihood this comes not from any shared intellectual beliefs, but from a shared experience in which there is exposure of the self to the natural elements. Put otherwise, their *experience of the world was similar*, consequently they came to view the cosmos and the workings of nature in similar ways. And therefore, not surprisingly, both traditions were major influences in the early formative years of what has come to be known as ninjutsu.

From Seeking Enlightenment to Fighting for Survival

As the society changed, the worldview of the early ninja became threatening to the established powers. Particularly noxious was the notion that each person could be his or her own priest (Hayes, 1980). Contention grew between shugendo and various governments in feudal Japan which, utilizing their far superior military power, attempted to subjugate the yamabushi. The shugenja practitioners were stripped of their right to defend their territories, and they were prevented from continuing their spiritual practice, i.e., temples, shrines, and retreats could not be built or staffed (Hayes, 1984b). Consequently, ninjutsu developed a clandestine "martial art" or "military" aspect (Hatsumi, 1981; Hayes, 1980).

In time ninjutsu became a specialized set of skills. However, it was not characterized as a unified body of knowledge. In fact, *ninjutsu* was refined and perfected by more than seventy families in the Iga and Koga regions of Japan. And each family had its own unique methods, as well as its own motivations and ideals (Hatsumi, 1981). What unified these families, and what brought about the rubric "ninja" to describe them, was their "personal-spiritual" orientation and their continual harrassment by the feudal lords for their beliefs.

The Distorted Image

To many the image suggested by the early history of the ninja families is unfamiliar. Most people are unaware of the spiritual root of *ninjutsu* and the reasons for why the combat techniques were developed. In many respects the naturalistic beliefs of the ninja forerunners were similar to the "witches" (from *wica*, meaning "wise one"), of medieval Europe, a parallel Shidoshi Hayes often alludes to in seminars. But the similarity ends where the ninja families of Japan found psychological, political, and military means of assuring their survival and the survival of their belief systems.

At the heart of ninjutsu, therefore, is the search for enlightenment and development of personal power. The all-too-often glorified and sensationalized martial arts facet of ninjutsu is but a part of the total picture, a part which serves the purpose of protecting the right to strive for, and attain, harmony with the universe. To focus exclusively upon the ninja as commando or underground resistance fighter is to make the mistake of seeing an egg as only comprised of the shell. In actuality the shell merely protects what we regard as the "essence" of an egg. *The shell, without the yolk and white, is hollow and empty.*

Daisuke Nishina of Togakure

If the origins of Togakure ryu ninjutsu can be ascribed to any one person, that person is Daisuke Nichina of Togakure. According to available sources, he studied the ways of Togakure Mountain shugendo with the yamabushi. In 1181 Heike troops attempted to put an end to resistance in and around Nagano, the birthplace of Daisuke. Daisuke sided with Kiso Yoshinaka, but after three years they were defeated, and Daisuke was forced to flee (Hayes, 1983). In leaving, Daisuke lost everything he had, including his samurai status (Hayes, 1981a). He escaped to the remote region of Iga (Hatsumi, 1981).

On the Kii Peninsula, Daissuke met the warrior-priest Kain Doshi. He studied for many years with this mystic in the mountains of Iga Province. Daisuke was taught how to make practical use of the "balance of elements" in a variety of spheres, including diet, combat, and in the regulation of thought and emotion. He also learned how to channel the forces and cycles of nature to his advantage (Hayes, 1981a). What he learned was not in opposition to his shugendo training with the yamabushi of Togakure Mountain, but complementary with it. In particular Daisuke learned the "*omote* (outer) and *ura* (inner) manifestations of wordly perspective" in his training under Kain Doshi, a training which led him to encounter both the powers of light and the powers of darkness (Hayes, 1983).

The founder of Togakure ryu ninjutsu took the name Daisuke Togakure in order to signify his "rebirth" into a new sphere of knowledge and to reflect his "roots" (Hatsumi, 1981; Hayes, 1983). The ninjutsu ryu of the Togakure family was "formalized" some three generations later on. Hence, from the teachings of Kain Doshi, as absorbed, integrated, and combined with the ways of the yamabushi in the person of Daisuke Togakure, ninjutsu was born.

Daisuke as the First Ninja

In determining the "essence" of any organization or institution one of the most important steps to take is to look at the founder. In Daisuke we find the founder of Togakure-ryu ninjutsu, and as such he is the cornerstone of our growing image of the ninja and their secret art.

Daisuke was clearly a man drawn to the mystic path, as evidenced by his training with the yamabushi of Togakure Mountain. When this tradition of knowledge was threatened by the Heike troops, he personally took up the fight to preserve a way of life he regarded as sacred.

The next stage in Daisuke's life is tremendously important. Daisuke set out on a quest. This quest is an important theme, and one that will be discussed at length in the second section of this book (see Chapter 7). For the moment, it is crucial to see that part of the ninja experience involves leaving what is known and journeying into that which is unknown. As is commonly reported in myths and legends around the world, the traveler gains secret knowledge, usually given to him by a numinous or divine figure. This knowledge changes the life of the seeker in fundamental ways and permits a deeper connection with both the inner and outer worlds.

Hence, the foundation of ninjutsu rests upon the *musha shugyo*, the warrior's journey. Again, our image of the ninja is made considerably more complex by integrating this fact. The image is not a static one in which a man or woman in a black suit embodies awesome destructive powers. Instead the image is an active one, one of moving through time, leaving the known, entering the unknown, and gaining knowledge.

Early History of the Ninja Families

What is known of the early history of ninjutsu is largely restricted to the development of the art within the various ninja families, or clans. According to Hayes (1981a) most of the traditions developed in the mountainous regions of south central Honshu island. The two largest traditions were the Iga-ryu and the Koga-ryu. The Iga-ryu was under the control of three major clans: the Momochi, the Hattori, and the Funibayashi. They operated out of Iga Province (within present-day Mie Prefecture). The Koga-ryu operated out of Koga Province (present-day Shiga Prefecture) and was comprised of fifty-three lesser-known families including: the Nakai, the Ukai, the Mochizuki, and many others that adopted the name Koga.

In addition to the major ryus were many smaller schools, each known for their own specialized subdiscipline of ninjutsu. Among them were the Koto-ryu, specializing in koppojutsu; the Fudo-ryu, who perfected the art of shurikenjutsu; the Kukishin-ryu, known for their vast network of spies; the Gyokko-ryu, experts in koshijutsu (attacking the nerve-centers of the body); and the Togakure-ryu, adepts at the use of the *shuko* (spiked iron band worn around the hand, used to stop sword blades and for climbing) and tetsubishi. Other ryus included the Mori-ryu, the Avbe-ryu, the Toda-ryu, the Taira-ryu, the Izumo-ryu, Sakaua-ryu, and the Kashihara-ryu.

It is interesting to note that the oldest of the traditions that currently make up the curriculum of the Bujinkan Dojo training of Dr. Hatsumi is that of the Gyokko-ryu. This ryu was named after Cho Gyokko, the famous Chinese warrior who first brought unarmed fighting techniques to Japan.

A More Familiar Image

The listing of the ninja families to be found in *The Ninja and Their Secret Fighting Art* (Hayes, 1981a), together with their specialties, adds to our image the tremendous diversity and complexity of the art of ninjutsu. Although the image of the "weapons master" is commonly found in the stereotyped renditions of ninja in films and books, what is often missed is the history behind this. For example, the bone-breaking techniques of the Koto-ryu took a considerable amount of time to develop, as did the ability to attack nerve centers with pinching or striking finger drives perfected by the Gyokko-ryu. We are also safe in assuming that the education, deployment, and maintenance of a vast spy network was the product of decades, perhaps even centuries, of work.

It is important to remember that each of the ryu developed its specialty under the intense military pressure from the established feudal lords, not in the luxury of peacetime. Hence, these specialized warrior skills are the product of persons able to concentrate and focus on highly complex problems while under the stress of life-and-death situations. This continued to occur for nearly 900 years; it is perhaps even more remarkable that the variety of combat forms developed.

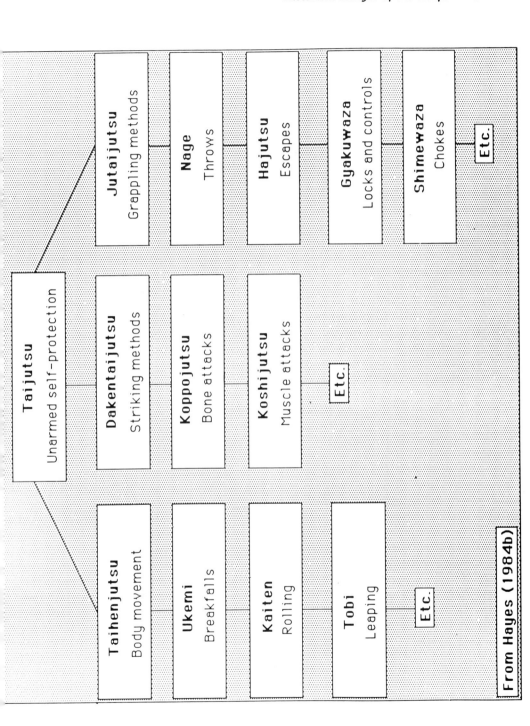

Taijutsu
Unarmed self-protection

Taihenjutsu
Body movement

Ukemi
Breakfalls

Kaiten
Rolling

Tobi
Leaping

Etc.

Dakentaijutsu
Striking methods

Koppojutsu
Bone attacks

Koshijutsu
Muscle attacks

Etc.

Jutaijutsu
Grappling methods

Nage
Throws

Hajutsu
Escapes

Gyakuwaza
Locks and controls

Shimewaza
Chokes

Etc.

From Hayes (1984b)

Organization

Our knowledge of the early history of the ninja is increased by references to the structure of the various ninja schools. The need for secrecy and invisibility was paramount given the political climate in which the ninja operated.

As Hayes (1981a) has noted, each school was comprised of three distinct ranks or levels. In charge of the major decisions and controlling the various activities the ryu was involved with was the *jonin*, or "high man." In the larger schools he was usually a man of great wisdom. The jonin's decisions were based not on the perspective of the material realm, but, instead, upon his understanding of the "scheme of totality." His concern when considering who to aid was guided by what appeared to be appropriate within a larger context.

In essence, the jonin was half-warrior, half-philosopher (Hayes, 1980). As the son of the previous generation's jonin, each generation's jonin had been raised to view the world in this philosophical manner. He was also taught how to run a highly complex, clandestine organization. By and large, the jonin was the only person with a true appreciation of the whole picture. Consequently it was he who decided who would receive the aid of his school, and who not, and at what price. Perhaps not surprising is the fact that the jonin was anonymous to most agents and operatives. This practice was maintained in order to protect the head of the school.

To inspire our imaginations amid this historical information we might consider Tulku's Hitoshi Matsutani, the head of the Matsutani family and president of Matsutani Shoji, Ltd. as a jonin. It is to him that all information flows, and it is from his position, and from his perspective, that decisions are made and passed on to those who will carry them out. This is the role of the jonin, to comprehend the whole picture, to view it in the context of the "scheme of totality," and then to instigate actions to correct imbalances or to prevent disruption of the "natural order."

Immediately beneath the jonin were the *chunin*, or "middle men." It was at this level that operations were organized. The chunin had the task of selecting the right men and/or women for a task, and deciding upon the most effective means of achieving the desired goal. According to the historical sources the chunin rarely took an active role as operatives; rather, their role was that of planning strategy and the effective management of the field operations. Apparently their primary training included time and logistics management, personnel motivation, as well as contemporary and unconventional methods of conducting warfare (Hayes, 1980).

In *Tulku*, certainly Teruo Ozawa, the Director of Field Projects Operations Matsutani clandestine operations group, and perhaps Toru Kitagawa, the chief trainer of ninja operatives, could be considered chunin. These men were well-connected at each end of the hierarchy. They were close to the head of the family, but also in close contact with the actual men and women who had trained under them and who would carry out the jonin's directives. Clearly their blending and integration of the philosophical directions set by the head of the family with what was possible in a given situation with the current personnel at hand was the genius of these men.

Finally, the field agents, or operatives, were known as *genin*, or "low man." It is the genin who we usually think of when we think of a ninja. It is this level of the ninja hierarchy that was particularly expert at espionage and infiltration, and utilized the shinobi shozoku black night suits and disguises to achieve their ends. When not on a mission, the genin lived in inaccessible, secret villages.

The genin were born into a family and tradition that was committed to the directives of the unknown jonin. At the same time, however, both philosophically, as well as through the adherence to the jonin's view of the scheme of totality, the genin also dedicated themselves to the welfare of the entire nation (Hayes, 1980). In many ways theirs was a life of faith in the wisdom of the jonin and his ability to manuever through the difficult and dangerous political waters of feudal Japan to effect the survival of the ninja family.

Taichi Nakamura, the ninja we meet in the opening pages of *Tulku*, Kenichi Odate, and the other ninja operatives in Hayes's tale are clearly genin. Their roles within the ninja family hierarchy was the realization of the jonin's directives in the material realm. To them fell the tasks of espionage, infiltration, and action.

Training

The ninja's training included constant exposure to new experiences. In essence, the ninja's training had to be comprehensive enough so that any situation could be appropriately handled (Hayes, 1980). When we consider that the ninja families were always outnumbered, it should be clear that each individual was crucial to the survival of the group. Hence, their education was geared toward providing them with information and experiences that would keep family members alive. With such a goal in mind it is understandable why training would begin in childhood.

Hayes (1981a) notes that at about the age of five or six, children's games began to become training exercises. In particular balance and agility were stressed. At about the age of nine, body conditioning was started. This was achieved through the ninja's yoga-like movements known as *junan taiso*, jumping, and rolling, and exercises to bring about muscle limberness and joint flexibility.

As the child matured he or she was taught the fundamentals of taijutsu, the ninja's unarmed practice that also formed the basis for all weapon's use. Added to this was training in the use of the sword and staff. The growing adolescent was taught how to employ the weapons of his or her ryu. Many of the other trademarks of the ninja were also introduced at this age: underwater tactics, using nature as an aid, building stamina and endurance, silent movement, distance running, and leaping. Finally, in the late teens, the young warriors developed the skills of acting, practical psychology, and medicine, as well as specialized combat techniques.

Philosophical Orientation

Hatsumi (1981) describes the basic philosophy of the ninja as *kyojitsu tenkan ho*. He notes that in a combat survival situation, it was necessary to take advantage of all factors that might permit one to achieve victory—including the actions and reactions of the mind. Part and parcel of this philosophy was the ability to "interchange falsehood and actuality," thus allowing the antagonist to be deceived. But to venture into the world of falsehood and deception the ninja had to be *firmly rooted in his or her own concept of reality*. This was, and continues to be, achieved through seishin.

Seishin is translated as "purity of heart," and embodies the sense of "completeness." When the ninja achieved this purity of heart he was able to enter the realms of darkness and falsehood without losing sense of his completeness. As Hatsumi (1981) put it, the realization of seishin prevents the defilement of the spirit. One can walk in darkness without fear of losing oneself *only if one is capable of carrying one's own "inner light."*

The ninja also chose to work in the darkness in another sense of the word. As Hayes (1981a) notes, the ninja chose to avoid overtly powerful and active means of accomplishing their ends, choosing instead to follow a philosophy of quiet and subtle action in the "darkness" (unseen). What this amounted to was a method of intervention that sought to preserve the natural order as much as possible. The ninja chose suggestion rather than force, deception rather than confrontation. By creating "win-win" situations in which the ninja's enemies believed they had won, humiliation of the enemy was avoided and, with it, the negative repercussions sidestepped.

The Darkness

From our childhood fears of having the light put out, to the adult fears of death, from the depths of depression to the religious struggle with "evil," darkness presents a problem for humankind, especially those raised in the Western cultural tradition. And yet, we find in the way of *ninjutsu* not only an acceptance of darkness, but an active working with it on a number of levels.

Turning to face, and integrate, our own darkness is a theme we will pick up again in the second section of the book (see Chapter 5). Without examining the psychological significance of looking into the darkness, however, we still add to our image of the ninja. Fearlessness—or an acceptance of fear—and the courage to enter areas of experience that are terrifying to most, is a trait of the ninja, and one to which we are drawn. Even at this superficial level the ninja become symbols for us of conquering our own darkness and facing the dark world.

But the ninja accomplish even more than walking into the darkness and using it—*they are able to preserve their inner flame*, their foothold in the light—and to hold onto it amid dark storms and periods of uncertainty. In short, the ninja were not taken over or polluted by the darkness. It should be emphasized that the ninja did not deny the many "dark" aspects of existence. Instead, they found ways of preserving who they were in the face of that darkness.

Ten Thousand Rivers Collect in the Sea

Yasuyoshi Fujibayashi, in his seventeenth-century encyclopedia of ninjutsu, takes up this theme of light and darkness. He notes that the "core" of ninjutsu lies in the dropping of attachments to the ultimately

unimportant aspects of existence. In this way the ninja realized a
"base state of spiritual purity." And it was this rockhard, experiential
foundation within the ninja that allowed them to move freely in light
and darkness, truth and untruth, reality and distortion. As members of
a tradition intent upon working within the scheme of totality and
maintaining optimum naturalness and harmony, this freedom made
them considerably more effective than those who were limited in what
they would allow themselves to experience, or what methods they
would employ to attain their goals (Hayes, 1981b).

During the reign of the fourth Tokugawa Shogun, Yasuyoshi Fujibayashi compiled the *Bansenshukai*, literally translated as "Ten Thousand Rivers Collect in the Sea." This encyclopedia is a collection of
knowledge and attitudes from many ninja families and allows us a
glimpse into the core of *ninjutsu*. It is also one of the few sources that
paints a picture of the ninja during that early historical period. What is
known of the *Bansenshukai* is revealed and commented upon by Hayes
(1981b).

The *Bansenshukai* is comprised of ten handbound volumes, each
volume covering certain aspects of the art of ninjutsu. The first of the
ten volumes is entitled *Jo* and deals with means of successful warfare
and military strategy. One of the central ideas expressed here is that
a single person can defeat considerably larger numbers of persons.
The way to achieve this most effectively is through ninjutsu.

The second volume, *Shoshin*, dealt with many of the spiritual
qualities that the ninja needed, including sincerity, motivation, and
moral strength (Hayes, 1981b). *The ninja are not common terrorists or
mercenaries.* Rather, they see and operate with respect to the "larger
totality," a spiritual-philosophical perspective that terrorists certainly
do not, indeed *cannot*, share. Hayes emphasizes that prior to any
discussion of techniques, Yasuyoshi Fujibayashi makes a statement
about intention. Clearly to this compiler of ninja tradition the nature
of the person was more important than the skills of knowledge he
possessed.

The third volume, *Shochi*, is concerned with methods of most
successfully utilizing ninja. Also included here are methods of orga-
nizational management and means of preventing the ruling powers
from infiltrating the ninja families.

The next volume, *Yo-nin*, takes a step into the more philosophical
aspects of ninjutsu. It deals with the *yo* (*yang* in Chinese), or masculine,
bright, and firm side of the ninja's power. How the intellect can be

used in its dynamic and creative dimensions is discussed. Also mentioned are five means of obtaining information without direct involvement.

The fifth, sixth, and seventh volumes are collectively referred to as In-nin. These deal with the in (yin in Chinese) aspects of the ninja's power, those aspects that might be metaphorically described as dark, motionless, or feminine. Not surprisingly this is where such methods as stealth, the use of disguise, night fighting, infiltration, and deception are dealt with. These means were considered "dark," or dishonorable by the samurai and were labeled cowardly by the ruling elite.

Hayes notes that the ninja techniques are presented in an esoteric way. For example, jargon and code words are utilized as reference points for various aspects of the ninja combat method. This desire to be cryptic served two purposes. First, it meant that the document was understandable only to the ninja families, and was incomprehensible to the samurai. Second, its goal was to remind ninjutsu practitioners of certain elements of the tradition, not to be an all-inclusive instruction manual. Hence, to make use of the document also meant that one had to be in the proper setting, i.e., one had to be in training with a genuine ninjutsu instructor who could read between the lines to make sense of the contents.

The eighth volume, Tenji, is much concerned with understanding the workings of nature. Included here are methods of calculating tide tables and moon phases, weather forecasting, and utilizing stars for navigation. The basis for these techniques lie in gogyo setsu (the theory of five elements), in-yo do (taoist principles), and ekkyo diviniation (e.g., use of the I Ching Book of Changes).

That section of the encyclopedia known as Ninki begins in the ninth volume and goes on to the tenth. Included are descriptions of ninja gear such as toki (climbing gear), suiki (water gear), and kaiki (tools for entering fortified installations). The tenth volume, known as the "tail volume," is often referred to as an appendix, or additional text. It includes part of the Ninki, as well as a description of kaki (fire gear). Information pertaining to explosives, smoke bombs, medicines, sleeping potions, and poisons is to be found here.

Cryptic and Poetic Secrets

The Bansenshukai is one of those sources of knowledge that, like the Tibetan Book of the Dead or the secret teachings of the sorcerer Don Juan

(Castenada, 1974a, 1974b), inspires a certain curiosity about esoteric traditions. The feeling is one of, "If I could just get access to it I would be empowered and know the path to wisdom." And the thought of a secret ninja document settles well into our fantasies.

However, as Hayes (1981b) repeatedly points out during his presentation of the *Bansenshukai*, the uninitiated reader would be unable to comprehend it. Trying to understand this document would be similar to attempting to comprehend a newspaper headline like "*One Flew Over the Cuckoo's Nest* wins Oscar" 1,000 years from now. Without knowing that *One Flew Over the Cuckoo's Nest* was a film, and that the Oscars were awards, the headline would be incomprehensible.

With this in mind our image expands to include the idea of ninjutsu as a highly complex tradition. Comprehending the ninja combat system out of its context is like trying to understand a living plant by uprooting it and examining it on a laboratory bench. Ninjutsu is not a set of skills that can be written down in a book and thereby effectively transferred to another person, although some books on the market promise to do just this. Instead, ninjutsu is a *living body of knowledge* that is passed down from teacher to student. Living in the tradition is not only a prerequisite for proper learning of the techniques, but is infinitely more important. As noted earlier, ninjutsu is not just a combat system. Rather, it is the combat system developed to protect an inner core of knowledge, a way of life. And that way of life, that philosophy of existence, can only be communicated and passed from one human to another by personal example.

Chuang Tzu illustrates this well in a story. He tells of Duke Hwan of Khi who is sitting under his canopy reading philosophy. Phien, a wheelwright, is in an adjacent yard making a wheel. After a time the wheelwright puts down his hammer and chisel and walks over to the Duke. He asks him what he is reading. The Duke replies that he is reading "The experts. The authorities." Phien then asks him whether these persons are alive or dead, to which the Duke replies, "Dead a long time." The wheelwright then states that the Duke is simply reading the "dirt they left behind." The Duke is angered by the man's insinuation and demands an explanation, stressing that it had better be good since death was his alternative. Phien then describes wheelmaking. He notes that if he is easy the wheels fall apart, if he is too rough the wheels do not fit. Only if he is neither too easy nor too rough does the wheel work properly. He then makes his point. *This process of finding the correct way cannot be put into words—it comes from experience.* "The men of old took all they really knew with them to the grave" (Merton, 1965). This is why the Duke is, in actuality, reading the "dirt they left behind."

Our image of the ninja and their art has been expanded in other ways, too. The idea that one person can defeat thousands is central to ninjutsu. This is not surprising given that the entire system developed in response to surviving overwhelming political and military powers. The fact that ninjutsu worked, and that it allowed the ninja families to survive, attests to its effectiveness. But this way is alien to our worldview.

We tend to think of our roles in the scheme of things as insignificant. Gandhi is reported to have once said, "Anything you do is insignificant, but you must do it anyway." In the present nuclear age many people have the feeling that nothing can be done, and this leads to apathy and depression. What ninjutsu represents is a means of making even small actions significant. However, to do so means to understand the forces one is up against. But by gathering information and coming to terms with one's foes, one begins to see that like giving a small shove to an off-balance boulder to create a landslide, one person's actions can have dramatic and far-reaching effects. This aspect of the ninja is probably one of their most appealing and important sides, and the reason many people have become attracted to their ancient, but effective, methods.

The *Basenshukai* also reaffirms our notions of a philosophical basis to ninjutsu. Again we see that being in touch with the larger scheme of things is essential to effective action. To find where one person's action will be effective requires understanding how the present situation fits together on a variety of different planes: military, political, psychological, cultural, historical, spiritual, etc. Action that occurs without an appreciation for the totality may result in negative or unwanted effects.

Ninjutsu also operates in a total way. The ninja's use of darkness has already been discussed, and the *In-nin* comprises three of the ten volumes of the *Bansenshukai*. But the ninja way also incorporates the lighted path. Indeed, the *Yo-nin* preceeds the *In-nin* in the seventeenth-century encyclopedia. The point is this, unlike the samurai who only employed ways that were culturally accepted as "right," and unlike various underground groups that were consumed by the dark path, the path of ninjutsu employed both, and was free to choose either, depending upon circumstances.

This idea of wholeness or completeness is one we shall look at more deeply in the chapters ahead.

The Height of the Historical Ninja Period

According to Hayes (1981a) the ninja families were powerful influences in both Iga and Koga Provinces by the 14th century A.D. They were able to maintain this position until the 17th century A.D. Not only were they able to control their own lands, but they were also protectors of the mikkyo temples. What is more, their services were hired out to those who sympathized with their philosophical and political orientation. It is during this time that ninjutsu developed its powerful combat effectiveness, embodying not only advanced and innovative techniques for wartime situations and intelligence operations, but also spiritual development.

One significant landmark in the history of *ninjutsu* is the battle of Onin no Ran in 1467. Immediately following this event certain ninja were employed by Shogun Yoshihisa Ashikaga, as well as lesser warlords. As Hayes (1981a) notes, the ninja could often accomplish through their silent, subtle, and unseen actions that which would have taken hundreds, perhaps thousands, of soldiers to accomplish with bold, aggressive methods.

Hatsumi (1981) indicates that during this period the ninja were trained in as many as eighteen basic areas of expertise. These included the use of many different weapons and fighting techniques as well as strategy, stealth, espionage, disguise, and explosives, even meteorology and geography. The foundations of these areas of expertise are junan taiso and taijutsu.

Junan taiso is the ninja's body conditioning method. As Hayes (1984b) notes, "The ninja's *junan taiso* body flexibility training provides for the structural freedom, suppleness, and speed required for the effective application of the techniques typical of the *ninjutsu* combat method" (p. 20). It should be stressed that these exercises are more than simply stretching out. As Hatsumi (1981) stresses, junan taiso forms the basis of "healthy living" by granting the practitioner the chance actually to *experience* the totality of the body working in an integrated and harmonious manner.

"The foundation of all aspects of the *ninjutsu* combat method is the practice and perfection of *nin-po taijutsu*, or the ninja's 'art of using the body' " (Hayes, 1984b, p. 53). Taijutsu is a means of developing the body's natural movement, and as such serves as the basis for ninja-ken, shurikenjutsu, and all other weapons fighting. It is a method designed to be effective against any opponent, regardless of height, weight, speed, expertise, etc. Through appreciating the unique aspects in a fight one can discover ways of turning these factors to one's advantage.

Taijutsu is based upon the five element theory. It is comprised of kamae, or "attitudes," each of that corresponds to one of the elements. Unlike stances that are static, the *kamae* are fluid. Since each reflects an emotional attitude (e.g., earth = confidence, or water = defensiveness), one moves into these *kamae* when it seems natural to do so in the course of the fight. The *taijutsu* basis is aimed at real, life-or-death situations. Historically it should be recalled that the samurai were also deadly and fearsome fighters. Through taijutsu the body's natural responsiveness is enhanced and turned to the advantage of the defender.

Flexibility and Naturalness

Junan taiso promotes *flexibility*; taijutsu is concerned with freeing the body up to move in *a natural way*. Therefore, even when viewing the ninja in purely combat terms, we see that flexibility and naturalness are the basis of ninjutsu, not heightened aggressive drives or superhuman strength. At the same time that it jars the image that many have of the ninja and their fighting art, it adds a dimension that belies its apparent simplicity.

The ninja were, and are, flexible in the physical realm, and this flexibility was used to overcome opponents in hand-to-hand confrontations. But the ninja were also flexible at other levels. Flexibility in terms of methods gave the ninja a greater choice of options for how to handle a certain political or military encounter. Flexibility in the realm of so-called ethics permitted the ninja to see events against a larger backdrop, and not just in relation to Confucian moral standards. The tree that cannot bend in a fierce wind breaks. And yet, rigidity in physical, psychological, and spiritual matters is a difficult demon to exorcise.

Like flexibility, naturalness is often lost as we emerge from childhood. Much that is part of our culture is unnatural. The highly structured culture of feudal Japan curtailed natural responses, and it was for this reason that the ninja philosophy was so despised and feared.

The Kunoichi of Feudal Japan

During the height of the historical period, *kunoichi*, or female ninja, were used in a variety of ways. According to Hayes (1984a), Chiyome Mochizuki, the wife of warlord Moritoki Mochizuki, set up one of the most extensive networks of female ninja agents established during the Warring States Period of Japan. This particular organization was founded shortly after the battle of Kawanakajima (1561) when Moritoki Mochizuki was killed. The Shingen Takeda requested that Chiyome provide him with spies, observers, and messengers—and she obliged.

Chiyome arranged for her operatives to be shrine attendants, or *miko*. In this role they could move freely within their respective communities and gather intelligence without attracting attention, much in the same way a parish priest might today. Not only was this network extensive, but it was also undetected. As Hayes (1984a) notes, women were, because of their social standing, often able to operate in situations that would not have been possible, no matter how silent or well-disguised, for male genin. Hence, the kunoichi were regarded as very valuable agents and resources for the ninja, well able to generate intelligence information that would enhance the possibility of survival for the family.

The particular kunoichi in question were trained in an underground academy that appeared to be nothing more than a home for young, unmarried girls orphaned and homeless as a result of the many wars of this period in Japan. Naturally they were instructed in the ways of their future guise: the various ceremonies required of miko. They were also taught how to gather information, analyze it, ensure that it reached its destination, etc. In short, they were extensively trained in the field of intelligence operations.

Like her male counterpart, the kunoichi received extensive training in all the ninja combat methods and uses of weapons. Her training was different in emphasis. Since commando tactics would be of little use, and personal one-to-one techniques considerably more relevant to the kunoichi's work, the later were stressed. Maximizing the kunoichi's ability to use psychology, manipulation, and intuitive means of survival were other important aspects of her training.

As noted earlier, the ninjutsu combat method is designed to handle any situation. Consequently, the kunoichi were well-prepared to face larger and stronger male opponents should confrontations arise in the course of intelligence work.

The Feminine Aspects of Ninjutsu

Ninjutsu is stereotypically seen as an entirely masculine discipline, in accordance with our cultural bias toward what a man and a woman can, and should, do. However, ninjutsu emerged against the backdrop of family survival. Part and parcel of survival thinking is turning all possible disadvantages into advantages. Put otherwise, it is a means of thinking that uses whatever tools are at hand to achieve what must be done.

At first glance women might appear to be at a disadvantage—after all, they are usually physically weaker. But it is precisely this type of thinking that the ninja turned to their advantage. Few would suspect a single woman working deep within a warlord's territory, or even in his castle, of carrying out clandestine intelligence operations that would result in instant death were she discovered. And if her true profession were unveiled, in the moment that a male might hesitate to act, not suspecting a woman capable of fierce hand-to-hand combat, the kunoichi might prevail. Sometimes being thought of as weak and harmless is the greatest advantage an intelligence agent can have.

To our image of the ninja, then, we must add the female component. Not only that, but we must accord that element high status and see it working in concert with the more obvious male side of operations. It should be noted that ninjutsu is probably one of the best disciplines for a woman to learn since, as a system, it is not based upon power punching and kicking, but upon flexibility and the natural movements of the body.

Historical Ninja

As noted in the beginning, historical information pertaining to the ninja is scarce. However, a number of important individual ninjas are known largely due to the research by Urata (1985; see also Hayes, 1985a). These include:

- **Hanzo Hattori**, one of the most successful jonin in the Iga-gumi organization. Aided Shogun Tokugawa Ieyasu in crossing dangerous territory in Japan circa 1582 (see page 128 for more details). Died in 1596.
- **Sandayu Momochi**, known as one of the founders of Iga-ryu ninjutsu. Various theories surround this man, including that he was the same person as Nagato Fujibayashi.
- **Nagato Fujibayashi**, one of the heads of Iga-ryu ninjutsu, together with Tanba Momochi. He was an important part of the battle of Tensho Iga no Ran, 1581, when Iga was invaded by Nobunaga Oda.
- **Chiyome Mochizuki**, the kunoichi jonin who, circa 1561, set up an extensive intelligence network through miko.
- **Kotaro Fuma**, fifth-generation head of Fuma-ryu ninjutsu. Best known for his forays against Takeda troops in 1581. In support of Hojo Odawara's family, he attacked the enemy by night with his ninja *rappa* (battle disrupters).
- **Magoichi Saiga**, head of the Kishu Saiga ninja group and master of Tsuda-ryu kajutsu (explosives and firearms methods) and Saiga-ryu ninjutsu. Utilized *shaki no jutsu* (flag discarding method) against

Nobunago Oda in which his agents were disguised as Oda's allies. It should be noted that Saiga was a Buddhist, and Oda an oppressor of Buddhism.

- **Minsan Suginobo**, born as Minsan Kanmotsu Tsuda. Thought to be the founder of Negoro-ryu ninjutsu and highly skilled at using firearms. In 1585 Hideyoshi Toyotomi successfully attacked Negoro temple with 25,000 troops in response to a previous defeat.
- **Danjo Kato**, considered a master of ninjutsu leaping and jumping methods. Also highly skilled at ninja *genjutsu* arts of illusion. In attempting to gain a high position among Kenshin Uesugi's troops, Danjo successfully removed a valuable scroll and servant from one of Uesugi's top general's castles.
- **Yazaemon Kido**, was an Iga-ryu firearms expert. He organized an unsuccessful assassination attempt against Nobunaga Oda, the fierce enemy of the ninja.
- **Dojun Igasaki**, is thought to have been the founder of the "forty-nine" ninjutsu-ryu of Iga. Yoshitaka Rokkaku employed Igasaki against Dodo. Utilizing forty-four Iga ninja, and four Koga ninja, as well as *bakemonojutsu* (ghost arts), achieved success.
- **Kumawaka** (young bear), was thought to be a Koga-ryu genin and a master of stealth and running methods. Various feats of speed and secret entering skills are attributed to him.
- **Goemon Ishikawa**, a notorious bandit hero thought to have originally been an Iga-ryu genin. Utilized ninjutsu for own personal gain. A popular character in novels and theater, he is often portrayed as the "greatest thief in the history of Japan."

A Glimpse at Individuals

By and large our visions of feudal ninja are confined to sterotyped images of black-clad genin, stalking through the night, destined for some guarded installation. They never have names, as if every ninja were the same, stamped with identical personalities, and possessing a prescribed stock of skills. Urata (1985) and Hayes (1985a), through the research presented above, allow us to penetrate this superficial image and glimpse something about certain individuals during this historical period.

What is added to our increasingly complex image of the ninja is the sense that on the one hand there is a system, or collection of related systems, known as ninjutsu, and on the other hand there are various people, each an individual with particular strengths and weaknesses.

A ninja is the result of the interaction between the ninjutsu system and a person. We see that some ninja, like Kotaro Fuman, were skilled at commanding small commando-type units, whereas others, like Danjo Kato, operated most effectively alone. Ninja also varied in terms of personal skills. Dojun Igasaki was a master of the ninja's ghost arts, whereas Magoichi Saiga was an explosives and firearms specialist. Finally, we see that many ninja were dedicated to the preservation of certain sects of Buddhism, whereas others, such as the famous Goemon Ishikawa, turned the ninjutsu teachings to their own financial benefit. In short, despite our often castiron stereotypes, there were as many types of ninja as there were people who could legitimately call themselves ninja.

The Decline

In terms of the "historical period" for the ninja, the beginning of the end was the battle of Tensho Iga no Ran in 1579 (Hayes, 1981a). Although Nobunaga Oda's attacks against the ninja were repulsed by Sandayu Momochi, a massive invasion of Iga in 1581 resulted in a ninja defeat. Outnumbered ten-to-one, many of the ninja mikkyo were slaughtered, and the surviving families were forced into the mountains.

Although this period is generally known as "the decline," it is not without various successful ventures. For example, following the murder of Nobunaga Oda in 1582, Ieyasu Tokagawa, the future shogun, employed the services of Hattori Hanzo (Hayes, 1981a). Hanzo was head of one of the most powerful Iga families (Hatsumi, 1981). The future shogun needed to get to Okazaki Castle from Sakai without passing through Honnoji territory, where Oda had been killed. This necessitated passing through the mountainous areas of Iga and Koga, areas of Japan controlled by the ninja. Hanzo was asked to assure safe passage for Ieyasu Tokugawa, and did so by organizing several of the Iga-ryu.

In time, Hattori Hanzo became Ieyasu Tokugawa's director of ninjutsu, although in most historical texts he is referred to as bushi or samurai (Hatsumi, 1981). Hanzo established an extensive network of agents who watched the movements and actions of regional daiymo (military rulers). In addition, he was appointed head of rear gate security at Edo Castle (Hayes, 1985a).

The presence of the Tokugawa Shogun in 1603 brought an end to the Warring States Period in Japan. Not all families had aided the future shogun; many, in fact, had preferred to retreat into total secrecy (Hayes, 1981b). But what the unification of Japan meant for most of the ninja families was a decline in the area of combat skills since these were no longer required in relative peacetime (Hayes, 1981a).

Many of the jonin and chunin went into police work and the military. Crime also attracted various ninja and included such famous bandits as Goemon Ishikawa, Saizo Kirigakure, and Sasume Sarutobi (Hayes, 1981a). The vast majority of the ninja ryu died out long before the Meiji Restoration in 1868 (Hayes, 1984a). This is evidenced by the fact that most of the scrolls belonging to the various grandmasters were donated to museums in Japan.

The Ninja—Rooted to the History of Japan

In our imaginations, in our novels, and on the screen, the ninja seem to "float free" of any historical context. What the post-1603 period emphasizes, however, is that the ninja grew as a result of political and military pressures—various threats to their way of life—but also declined when those pressures were removed. Ninjutsu was developed as a means of survival, and it fulfilled its function during the Warring States Period. The goals of the ninja families did not include large scale political victories or military conquests, nor the establishment of extensive underground crime rings. It may be presumed that the ninja, like ourselves today, *welcomed peace* and appreciated it as a time in which family members would not be killed or tortured a time in which the ability to pursue the lifestyle they wanted was permitted.

If our image of the ninja is one that is entirely focused upon its aggressive and combative shell, then this historical turn of events takes the wind out of our sails. However, if we return to our original goal of fleshing out a more accurate picture of the ninja we must integrate this information, especially the idea that the ninja were families, and, as such, desired little more than the survival of family members and the ability to raise children and live lives that were in accordance with their belief systems. And as noted earlier, the goal of ninjutsu was not primarily offensive, but, rather, protective. Hence, the ninja are not pure manifestations of aggressive energy at work upon the world's stage, but are real, flesh-and-blood persons, with spouses, children, and interests quite apart from military strategy, however disappointing this may be to our fantasies.

The Survival of Ninjutsu

Ninjutsu did not die out completely. As evidenced by the continued teaching of ninjutsu in Japan, and now elsewhere, it is clear that this body of knowledge was preserved. As Hatsumi's teacher, Toshitsugu Takamatsu, said to him, the core truths of the ninja warrior arts would live on forever. Given that Togakure-ryu ninjutsu survived through the early 1600s and down through the First and Second World Wars, and survived while other ryu died out, it may be appreciated that this was accomplished by a small group of highly committed men (Hayes, 1981a).

Toshitsugu Takamatsu

Toshitsugu Takamatsu was the grandson of Shinryuken Masamitsu Toda, the 32nd Grandmaster of Togakure-ryu ninjutsu. As such he was trained in Koto-ryu and Shinden Fudo-ryu methods. He was also trained by Taka Matsutaro Ishitani, the 26th Grandmaster of the Kuki Shinden-ryu *happo hiken* (secret weapons art) of ninjutsu. Ishitani was descended from chunin who had worked under Hattori Hanzo. During the Meiji Restoration he refused to dilute the teachings that had been passed down to him. However, when he met Takamatsu, already a practitioner of Koto-ryu koppojutsu and Shinden Fudo-ryu dakentai-jutsu, he realized no dilution of the art was necessary (Hayes, 1984a).

At 21, Takamatsu went to China. During the early 1900s he studied with many of the best Chinese boxing masters, and earned the name "Mongolian Tiger" (Hayes, 1981a). In 1919 he returned to Japan and was ordained as a *mikkyo* priest of *Tendai-shu* (Hayes, 1984a). In addition to carrying the scrolls as the 33rd Grandmaster of Togakure-ryu Ninjutsu, Takamatsu was also granted the scrolls declaring him 27th Grandmaster of the Kuki Shinden-ryu.

Toshitsugu Takamatsu passed on his knowledge to the present Grandmaster of the tradition, Dr. Masaaki Hatsumi.

Dr. Masaaki Hatsumi

Hatsumi began his martial arts training at the age of seven. As an adolescent he attained teaching ranks in karate, aikido, and judo.

However, according to Hayes (1984a), Hatsumi was disturbed by how easily the American occupational soldiers picked up traditional Japanese fighting arts. In large part this was simply due to size. Through his ancient weapons teacher, Hatsumi learned of Toshitsugu Takamatsu and went to study with him.

During the 1950s and 1960s, Hatsumi studied with the 32nd Grandmaster of Togakure-ryu ninjutsu. He eventually inherited the title of *soke*, or "head of the family," from Toshitsugu Takamatsu. Hatsumi acquired the authority and headmastership of the following traditions (Hatsumi, 1981):

- 34th Soke of Togakure-ryu ninjutsu
- 28th Soke of Gyokko-ryu koshijutsu
- 28th Soke of Kukishin-ryu happo hikenjutsu
- 26th Soke of Shinden fudo-ryu dakentaijutsu
- 18th Soke of Koto-ryu koppojutsu
- 18th Soke of Gikan-ryu koppojutsu
- 17th Soke of Takagi yoshin-ryu jutaijutsu
- 14th Soke of Kumogakure-ryu ninpo

Hatsumi currently supervises the Bujinkan organization. Although he no longer accepts personal students, training in the Bujinkan Dojo system is available from shihan and shidoshi both in Japan and in various countries throughout the world.

Of particular importance to the West was Hatsumi's decision to accept Stephen K. Hayes as a personal student. Now that Hayes is a *shidoshi* ("teacher of the warrior ways of enlightenment"), his writings, seminars, and lectures have brought Hatsumi's teaching to a new soil.

Shidoshi Stephen K. Hayes

Hayes's importance in the history of ninjutsu as it has been presented in the West cannot be understated. With the exception of Hatsumi's two sources, this chapter has been based exclusively on Hayes's writings, and, in terms of the presentation of an historical image, his position is unequaled. He is the only American to have ever been granted teaching credentials by the Grandmaster and is the only ninjutsu teacher in the U.S.A. who holds the high rank of shidoshi. What is more, he is the only American ever to have passed the test wherein the student sits with his back toward the Grandmaster and successfully avoids the descending sword.

In nearly a dozen years, Stephen K. Hayes has produced a small, but solid body of work recounting his experiences and knowledge of ninjutsu, including a book of poetry and photography, and a novel.

Stephen K. Hayes was also given permission to establish an American ninjutsu family, The Shadows of Iga Ninja Society.

Hayes's journey to Japan, his musha shugyo, is beautifully chronicled in *The Ninja and their Secret Fighting Art* (Hayes, 1981a). Since his return, he has published six technical manuals on ninjutsu (Hayes 1980, 1981b, 1983, 1984a, 1984b, 1985a), a book of poetry (1984c), and a novel (1985b), as well as numerous magazine articles (e.g., Hayes, 1985c). He is in constant demand as a lecturer and teacher and frequently returns.to Japan for further study with Dr. Hatsumi. He is the foremost authority on ninjutsu in the West.

To summarize the wealth of information available in Hayes's writings would be impossible in a short space and unnecessary given their ready availability. However, there are several themes stressed in both his teaching and books which will be briefly mentioned here.

The first is the idea that ninjutsu is now in a position to "return to its roots." Since there is no longer a political or military need for ninjutsu, the art of ninjutsu can return to its emphasis on the original purposes of its founding ancestors. Hence, the system is now taught as a method of personal enlightenment and mind-body-spirit harmony (Hayes, 1980). This is in keeping with Hatsumi's (1981) position that the Togakure ryu (style) exists today as a body of instructors and knowledge whose goal is teaching effective methods of self-development and awareness.

The second idea often discussed by Hayes, and perhaps the most important, is the idea of the *warrior*. Indeed, ninjutsu is commonly referred to as the ultimate warrior's art and in the majority of Hayes's publications the word "warrior" is used in the title. He regards the warrior's way as a means of interacting with the environment such that the experiences needed for enlightenment may be encountered (Hayes, 1983). He describes the ninja warrior as " . . . the epitome of spiritual freedom and power, able to tread confidently when necessary on either side of the nebulous line that separates the light from the darkness" (Hayes, 1985a, p.9). Finally, "Unlike the conventional sport or exercise martial arts so popular today, the ninja warrior's art knows no inherent limits because it was conceived of as a means of surviving the insidious onslaught of powerful oppressors" (Hayes, 1984b, p. 149).

Third, the idea of "personal responsibility" is inherent in the ninja

Jack Hoban came from a military
background to learn ninjutsu from
Shidoshi Hayes. He travelled to
Japan for further training and has
written many articles and a book,
Tantojutsu: A Ninja Defense Technique.

The Shadows of Iga Ninja Society is more like a club than the more common military-like martial arts organizations. Members, male and female, are from every walk of life and the feeling of a large extended family is the rule rather than the exception.

tradition. To become a true warrior means taking responsibility for our thoughts and actions and avoiding the all-too-human tendency to blame others or to see them as in charge of our lives.

Finally, the warrior's path involves the realization of intentions in the world. Given the overwhelming odds against which the ninja families were pitted in feudal Japan, the importance of this may be easily appreciated. Each Annual Shadows of Iga Ninja Festival ends with a ritual concerned with realizing intentions. Hayes has also spoken of "visualizing, verbalizing, and vitalizing" intentions as a means of bringing about their manifestation in the world. In short, the warrior must be able to achieve his ends within the confines of his or her situation.

Final Additions to the Historical Image

In Toshitsugu Takamatsu, Dr. Masaaki Hatsumi, and Shidoshi Stephen K. Hayes, we see the manifestation of the ninja warrior tradition in our lifetime. And in many ways, they most effectively shatter the images created by the film industry, martial arts arena, and fiction.

All three of the areas discussed in the first three chapters make up ninjutsu. Most of the stunts seen on the screen are drawn from karate and tae kwon do traditions; many of the supposedly true ninja teachers have merely recreated other martial art moves dressed in black; and the majority contributing to the fictional sphere have simply allowed their imaginations to invent, adapt, and combine. But the art of ninjutsu, in reality, is the product of centuries of development. We can appreciate that ninjutsu is a tradition by reference to the lineage of Grandmasters. And like other Japanese traditions such as Zen Buddhism, the samurai, and the tea ceremony, ninjutsu did not develop overnight and may be easily differentiated from rootless contemporary imitations.

Fundamental to this separating reality from the fantasy is deeply understanding that ninjutsu focuses on what is beyond the physical by moving through the physical. Put otherwise, it involves the spiritual aspects of reality. And, "in the sense intended by the original *shugeja* forefathers of the ninja, spiritual study implies exploring the subtle realm that seems to be beyond the physical in order to transcend the limitations of the mechanical" (Hayes, 1984b, p. 151). Almost all other martial arts pay lip service to the spiritual side of the physical techniques, perhaps suggesting students meditate; ninjutsu regards it as vitally important. Indeed, enlightenment, not physical superiority, is the ultimate goal of the ninja warrior.

Although our fantasies may wish for ninjutsu to be a black assassin's art—the success of films, martial arts publications, and ninja fiction would support this—ninjutsu today is returning to its roots. The ninja warrior walks on three planes: the physical, the psychological, and the spiritual. He or she takes personal responsibility for thoughts and actions, and the difficult task of realizing intentions in the real world is undertaken.

At first we may be disappointed at this image of the actual ninja. However, as will be demonstrated in the following sections, our attraction to the more superficial and less accurate images of the ninja point us toward the deeper historical image. It is as if we are drawn in a certain direction, but do not fully understand the attraction, nor the ultimate goal. Our next task, therefore, is to understand why we are attracted to ninjutsu, and to see the historical image to be the image we are, in fact, imperfectly seeking through lesser stereotypes.

5

The Shadow Warriors and the Warrior's Shadow

"How can anyone see straight when he does not even see himself and the darkness he unconsciously carries with him into all his dealings?"—**C. G. Jung** (1969)

"If they feared the ninja's power and the wrathful deities said to be in league with the ninja, common warriors could actually inflict destruction upon themselves through the self-engendered powers of their own minds."—**Stephen K. Hayes** (1983)

"Once a band of strangers have been identified as threatening, the archetype of evil is automatically projected onto them and they become *Untermenshen* to be destroyed: the projection is the justification of the act."—**Anthony Stevens** (1982)

"Suffering accepted, darkness recognized, and sorrow understood are great assets to the authentic life of the spirit. Composure, serenity, and authentic psychic strength all arise from the recognition and acceptance of the reality of evil and darkness, and not from their denial due to false optimism."—**Stephan Hoeller** (1982)

Now THAT WE have a good sense of the image of the ninja our task is to turn to the psychology of that image. Clearly "the ninja" intrigues us, whether we are going to the movie theater or watching television, reading martial arts magazines, enjoying "ninja thrillers," or actually training in authentic ninjutsu. And since "we" are all Westerners, Western psychology provides many interesting insights into the richness of the image and the reasons we are attracted to the ninja of ancient Japan.

Our first task is to look at the "dark image" that the ninja had in ancient Japan and continue to have today (Chapter 5). From there we turn to the notion that ninjutsu is a path of wholeness leading toward increased self-knowledge, greater knowledge of the world, and the realization of our limitless potential (Chapter 6). In addition to the fact that ninjutsu can connect us more deeply with ourselves and with the universe around us, the many channels for psychic energy within ninjutsu give it a tremendous richness. This we will look at in some detail (Chapter 7). Finally we will reach the point where our psychology ends and look at what lies beyond. We shall take a look at nin-po mikkyo, part of the ninja's spiritual heritage, as Steven K Hayes has presented it in the West (Chapter 8).

The Demonic Ninja

From their origins in feudal Japan to the present, the ninja have been regarded as malevolent. As stated earlier, the superstitious people of Japan's past thought the ninja were descendents from *tengu*, mythical demons, half-man and half-crow. They were accused of being in league with dark powers. The ninja were seen as evil sorcerers and powerful wizards able to summon spirits to aid in the realization of their dark intentions.

The fantasized beliefs suggested by the media of Western culture about the ninja, which many people consider *absolutely accurate*, is widespread. Certainly this image is prevalent among those seeking to put stringent restraints upon martial arts activities in the United States. If anyone is blamed for the "dark side" of the martial arts in the 1980s, it is ninjutsu practitioners. Despite the fact that the film images, martial-arts images, and most fiction images of the ninja are fabricated and inaccurate, they persist in the minds of lawmakers. Ninjutsu is dangerous. It must be controlled.

The Ninja as "Shadow"

On the one hand we know that the ninja are seen by many as incarnate evil. On the other hand, as we have seen in the first four chapters, much of this is erroneous. So what is happening here? Why is it that even when correct and authentic information about the ninja is made available the negative image persists in a disturbingly tenacious way?

Put simply, most people *want to see the ninja negatively.* To be even more accurate, most people *need* to see the ninja as demonic. But why? To answer this question we must dip into psychological theory, for it is here that we find many of the clues we need.

From the ancient mythologies of the world to the more recent *Star Wars* films, there has existed the notion that there is a "dark side" to all things. Wherever there is light, there is also shadow. And each of us has a dark side, or, as the eminent psychologist Carl Jung termed it, the *Shadow*.

But what is the Shadow? And how does it relate to the ninja? The Shadow of any person is comprised of those qualities that he or she considers negative. These negative parts of ourselves are usually those parts that do not coincide with how we would like to think of ourselves. And these unacceptable aspects of our being are pushed out of awareness, or *repressed*. They become unconscious, and so we are no longer aware of them.

With our negative and inferior qualities repressed, it would seem we would be done with them. But this is not the case. As Jung (1968) wrote, even *potentially positive* tendencies are transformed into *demons* when they are repressed. In other words, the moment we fail to acknowledge certain aspects of ourselves they become negatively charged. They become part of our Shadows.

And the process does not end there, either. What is repressed, and no longer attributed to ourselves, is *projected* and experienced as a *part of others*. Indeed, we will never find our Shadows if we look inside ourselves. We find them when we look at others and experience types of people whom we have strong negative reactions to. Of course, most people are not interested in discovering their dark sides. They are only interested in making absolutely sure *they* are right and others are wrong.

Already it should be clear how this ties in with the ninja. For most people the ninja are not "us" but "them." And what are the particularly negative qualities the ninja are accused of possessing? In

essence they are accused of carrying a great many of the most negative aspects of our culture, which we do not want to admit we have—violence, aggression, misogynism, a lack of compassion, etc.

The ninja have become carriers of our Shadow qualities. They are seen as negative, evil, morally inferior, scum.

Distorting the Reality of the Ninja

It is obvious that the reality of the ninja *cannot be seen* if we are looking at the ninja but actually seeing parts of ourselves that we do not want to acknowledge as our own. When our emotions are stirred by the negativity we see "out there," *in* the ninja, our vision is blurred and we are no longer able to see objectively and relate to what we see humanely. It is not the ninja who become less human, even "inhuman," in the process, it is those who insist upon the Shadow image of the ninja. Given that many need to see the ninja in this manner, to maintain their own psychological equilibrium and to bolster their own sense of righteousness, it should be clear that the question of who the ninja really was is asked by a very few.

In short, when a Shadow projection takes place, there occurs a blurring of reality and fantasy. We become *unable* to separate what we are seeing of ourselves (projected onto someone else), and the reality of the other person. When people consider the ninja as nothing but "evil," they cannot separate who they are from who the ninja really are. They are *convinced* of the accuracy of their perception! However, as we have seen in our examination of the image of the ninja in the West, most of what is presented to us is fantasy—not reality. The two are blurred, but most people neither see the distortion, nor want to see it.

"Eliminating Shadow"—Killing Ninja

In order to appreciate why the ninja were, and are, seen as so negative that they are attacked on a variety of different levels, we need to get a little complicated for a moment. We need to see that there are two types of Shadow projection. The first is the one that we have been considering all along: the individual's Shadow. Here the other person, tradition, or institution becomes the carrier of all the "evil" that we refuse to accept as part of ourselves. But there is an even more powerful type of Shadow projection.

The other type of Shadow projection is a "collective projection." By "collective" we mean something that we do *as a group of people*. For example, there are groups of people whose similar personal Shadows combine and get projected onto the ninja. Here we have one group claiming to be "the righteous" (e.g., the feudal samurai) and accusing another group of being "the Enemy" or "the personification of Evil" (e.g., the ninja). Here we find the seemingly common need to find a scapegoat. People in groups find something to blame, *and attack*, in order to feel that they are somehow free of any negative qualities (especially those in the scapegoated person, tradition, or institution). Here the "other" becomes the *Enemy*. It goes without saying that those who engage in scapegoating are *completely unaware of the fact that they have never adequately dealt with their own problems*, especially the "problems" associated with their own personal and collective evil. They fail to realize that their overreaction to the "Shadow warriors" is a manifestation of their own unresolved darkness.

It is the projection of the collective Shadow that is at the root of social, racial, and national discrimination. It is the projection of the collective Shadow that motivated the witch hunts of medieval Europe and the Ku Klux Klan's operations. The projection of the collective Shadow has involved us in the bloodiest of wars. As Jung (1968) said, when we look across the Iron Curtain it is our own face we see grinning back.

And this leads us directly to the highly repressive attitude that the warlords of feudal Japan took toward the ninja families of the Koga and Iga regions. To paraphrase Jung, it was their *own evil face* that the samurai elite saw grinning back at them from the Iga and Koga regions of Japan. The samurai were "right and good." The mystic teachings of the ninja threatened all of that by viewing reality from an entirely different perspective and pointing beyond concepts of good and evil. In essence, the *samurai* response was to categorize the ninja as evil. And, as Stevens (1982) has written, every society decrees that while it is morally indefensible to kill a member of your own "righteous" group, it is entirely justifiable to kill those who are outside of the group and who threaten it in whatever way they do. Hence the ninja, who "threatened the samurai group," could be *justifiably* and *without moral compunction*, slaughtered.

This is precisely what Nobunaga did. He had a mission to rid Japan of the ninja. They were "the Enemy," they were "Evil," and so he was

able to murder men, women, and children without any disapproval from the society at large. If you have read Clavell's *Shogun*, or Endo's *The Samurai* and *Silence*, you will quickly realize just how ruthless the warlords of feudal Japan could be. The tortures inflicted upon prisoners and the phenomenally cruel methods of execution commonly used in those days are spine-chilling. And it was this type of repressive power against which the ninja struggled for survival.

Today, while our society precludes such actions, the ninja are still maligned, and the forces of local and federal governments are already at work to curtail the practice of ninjutsu. For some officials, the ninja are directly responsible for the tremendous interest in exotic martial arts weapons such as the shuriken, and for the "perversion" of "our youth." And these comments can all be made without any whisper of conscience, for the ninja are Shadow. As in ancient Japan, they are the Enemy, they are Evil.

Our first response to Shadow, as people or as groups, is to *eliminate it*. This may involve purposeful distortion, legislative action, political attack, or even, as in the past, outright and highly flaunted attacks. And there are ethics, morals, and supportive others encouraging this "elimination"—even if it involves murder. What is at work here is a symbolic acting out of dealing with the Shadow. As we have noted all along, it takes tremendous courage to face our own darkness. It conflicts with how we like to think of ourselves and involves radical changes in the way in which we see ourselves. It is far easier, particularly when surrounded by others who also do not wish to look at their Shadows, for people to attack something external, something that is (unconsciously) seen as the Shadow.

The Ninja: Different, Remote . . . and Feared

The question arises: why were the ninja "chosen" to be scapegoats—in both ancient Japan and twentieth-century America? Again, the answer to this is both simple and complex.

First and foremost, the ninja families of feudal Japan were a minority within the population at large. In addition to this, they lived in some of the more remote parts of Japan and had an established culture of their own, which differed from that of mainstream Japanese life. What is more, the ninja families did not seek integration with the culture at

large, but sought the maximum amount of independence and freedom possible from it. So the ninja were "different," they lived in "the
wilds," and they "resisted" or "refused to accept" Japanese culture at
large.

It is inherent in human nature that whatever is "different" is feared.
Although this comes from our distant evolutionary past, and was
"designed' to aid our survival, it has persisted as a fundamental
aspect of human psychology. Since the ninja were not readily understandable, they developed a negative reputation. Also, another well-
established fact from anthropological studies is the fact that the
"wilderness" regions of the world are frequently inhabited with
demons and monsters. What happens is that the wilderness becomes
a "projection screen," upon which we can project what we as a culture
dislike in ourselves.

So, by virtue of their differences and the place where they lived, the
ninja came to be feared. They became the carriers of Japan's worst
fears and most rejected qualities. Worse still, when the "just" society
moved to conquer and control them, the ninja families did not accept
this lying down. From the various cultural influences that shaped ninja
traditions *ninjutsu* arose—a combat method designed to protect the
way of life they believed in. To the samurai-dominated society there
could be no better "proof" of the inherent evil of the ninja than the
fact that they fought back, especially when they used techniques the
samurai rejected. Since the samurai *needed* to see the ninja as the
Enemy (so they would not have to admit to themselves that they
possessed the very negative qualities they attributed to the ninja), it
never really occurred to them that the survival tactics of a minority
struggling against a repressive majority had to be different. It was
simply confirming evidence that the ninja were cowards, scum, and a
people lacking the esteemed bushido way of life.

Ninjutsu as a "Projection Screen"

There are other reasons why the ninja, and not another group, were
"selected" as the group upon which the collective Shadow of samurai
society would be projected. First and foremost, the ninja were a threat
to the ruling elite for a variety of reasons ranging from spiritual to
political. Hence, they were a thorn in the side of samurai rule. But
more importantly, they offered a "hook" for the projection of the
collective Shadow.

When the Shadow is projected it is not usually projected indiscrim-inantly. If you are arrogant, for example, but wish not to admit this to yourself, you will not project your arrogance onto someone who is humble, but someone who also manifests arrogance in their lives. Put otherwise, the projection needs a "hook."

But projection is *not* accurate perception. Indeed, as we have already seen it leads to a blurring of fact and fancy. It prevents us from seeing the Other clearly. Although the person onto whom your arrogance is projected may indeed be arrogant, the extent of his arrogance may be slight compared to your own. However, the aware-ness of any difference in magnitude is lost in the projection. Hence,

the mildly arrogant Other may appear to you as terribly inflated and bigoted. Such is the nature of projection that you do not realize that you are actually looking at your own rejected face.

The ninja, then, did provide the samurai with hooks for their projections. But these hooks were distorted by the samurai out of all proportion. Certainly the ninja fought to protect their families and their way of life, but this defensive action was seen as violence pure and simple. Hence, the repressed violence of samurai society was projected onto the ninja. The ninja became every bit as violent, in the eyes of the *samurai*, as the samurai were themselves. By projecting this violence, not only did the samurai feel that they were then free of this negativity, but they found they could also fight it in the hopes of vanquishing it forever. And since it was experienced as inherently "ninja," the ninja became the targets for the samurai's own misguided attempts to deal with their own psychic violence.

There were many other hooks also, enough, in fact, for the ninja to make ideal targets for the samurai elite. Hence, there emerged the sense that the samurai were "righteous" and "good," following the codes of bushido with reverence, while the ninja were "evil," those who would defile the fundamental goodness of the samurai's code of honor.

The Ninja's Higher Plane of Awareness

There is yet another important reason why the ninja were so feared and so despised which, if not more important than the above reasons, certainly adds a new dimension to them. Stated simply, the ninja families tended to have a higher awareness of reality than the ruling samurai elite. This should not seem entirely surprising since ninjutsu had its origins in a pragmatic realization of enlightenment. But why should this evoke the powerfully negative response that it did?

In essence, the psychological/spiritual battle between the ninja and the samurai was not only over different perspectives of reality, but *different levels of consciousness with which reality was viewed*. The ninja's perspective was more "adult," so to speak, the samurai's view more "childlike." To the proud ruling elite this was intolerable, and so they moved against the ninja families. To appreciate why the samurai were so uneasy about the ninja's view of reality we must look at the nature of consciousness itself.

Conscious awareness is not of one dimension, but many. This is clear if we consider how differently a child sees the world from an adult, and remember how many stages there are along the way to adult consciousness. But the *"ladder" of increasing awareness does not end with adult consciousness*. Indeed, an enlightened person may look back at an adult level of awareness and see it in the same way we might see a child's level of awareness. And, as we have already noted, this was equivalent to the way the ninja, from their level of awareness, looked at the samurai and their level of conscious awareness.

Wilber (1980, 1981) has outlined the hierarchic layering of consciousness in a way that can help our present discussion. Consciousness originates in Nature, in the unconscious, prepersonal realm. Awareness in this realm is simple animal-like "body" awareness. This is not the awareness of the body that a highly trained martial artist has, but an awareness of the body that lacks any involvement of thinking—a two-year-old's body awareness, not that of someone who has trained for years. "Mind" as we know it begins with the development of language and the sense of belonging to a community. This "early mind" stage, on the border between subconscious/pre-personal and self-conscious/personal, eventually gives rise to "advanced mind," the development of a strong ego (or individuality), rationality (e.g., science), and an ability to reflect on oneself (e.g., psychology). This is "adult consciousness" as we know it in the twentieth century.

But the layering goes on. Once "mind" has been created and established it can be integrated with the body. This leads to what Wilber calls the Centauric realm, and it is this level that corresponds to the advanced martial artist—mind and body as one. At the border between the self-conscious/personal and superconscious/transpersonal lies the "subtle" levels of awareness. Here clairvoyant perception begins, as do transpersonal sensitivity and extrasensory awareness. This, in turn, leads to "actual-intuition." From here consciousness emerges into the "causal" realms or final illumination realm and the total awakening to the original condition consciousness.

As complex as all of this sounds, it provides us with a framework for understanding why it is the ninja were so feared. To move from one layer of consciousness to the next involves "dying" to the way you used to conceive of yourself in order to be "reborn" on a higher level of awareness. Since none of us wishes to "die" we resist any movement upwards, *despite the fact that we have an intuitive sense that we are "one with the universe"* (the higher realms).

Now, Hayes has often noted, many of the fantastic tales about the ninja have a core of truth. The ninja's ability to read men's minds, to predict the future, or to realize their intentions in the world against overwhelming odds all point to realms of consciousness beyond that of the normal adult. So, as we noted earlier, the ninja viewed reality from a higher plane.

The effect of this upon the warlords and samurai elite was disturbing. In essence, simply by existing in the numbers that they did, the ninja pointed out to the society at large that bushido was superficial and illusory. They were pointing at the warlords' insatiable quest for power and wealth and seeing it for what it was—a means of touching the universe's "power" and "richness" without having to "die" to a new level of awareness. The ninja were also a stark contrast to the samurai's excessively rigid way of life and revealed bushido as cutting the samurai off from a deeper sensitivity to the world.

In short, *the very presence of the ninja confronted the society at large with the frightening vison of death—not because the ninja were death's envoys, but because rebirth on a higher level of awareness involved "dying" to the previous level. The* ninja did this primarily by refusing to partake in a society that did not understand them and that sought to destroy them. They also saw through the samurai's, daiymo's, and shogun's lust for power and, therefore, did not feel that they were subject to someone else's means of escaping growth.

This is another piece of the answer to why the ninja were so feared. They did indeed represent "death"—not the death of the Grim Reaper, but, rather, the death to a way of conceiving of "self" such that there is rebirth at a higher level of awareness. But most samurai did not want to face this. It was easier to kill ninja, to "eliminate death," than to "face death."

Also of importance with reference to the different levels of consciousness is that when the samurai attempted to attack the ninja, they were fighting, essentially, at a disadvantage. The ninja were able to turn their greater level of awareness to their advantage when placed in a confrontational situation. With their vastly more developed intuitive powers, they not only found means of "winning against the odds," but the way in which they did it pointed out the inadequacies of the samurai's perspective of the world. And the response of the samurai was predictable: even greater anger at the ninja, and an even greater desire to have them eliminated.

The Ninja's Use of Shadow

The ninja were known as "Shadow warriors," principally because they worked literally, and metaphorically, in the shadows. But there is another way in which the ninja made use of Shadow: as a means of protection.

Hayes (1983) has noted that those with insight and advanced knowledge can turn fear and superstition into powerful tools to use against those who attack them. The ninja were able to create such "tools" by *allowing the Shadow projection onto them stand*. The ninja, in fact, furthered their distorted image for the purpose of intensifying the fear that surrounded them. They turned the samurais' own Shadow back against themselves.

Had the ninja been, in fact, no different from Japanese society as a whole, they might have found it a fairly easy task to correct the misperception and thereby do away with the Shadow projection. To begin with, for instance, the ninja could have willingly subjected themselves to the warlords and accepted the power of the daiymos

and shoguns as absolute. But the ninja were different from the samurai society developing around them. And they were different in a way that really mattered: they viewed reality from a higher level of awareness, without "rigidity," and with power invested within each and every individual. Consequently, the ninja knew, both intuitively and realistically, that a peaceful coexistence between themselves and the samurai elite was not possible. Not because they wished to make war on the samurai, but because the samurai were threatened by them and *needed* to eliminate the ninja.

With little or no possibility of peaceful coexistence with vastly more powerful economic, military, and political forces, the ninja were in need of harnessing every possible means of protection. And *what better means of keeping their opponents away than their opponent's own worst fears?* Since the energy for the Shadow projection came from the samurai, by simply "confirming" this projection in small ways, the ninja were able to turn this energy back on their oppressors. As the quote by Stephen K. Hayes at the beginning of this chapter indicates, common warriors fought not only real, flesh-and-blood ninja, but also, their own worst fears. Needless to say, this was a terrible, *but entirely self-inflicted,* disadvantage in potentially fatal situations.

Like the wrathful deity Mahakala in Tibetan Buddhism, who was terrifying to enemies of the faith but a protector of the initiated, and like the ninja's grid of nine-slashes which was both a curse upon enemies but a blessing upon allies, the Shadow image of the ninja was terrifying to the samurai, but "comforting" to the ninja. It not only discouraged the samurai from attacking, but also put them at the mercy of their own fears in confrontations.

The Ninja's Acceptance of Shadow

So far we have discussed the ninja's relationship to society's collective Shadow. It should be clear at this point why they were feared and how they turned that fear to their own advantage. But the ninja's relationship with the Shadow does not end here. There are the "Shadow Warriors," to be sure, but there is also the "Warrior's Shadow." As we noted earlier, every person, every group, every institution, every government has a Shadow side. This is simply a fact of life. Nothing can alter this. But *what a person, group, institution, or government chooses to do with his/its Shadow side is a different question altogether.*

Part of the ninja's "power" comes not from themselves, but from the fears of those around them. But another very important source of power comes from the ninja's own Shadow. Here, rather than "giving away" the energy of their own Shadow, like the samurai did, to their detriment, the ninja "kept" the energy of their own Shadow. And to do so meant *accepting* their own negative and inferior qualities (and we all have them) rather than denying them or pushing them away.

It takes *tremendous courage to face our own Shadow sides,* to admit that we have qualities of being that we wish we were free from, to acknowledge our inferior sides. We all want to be strong, powerful, and secure, not the opposite. However, as Stephen K. Hayes has noted in numerous seminars, genuine strength is not gained by ignoring our weaknesses, but by seeking them out, working with them, and "correcting" them.

Facing the Shadow does, indeed, take courage. It also takes genuine (not rigid) discipline, and it certainly does not include repression. However, as difficult as it is to face the Shadow, once it has been faced, an interesting thing happens. We see that the Shadow side of ourselves is not all negative. From our former, limited ego

perspective, we only thought it was. Indeed, we suddenly find that the Shadow also contains energies and characteristics that could be of tremendous benefit to us, only they are often in a form with which we are not entirely comfortable.

The important idea here is that *values, qualities, and energies that are needed by consciousness are in the Shadow*. And the ninja intuitively knew this. They knew that to survive they would have to marshal *all available sources of inspiration and strength*. This included the aggressive strength rejected and thrown into the darkness of the Shadow. True, such strength often conflicts with morality and is difficult to integrate with more peaceful tendencies, for it is often in an inaccessible form, but it is only salvageable if the Shadow is faced and accepted.

Ironically, not only does the Shadow contain strengths that have been rejected because they are viewed as negative, but it actually contains positive qualities that we have never realized. But, again, these aspects of psyche can never be approached and integrated with the personality if the Shadow is refused entrance to consciousness. It is only when we begin to realize that the darkness within us deserves to be listened to—indeed, needs to be nurtured and given appropriate expression—that we can begin to approach wholeness.

Indeed, it was wholeness, however one chooses to define it, that the ninja sought, for only through wholeness could they hope to survive against forces that denied vast areas of human awareness, strength, and creativity As many have noted, wholeness cannot be realized without an acceptance of personal evil.

The Shadow as Guide

It is ironic that the ninja should have been referred to as the "Shadow Warriors," for not only did they accept their Shadows, and use the strengths hidden therein to survive against overwhelming odds, but they actually took the Shadow as guide! They were, even in Western psychological parlance, "Shadow Warriors"—warriors courageous enough to follow the Shadow into the depths of their being. And there they came face to face with their own negativity and evil, as well as their hidden strengths and positive qualities.

The Shadow is "the doorway to all deeper transpersonal experiences" (Whitmont, 1969); when it is realized, it is the source of renewal. New and creative impulses do not come from our established, often rigid, conceptions of who we are, but from the nether regions of the psyche. In fact, the *only* access to our larger, currently unconscious potential is *through the Shadow.*

As Jung once said, you do not become enlightened by imagining figures of light, but by working with your darkness. Not surprisingly, however, few wish to follow this path toward enlightenment. Facing the Shadow is not popular, not today and not in feudal Japan. Hence, the ninja had a distinct advantage over the ruling *samurai* elite. They did look into their own darkness and found the added strength and ingenious creativity that permitted them to prevail.

Our Attraction to the Ninja

With all this talk of negativity and of the dark side of humanity, why is it that we are attracted to the image of the ninja, especially as they are portrayed on the screen and in the martial arts community? Why are we even attracted to assassins or highly aggressive super martial artists?

The answer is intimately connected with our relationship to our own Shadows. Like everyone else we find it difficult to face our dark side, we find it difficult admitting that many of our "enemies" are right in what they say about us, and that many of the negative things we see in those same enemies are really parts of ourselves that we deny. But, at the same time we run from our Shadows we are also, usually unconsciously, drawn to them.

What is the witch-hunter without the witch? Or the Ku Klux Klan without a minority to tear down? Or the hardened right-winger without commies to bait? Or the ardent communist without capitalists and imperialists to root out? To be sure, part of this is the desire to eliminate that which is unacceptable. But at the same time there is an intimate involvement with the Shadow. We just cannot leave the Shadow alone. We feel compelled to interact with it. Certainly this approach to the Shadow only results in further separation from the Shadow and ourselves, but it holds open the door for getting to know the Shadow and befriending the darkness within.

We are clearly drawn to that which we despise. *We want to know that part of ourselves that we have pushed out of the light.* But we are frightened. The Shadow is indeed the doorway to our individuality, to all deeper transpersonal experiences, to the dynamism of our total beings, but we are scared to open that door.

But the ninja, at the same time that they have become Shadow carriers in our culture, *also represent the ability to face, accept, and grow through the Shadow.* They represent the courage to look inward, the courage to befriend that which is unacceptable, the courage to take responsibility totally for themselves.

As noted in the chapter on the image of the ninja in the martial arts, although aggression is packaged in the form of ninja this is not necessarily bad. If that is what attracts us to the ninja that is what attracts us. But to move beyond the aggressive images of the screen, of martial arts publications, and of much fiction *we must follow the ninja-Shadow guide.* This path may lead to the writings of Dr. Hatsumi, 34th Grandmaster of Togakure-ryu ninjutsu and to the technical and fiction books of Shidoshi Stephen K. Hayes. Ultimately, however, if the path is followed further, it is necessary to drop all conceptions of the ninja, all of the images we create of the ninja, and *experience* the reality of the ninja tradition through ninjutsu training. We must move beyond what we think about the ninja and come to know what they really are through a combination and integration of mind-body awareness.

Violence and aggression are terrible problems for us in the West. We are very far from accepting these as part of who we are as a people, and as individuals. And we get little help from established religions and psychologies when we do face this aspect of ourselves. "Good" and "Evil," "God" and the "Devil," are *radically* separate in the Judeo-Christian tradition—to "befriend" the devil is sacrilege. If you are wedded to a Freudian perspective of the psyche you look into the darkness, but ultimately all you see is a morbid mixture of aggressive and sexual drives—nothing more.

Ninjutsu offers us a means of moving beyond both of these impasses. "Good" and "Evil" are radically separated only at the peril of the person who *needs* to separate them so absolutely. And there is more to the unconscious, and more to the superconscious, than aggression and sex within the ninja tradition. There are the higher realms of awareness that are accessible once the practitioner has worked through these baser aspects of being.

So ninjutsu not only attracts us because we are intimately involved with our own Shadow qualities, but because it offers us a way of facing and integrating those parts of ourselves. Aggression is not "bad," provided it is regarded as a doorway and followed wherever it leads. Only stagnant aggression results in destructiveness.

The ninja also have emerged upon the cultural scene at an important time in our history. As many writers have noted, we have

lost much of the mystery of life, much of what we might term "spirituality." We shall look at this more in Chapter 8, but of all the "martial arts" writers, Stephen K. Hayes is one of the *very few* who have addressed the spiritual side of the martial traditions. Whereas most pay only lip service to anything beyond the physical, Hayes makes spiritual practice a fundamental part of the way he presents the ninja tradition. Ninjutsu is not a tradition of mind-body development, but of *mind-body-spirit* development.

As Jung once said, the modern world is devoid of the sacred. In order to discover his deeper, spiritual resources, modern man *must* grapple with the Devil. The image of the ninja, from its aggressive and sexualized image in films, magazines, and some fiction, through to its deeper reality as contained in the writings from the historical tradition, provides an opportunity to not only grapple with the devil inside of us, but a chance to reawaken the sacred, to create a truer relationship to the world around us. *This is the ninja as Shadow, the ninja as inner guide.*

6

Ninjutsu as a Path Toward Wholeness

"The teachings of *ninjutsu* advocate the development of the total entity, with all its naturally endowed balances and polarities, and they reject as senseless and needlessly brutal any system, martial or religious, that demands suffering, repression, self-debasement, or abdication of the joy of life for the sake of attaining transcendent consciousness or so-called salvation."—**Stephen K. Hayes** (1980)

"The achievement of personality means nothing less than the optimum development of the whole human being . . . [However to] develop one's own personality is indeed an unpopular undertaking, a deviation that is highly uncongenial to the herd . . . Small wonder, then, that from the earliest times only the chosen few have embarked upon this strange adventure."—**C. G. Jung** (1954/1981)

"Because he is totally honest with himself at all levels of introspection, [the ninja] can venture into the realm of falsehood and untruth without defiling himself or his spirit. He can willingly plunge into the cold darkness, knowing full well that he has the power to create his own light from the brightness he carries in his heart."—**Dr. Masaaki Hatsumi** (1981)

A s WE HINTED at in the preceding chapter, much of the ninja's strength and personal power are derived from the ability to use that which others regard as useless or beneath their dignity. This included not only unconventional ways of viewing reality but also inner qualities that are part of Shadow. By facing their darkness, by accepting their inferior personality characteristics and weaknesses, the ninja came to know themselves in a way most people never do, for looking at the dark sides requires tremendous courage. This allowed them to take into account things in themselves that could have jeopardized a mission or distorted a viewpoint. It also provided them with the opportunity to overcome their weaknesses. And finally, as we have already noted, it allowed them to discover hidden light as strength.

To use psychological jargon for a moment, what the ninja did by uniting their egos (or "light sides") with their Shadows (or "dark sides") was to bring about a wholeness or totality. By not rejecting parts of themselves that the samurai elite would have regarded as undignified, cowardly, dangerous, or too mystical, the ninja attempted to repress as little of their psychic energy as possible. In other words, *complete acceptance and knowledge of oneself brings tremendous personal power—* a power that the ninja effectively employed in their centuries-long struggle for survival.

Images of wholeness are explicitly and implicity present in our best sources of reference about the ninja—the sources from the historical tradition and especially the writings of Dr. Masaaki Hatsumi and Shidoshi Stephen K. Hayes. We shall start, therefore, with a brief look at the images of wholeness generated explicity within ninjutsu. This will be brief since many of the concepts introduced will be more fully discussed and elaborated upon in Chapter 8. We shall then use psychological theory to crystallize many of the implicit images that we probably sense intuitively but for which many have no language to discuss. In this way ninjutsu as a path toward wholeness might best be examined.

Images of Wholeness Within the Historical Tradition

As Hayes's opening quote to this chapter stresses, ninjutsu is concerned with the development of the "total entity," including *all polarities.* This includes light and dark, good and evil, masculine and feminine, strength and weakness, etc. Indeed, it includes all of the pairs of opposites that make us uniquely human. Jung's conception of the structure of being consists of a great network of interrelated opposites, or *dual powers*, which extend from the most concrete and physical planes of existence to the most suble and transcendental levels of spirituality. Hence, when Hayes makes reference to developing "the total entity, with all its naturally endowed balances and polarities," he is describing the realization and empowerment of the very *structure of being in its totality.*

Mind and Body

We do not have to look far to see that ninjutsu is concerned with the harmonious and holistic functioning of mind and body. The combat aspect of the art clearly represents the body side, and the ability to use one's personal power the mind side. The important thing for us to realize is that body and mind are not used separately, as the situation might demand, but together at all times.

Jack Hoban has addressed this point in some of his seminars. He notes that many consider true martial arts ability to be an instinctual, animal-like responsiveness. In a fight you hope to become like a tiger or jaguar, naturally knowing what to do. If we hearken back for a moment to Wilber's Great Chain of Being, however, we see that this mode of functioning, for all its popularity and appeal, is at a fairly low level of conscious development. This is what Wilber calls the Typhon, a creature but half man and still dependent upon his lowest animal heritage.

Jack Hoban speaks of "fighting intelligently," where there is no giving in to pure animal energy and instinct but a *full use of the mental powers of the human level of awareness.* Hence we see, in the historical tradition, a unified model of warriorship, one that for all its physicality also *fully integrates the mind.* As Jack Hoban has said, this philosophy of combat effectiveness and lifestyle makes the most common sense.

Mind-Body-Spirit

The holistic, integrated functioning of the mind and the body is certainly one symbol of wholeness we see in the historical tradition. More important, however, is the fact that ninjutsu, *more so than any other tradition that is regarded as a "martial art,"* emphasizes the spiritual aspects of life and seeks to bring such experiences and insights into relationship with the harmoniously functioning brain and body.

Without examining *in/yin* and *yo/yang* in any great conceptual detail at this point, a task we shall take up more fully elsewhere in this chapter (but in a Western psychological guise), as well as in Chapter 8, we can still point out the inherent wholeness of ninjutsu by seeing how important this concept is. Far more important than the concept is the balancing, and bringing into harmonious relationship, the *in* and

the *yo*, not only externally, but internally as well. If we remember that this philosophical orientation is a means of conceptualizing *the entire cosmos*, we begin to appreciate the full power and extent of the ninja's vision of unity.

At its most base level, *in* and *yo* divide the world in two. This is certainly a tremendous advance upon seeing the world as the "ten thousand things," *but it is still divisive.* What the balancing, harmonizing, and bringing together of *in* and *yo* does, then, is heal the basic tendency within all of us to divide ourselves, the universe, experience, etc., into bits and pieces, instead of allowing these things and processes to retain their inherent relationship with the whole. The ninja did not see themselves as split off or divided from the universe but as an essential part only separated from the whole by improper thinking.

The Five Elements

Any reader of Stephen K. Hayes's books will be instantly aware of the importance of the five elements: earth, water, fire, wind, and that transcendent element, void. As taught at the physical level, the ninjutsu practitioner aims to develop each of these elemental attitudes and responses holistically such that all are available should a fateful confrontation occur. Not surprisingly elemental balance is sought at the psychological and spiritual levels also.

There is a rather interesting modern development of this holistic, five-element philosophy within the historical tradition. Stephen K. Hayes and Dr. Glenn J. Morris, a psychologist, have developed a psychological inventory designed to help people see where their strengths and weaknesses are from a five-element perspective. The goal of this inventory is to promote *wholeness*.

Uniting the Taizokai and Kongokai Realms

Stephen K. Hayes also addresses the unification of the *taizokai* material realm and *kongokai* cosmic realm perspectives in both his technical and fictional books. As with *in* and *yo* this is another fundamental way of dividing the One, but a way that is considerably closer to Oneness than the vision of "the ten thousand things." Without going into great detail here, this unification of perspectives allows the practitioner to view reality both as a fully developed human, with his feet in the everyday world of man, as well as to have the capacity to view reality with shin-shin shin-gan, the "mind and eyes of god."

Balance and Harmony

Fundamental to all that we have discussed are the concepts of balance and harmony, both of which are expressions of wholeness. Both internally and in world affairs, the ninja sought to bring about a harmonious, balanced reality. They sought to disturb the natural order of things as little as possible. And when there were imbalances, these were corrected as quietly as possible.

We have looked at a few of the ways in which the symbol of wholeness is expressed in the historical tradition. There are more. But if we bear in mind the idea that to bring about balance requires the harmonious functioning and interaction of all parts within the whole.

Bringing about harmonious relations requires finely tuned balance, then we will appreciate that beneath whatever superficial differences there appear to be between different ways of viewing the phenomenal world, an inherent wholeness underlies it.

Having established that wholeness is an inherent part of ninjutsu within the historical tradition, we now turn to viewing it through Western psychological eyes in order to more fully understand and clarify this idea of totality. It is no accident that the psychological theory we are drawing from is one that itself advocates wholeness—indeed, it places the striving for wholeness as one of the most fundamental of human drives.

Unifying Thinking, Feeling, Sensation, and Intuition

One of the most striking ways in which ninjutsu may be seen as a symbol of our path toward wholeness is in the striving to develop all aspects of psychological functioning equally. When one aspect of the person is developed to the exclusion or neglect of another, naturally, an imbalance occurs: In actuality it is almost uncanny how many of the principal tenets of ninjutsu fit into Jung's four categories of psychological functioning.

When we speak of "psychological functions" we are speaking of the way in which the psyche operates to make sense of the world. In fact, it is through our "functions" that we see reality. Not surprisingly, there are a number of basic functions. The four that predominate in Jungian psychology are thinking, feeling, sensation, and intuition.

Before we get into a discussion of what each of these is and how they relate to ninjutsu training, it is important to recognize two facts. First, the ability to use or have use of all functions simultaneously would be an expression of unified or holistic psychic functioning. To attain this requires tremendous effort and is, consequently, *very rare.* A vast majority of people have developed one, perhaps two, of these functions—and have ignored the others.

Second, these functions can be arranged and looked at in a consistent relationship one to the other. In fact, they exist as two sets of polarities. Thinking and feeling represents one pairing, sensation and intuition the other. What this means is that those people who are more inclined toward the thinking end will tend to repress and ignore their feeling function. Similarly with sensation and intuition; the preference for one leads to a relative neglect of the other.

The relationship between the functions can be graphically represented by a cross. People will tend to choose one function as their dominant function or characteristic way of seeing the world. For example, a professor might be "thinking dominant." Sometimes people will have access to an auxiliary function, one which they use at times or have access to. The professor might, for example, be intuitive. The opposites of the dominant and auxiliary functions will be largely unconscious and unavailable for use. Hence, the professor in our example will have difficulty with the feeling and sensation functions. Just from this simple example we can already see the great benefits of an equal development of the functions.

The Ninja's Accurate Perception of Reality

If there is one ability of the ninja that receives the most publicity on the screen, in the martial arts world, and in the majority of fiction, it is the almost uncanny perceptiveness of the ninja. They see and hear things that most of us cannot. Even if we hear or see the same things, the ninja somehow know how to interpret their perceptions more accurately. Add to this the highly developed senses of touch, taste, and smell, and the ninja are very much in touch with physical, concrete reality.

It is not just the ninja's powerful sense perception that is emphasized but also their physical abilities. The ninja are portrayed more often than not as super martial artists, gymnasts, and illusionists—all disciplines that require phenomenal skills in the physical dimension. The ninja, therefore, are not only aware of physical reality in a very intimate and highly developed way—they are also very much in touch with the hard and cold facts of their own physical existence.

Since ninjutsu is often portrayed in these ways it would make sense to begin our investigation of the functions with sensation. Put simply, *sensation* is the concrete perception of people and objects, including ourselves, through the five senses. This function provides the basic framework of our lives. It provides us with a sense of reality that we do not take for granted in everything we do, and that, were it not there, would leave us unable to make sense of our world.

Jung (1971) emphasizes that sensation is not just concerned with external stimuli but with internal stimuli as well, as in the organic processes of the body. Hence we see that the sensation function looks outward *and* inward in a concrete way: viewing the reality of self and world in a straightforward manner. To the ninja the facts of the body were every bit as important as the facts of the external world.

The role of the sensation function in ninjutsu is clear. We need simply look at the sophisticated techniques of escape and evasion to recognize that the ninja rely heavily on sensation. It was crucial for

their survival that the ninja be in *intimate touch with the facts of their esistence.*

The use of the sensation function also finds expression in the actual development of the ninja combat skills. As noted above, sensation is not only concerned with looking outward at the world, it is also connected with looking internally, too. *Body sense* is the result of utilizing the sensation function, and the acquisition of ninjutsu fighting techniques requires a highly developed sense of your physical being, what it can do, what it is not doing, and how best to use it.

It should go without saying that in the midst of a confrontation, the ability to judge where the other person is in relation to you is crucial. *All senses must be activated.* You must be able to see clearly whenever possible. Should your back be turned a sound may give you a lifesaving clue as to the position and actions of your opponent. Were you to be blinded by sand in your eyes or fighting in the dark, being able to feel the other, and make sense of those perceptions (especially anticipating a strike) would be invaluable. Being well-grounded in physical reality is a prerequisite for learning ninjutsu.

Clearly the development of the sensation function is important in the study of the ninja combat technique. However, this development *must be in balance* with the other psychological funtions. There are many dangers that result from being unbalanced in this area. Many people who are *sensation dominants* are extremely dry, matter-of-fact, and stuck in the mud. They may be too attracted to sensual (physical) enjoyments. In the martial arts world this could translate into an overemphasis of techniques, ignoring other aspects of training.

To the overly sensation-dependent person, people and belongings may simply be objects that he feels he can use; feelings and meanings may be totally disregarded. This would most certainly place such a person at a disadvantage in interacting with others to collect intelligence, as well as in interpreting the data. Often such *pure types* are conventional and unimaginative (hardly the mark of a "true ninja"). Hence we see that sole reliance upon sensation would be a dangerous thing indeed.

The Ninja's Intuitive Powers

At one extreme we find that the physical side of ninjutsu is very appealing. At the other extreme we find a fascination with the psychic powers of the ninja. Certainly on the screen these two aspects of ninjutsu have been placed side by side with great box office success. It is as if intuition were being viewed from a sensation-dominant perspective. Sensation-dominant people do not, indeed cannot, understand intuition, if they have not worked at developing this aspect of themselves. Hence, intuition seems incomprehensible, like magic. The result is that the intuitive dimension of the ninja is given a very primitive, shallow, and quite ludicrous presentation. Hence, the ninja of the screen are technical wizards, equipped with hocus pocus magic and mind-reading ability.

But what is intuition? If sensation is thought of as perception through your senses, *intuition* may be thought of as *perception through the unconscious*. As Jung (1971) has said, intuition operates in such a way that the awareness of something presents itself to us in consciousness as an already established whole. We are *suddenly*, and *clearly*, aware of something, just as we suddenly and clearly see a car coming toward us; except that this "seeing" is through the unconscious, not through the senses. We do not know how we know it—*we just know it.*

Consider what happened on one of Dr. Hatsumi's trips to the United States. A group of students asked him about the ninja's *kuji-kiri* and *kuji-in*. In reply he asked Shidoshi Stephen K. Hayes to punch him in the back of the head at any time he was ready. Hatsumi then went on talking to those around him. However, when Hayes did effect the punch, Hatsumi simply slid to the side before the strike could reach its target. As Hayes (1983) has noted, it would have been impossible for the Grandmaster to have heard the punch coming. And even if he had heard it, such information would not have given him sufficient time to react.

Lest we think that these tremendous powers of intuition are the exclusive property of the Eastern brain, it should be noted that Shidoshi Stephen K. Hayes has passed a similar test, the *go-dan* or sword test. As he reports it, "Twice I felt as though the blind blade behind me had begun its descent toward my head, but in reality I suppose it was merely a perception of the building potential of the sakki 'force of the killer' that slowly filled the room . . . [Then] I was suddenly aware of the fact that my body had moved, somehow collapsing sideways in a seemingly involuntary motion" (Hayes, 1986). Here we see not only intuition as a means of perception, but "intuition in action"—Hayes's body moved out of the way of the descending blade.

Had Hatsumi heard Hayes's punch coming or Shidoshi Stephen K. Hayes heard that the sword strike was coming, then these abilities to avoid danger would be due to a highly developed sensation function. But they had no such sense warning. Their perception was through the intuitive function. As Hatsumi (1981) puts it, the ninjutsu practitioner "refines" his perceptive abilities. This refinement takes him far beyond the level attained by most people. The ninja thereby become sensitive to information that does not come through the five senses, but from another source. Hatsumi emphasizes that there is nothing particularly magical about this. Just as we all see, hear, taste, feel, and smell the same things, so, too, we might also "know" things in the "thought realm." The point of this: it is not a question of this being possible or not—it is a question of whether *we can become sensitive enough to experience it.*

Clearly the ninja possess highly developed intuitive abilities. However, we must not lose sight of the fact that these abilities are not the single most powerful tool of the ninja, but *one tool in a balanced set of tools.* For again, the unbalanced intuitive dominant has many weaknesses. Although such people might have intuitive skills that could be classified as ESP, they may misjudge their position within the immediate situation. Overly intuitive people often ignore physical reality, including their own bodies. This can lead to situations in which they might actually court death. Also, such people may be quite detached from reality. Their seeming calmness is not connection, but disconnection.

It goes without saying that the ninja most certainly did not ignore their bodies, nor were they out of touch with the facts of their existence. The ninja's intuitive powers were always in balance with their sensation function—a symbol of holistic functioning in and of itself.

Clearly the pure "intuitive dominant" is not an accurate portrayal of the ninja ideal. Ninjutsu stresses "being in touch," not journeys into the extrasensory realms that may result in *losing touch* with basic, immediate reality. Intuition is vitally useful in avoiding danger—especially unseen danger—but in a swordfight or grappling situation you need to be in touch with concrete reality, the reality perceived through your five senses. You cannot afford to be detached. However, it should be noted that an intuitive sense of the fight, *provided it works hand-in-hand with the sensation aspects*, certainly gives the practitioner of ninjutsu a decided advantage over his opponents.

One final note on intuition. We in the Western world tend to neglect and ignore intuition. One of the reasons we are so fascinated with the kuji-kiri and kuji-in of the ninja is because they point toward unrealized potentials within us. This is also a reason why blatantly silly "intuitiveness" sells on the movie screen. It is no different than using grade school science to entertain primitive peoples who have not developed intellectual traditions to the same extent as we have in the West. But intuition is, in actuality, no more dramatic nor silly than any other function—it only seems so when it is viewed from an imbalanced perspective.

The Kamae or Basic Attitudes of Ninjutsu

A fundamental aspect of ninjutsu training is using your feeling state as a guide to the natural response to any confrontation. It is your confidence, fearfulness, or aggressiveness that is translated into body action. Clearly this brings us to the feeling function.

Feeling is related to what we do with what we perceive. In essence, the feeling function involves making a personal, subjective judgment about what we have sensed. We determine what the value of each thing is that we experience in the world, and this appraisal is one of *involvement, relationship, and interaction*, not objective distancing. Although the feeling function is, strictly speaking, a valuing function, it should be clear that it has an intimate connection with feelings and emotionality. After all, our emotions quickly respond to the world and evaluate it in terms of like or dislike, safety or danger, etc.

Hayes provides many examples in his books of the use of feeling. Usually these are closely associated with the basic elements earth, water, fire, and wind. We shall look at one example to consolidate our understanding of the feeling function in ninjutsu.

A good example Hayes (1980) provides is as follows. Imagine yourself in a small roadside diner alone. Two thugs enter, catch sight of you, threateningly approach, and sit down across the table from you. There is little doubt from the way they are talking that they intend to rough you up. If you respond to the situation from the earth center you

have the attitude of "I don't want to be bothered." You are confident and feel well grounded. Consequently you continue as though they were not there, finish your meal, and get up to pay the cashier, hoping that your nonchalance will defuse the situation.

If the thugs are considerably stronger than you, you might feel overpowered and defensive. In this case you would be responding from the water center. Using your nervousness you might joke with them and laugh off their threats. You might then "retreat" to the washroom. If you can escape, you will. If not, and they follow you in, you might use their assumption that you are running scared and ambush them in the washroom, then escape.

From the fire center you would respond with assertiveness or aggression. As they begin to make their move you would respond quickly and decisively. You may even move first to gain advantage over their two-to-one odds.

Finally, from the wind center, your response is one of intelligently using feelings to simply not be there for the thugs. They want someone to intimidate, but if you were to begin acting in a bizarre manner—knowing full well that mental illness makes even the most hardened criminal anxious—they might want nothing to do with you. You are not what they are looking for to satisfy their need. Consequently they might leave you so as not to have attention drawn to them.

It should be clear from the above examples that your feelings can guide you to a response that is right for you in a given situation—*provided you are in touch with your feelings.* So often in the West, especially among men, feelings are inaccessible. But it is crucial we see that feelings can be of tremendous help in guiding our relationship to reality. Indeed, the famous anthropologist Gregory Bateson (1972) noted that emotions have their own logic that is every bit as precise and as complex as the logic in rational thought. It's just that we have difficulty seeing this logic. Put otherwise, "The heart has its *reasons* which the reason does not at all perceive." Again it should be clear that the ninja, rather than repressing or discounting emotion, worked with it and integrated it into ninjutsu.

As with the functions already described there is always the danger of imbalance if one function too strongly dominates the others. In an extreme form the feeling-dominant person can be so externally focused that he loses touch with who he is. He cares too much what other people think of him. Feeling-dominant persons can often see things only in black-and-white and often have shallow, dogmatic, and prejudiced ways of thinking. It's obvious that if this function is out of balance serious consequences could result.

The Intelligent Ninja

The thinking function is quite familiar to us in the West, for it is the foundation of our scientific method. Thinking brings about the ordering of our perceptions, whether they are intuitions or sensations (although the latter functions fit the scientific method better). It also places these perceptions in a meaningful relationship.

The ability to think clearly, to be logical and rational, can be a tremendous asset to any person. However, if it is out of balance it can lead to trouble. One of the biggest difficulties a thinking type can get into is making his rationality a creed—existence is "only an abstraction." And this attitude allows such a person to be strikingly, and often cruelly, oblivious to the feelings of others—even close family and friends.

The ninja clearly made use of "logic." In fact ninjutsu is often described as a "scientifically" developed system. But to make the point again, the ninja were not enslaved to logic or science. These perspectives were but one in their arsenal of psychological functioning, powerful because they were in balance and could therefore be used most effectively and to their best advantage.

Striking a Balance

Striking a balance among the four psychological functions was clearly a goal for the ninja: they wanted to view reality and respond to it with the *maximum of freedom and appropriateness.* But striking this balance is not easy, just as looking at the Shadow and integrating our own negativity is not easy. But the rewards for so doing are tremendous. And if we only begin to bring balance to ourselves we at least know ourselves and our weaknesses better, and can appreciate the way someone of another type sees the world.

As we noted earlier the functions exist in two sets of polarities. The rational man will have difficulty with his feelings (a very common problem), the feeling type will evidence inferior thinking, the intuitive will often lack a good grounding in reality, and the sensation type may have little awareness of anything beyond the concrete. The reason for this is that we tend to use our strengths, and neglect our weaker functions. However, to quote Hayes again, it is necessary to find our weaknesses and work with them.

It is entirely normal to rely upon our dominant functions. We do so without even being aware of it. But as Jung has stressed, when we are considering totality, the rounding out of the personality, then it is imperative that we listen to our other functions as well, especially to our least-developed functions. It is only then that we can discover

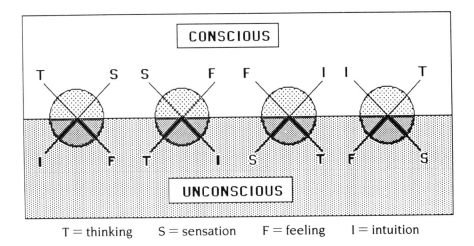

T = thinking   S = sensation   F = feeling   I = intuition

there are many situations in life we cannot possibly handle effectively with only our strongest function.

To approach life with one function only is to kill life. To decide to develop your potential, to accept your "fate" with all your strengths and shortcomings, and to walk your individual path in life is called *individuation*. Individuation is the drive within us to become whole—a drive we too often ignore. However, one of our attractions to the ninja is that they represent a way of life that does just that. They are living examples of persons who have embarked on this journey, the journey we all, at some level of our beings, wish to be on.

Balancing Inwardness and Outwardness

From our discussion of the four psychological types it should be clear that the ninja aimed at a wholeness that would make them at home both in external reality ("the world") and within themselves ("the psyche"). Again, *this was a necessity, not a luxury.* Outwardly there were the realities of the warlord's armies and powerful oppositon; inwardly lay many strengths that were difficult to get access to, but were part of the key to their success. In particular the ninja did not want to trip themselves up; instead, they let the *samurai* stumble over the obstacles in themselves. Therefore the ninja needed to balance these two approaches to reality.

Two of Jung's concepts, which are widely known even outside of psychological circles, are "introversion" and "extraversion." Each of these concepts represents a basic way, or attitude, of interacting with the world. Ordinarily a person is either an "introvert" or an "extravert." As with the psychological functions, people are strongest in one way of interacting and tend to use it more than the other. Again we are faced with a human fact that our weaknesses are pushed away and neglected, and again this was a phenomenon that the ninja were determined to reverse. They sought ease of movement both within and without.

Let's begin with a quick look at the extravert for this is the attitude that is most familiar to us in the West. The extraverted person centers his life around external demands and conditions in the world. These factors, not subjective factors, are important to this type. Inner life is "subordinated to external necessity." Often the extravert will ignore not only his psyche but his body as well, since the body is not "out there" enough. He is then left with a vague sense of imbalance, but does not know how to proceed in terms of correcting that balance. The danger for the extravert is that "he gets sucked into external objects and completely loses himself in them."

Such a basic attitude toward life, especially if extreme, would have been highly detrimental to the ninja. The ninja could not afford to rely solely on "one version of reality," because any version among many would be one-sided. The ninja's actions, therefore, could not be determind by external factors alone.

When we turn to introversion we find that within American culture the introvert is considered something of an oddity. Not infrequently such a person is regarded as abnormal in some way. But this is not so in other cultures, including those in the East. Part of the reason for this stems from the East's greater experience with, awareness of, and acceptance of the reality of the inner world. One of Jung's great contributions to our understanding of others was his assertion that an introverted attitude was every bit as valid as an extraverted one. Indeed, we all have introverted and extraverted tendencies. It is simply a matter of which we give preference to and which we reject.

The introvert tends to be subject-oriented. He is oriented toward the inner world of the psyche, and, to him, psychic reality is a concrete experience, every bit as concrete as the external reality of the extravert. The introvert is often directly in touch with what Jung would call *archetypes* or what Tibetan Buddhists might call "deities"—those parts of us which act autonomously within and which, if we can forge a positive relationship with them, can produce powerful changes in personality and awareness. Unfortunately the introvert, at the same time that he grants the inner world its due, often devalues the external world. Whereas the extravert feels ill at ease in matters of psyche, the introvert feels similarly in matters of external reality.

In sum, the introvert tends to fear or mistrust things out there; the extravert, of things in here. Each finds a lifestyle, which may become a prison, that will most easily accommodate his fears. Now it should be pointed out that neither will consciously admit to these fears, at least

The spirit must be trained to flow
and find balance just as the body
must be trained.

not easily. The tough-minded business executive who can run a multimillion-dollar company, follow the stock market, and invest wisely and opportunistically in real estate may not show any overt fear of the inner world, but he will avoid it. If he is involved in any religion, it will be with its surface aspects only. He will probably prefer thrillers and books about business to spiritual or philosophical texts. He will probably scoff at those interested in Eastern cults and be resistant to such practices as meditation. In short, he is unfamiliar with, mistrustful of, and sets no value in the inner world.

The introvert may well be found in an academic position, or as an artist. Whatever positon in life he takes it will likely be one that minimizes the interaction and involvement with the outer world and maximizes the value of the inner world. Certainly those who follow through with spiritual training, especially those attracted to a monastic way of life, are introverted in orientation. Like the extraverts, the introverts fear the other's domain. They feel uncomfortable in externally oriented situations. And like the extravert they discredit what is out there, claiming it is far less important than the vast inner horizons.

In times of relative peace and little persecution it matters little, in a life-or-death sense, which attitude you have. But for the ancestors of the ninja the luxury of constructing a life around one of these attitudes was not possible. Having briefly looked at each attitude it should be clear that ideally neither the external, nor the internal world, should be devalued. *Strength lies not in imbalance, but in balance.* The extraverted attitude with its strengths of knowing what is going on out there needs to be joined to the introverted attitude that knows what is happening deep within.

The easiest way to illustrate the ninja's emphasis on both attitudes is to note that they developed vast, highly effective intelligence networks, while at the same time, nurturing and developing their mystic heritage. "Information gathering," especially in times of social tension, is extraverted in orientation, as is the job of orchestrating such operations. At the very least the chonin and genin ninja had to have well-developed extraverted attitudes. Hearkening back to Chapter 4 it should also be clear that through the shugendo practices, and others, the ninja have, from the start, been very much involved in the inner world. As a symbol for the development of both attitudes we have the jonin, the head of a family, who are often described as "warrior-philosophers"—"extravert-introverts."

It should be clear that we have been describing yet another way in which ninjutsu is associated with wholeness. Indeed, just as the desire to balance your four psychological functions is an expression of the search for completion and totality, so is the desire to develop both an extraverted and introverted attitude. Hence, if you are interested in the nin-po lifestyle, if you are interested in affirming all of life, rather than selecting some parts and rejecting others, then you are on the path toward wholeness.

But as wonderful as that sounds there can be little doubt that this is not an easy road to tread. Most people are too scared to even begin walking on this path, and you are unlikely to receive much help from other people. *Wholeness is a dangerous thing—it points out the one-sidedness and imbalance of others.* Proof of this is easily found. Jung's psychology, a psychology that values the inner life in balance with the outer life, is discredited and maligned by the more popular, extraverted psychologies. More to the point, the ninja families of ancient Japan were ruthlessly attacked by the samurai elite, who advanced a rigid way of life that trained the mind to think in one way only. As we noted in Chapter 5, attack is the first response to catching a glimpse of the Shadow. Just as the Jungians carry the Shadow projections from the Freudians and were "attacked" in numerous scholarly papers and books, so, too, were the ninja attacked, literally and militarily, because they carried the Shadow projection from the samurai power structure.

The Sun and the Moon, the Firm and the Yielding

Time and again we have pointed to the ninja's ability and courage to face what is inferior, rejected, or spurned by the culture at large, and realize the potential contained in it. So far this has seemed relatively straightforward: confronting shadow, integrating psychological functions, balancing outwardness with inwardness. At least, in thought, these are fairly easy to accept (although in practice they are exceedingly difficult). But we now turn to another set of psychic polarities that even in thought are threatening to us—particularly those of us in the West. This polarity is that of masculine and feminine.

From the screen to the ninja magazines and to most of the novels about the ninja we have a fairly standard image of the real ninja. He is the epitome of all that is male. He is strong, decisive, aggressive, forceful, and virile. In short, our conception of the ninja is macho. Curiously, many of these images even show "male extreme" psychopa-

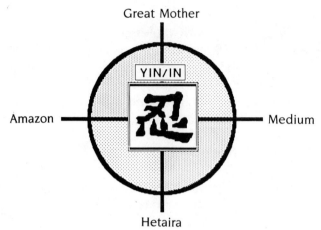

thology, especially schizoid aloofness and alienation, an inability to cope with feelings and an ineptness in interpersonal relationships.

In the face of the public image of the ninja as the macho male comes our assertion that the ninja sought completeness, wholeness, and totality. Although this probably makes us uncomfortable, especially those who are wedded to such an image of the ninja, this also includes the *unity of our masculine and feminine qualities*. Strength lies in unity of self, not in divisiveness, and we must have the courage to face all of who we are, not just those parts of us that we want to, those parts that fit in with who we would like to be.

As we mentioned earlier, ninjutsu philosophy contains the Eastern concepts of In/Yin and Yo/Yang. It is important to realize that the ninja did not just apply these concepts to the world "out there," but also to the world "in here." We shall look more closely at these concepts in Chapter 8, but to understand the male–female polarity we need to sketch out what these mean.

The first hurdle we must get over is thinking that maleness and femaleness are associated with men and women exclusively. This is not so. "Masculine" or "feminine" are labels we put on types of psychic energy. And we all contain and exhibit *both types of energy*. We must remember that In/Yin/Female and Yo/Yang/Male are *symbols*; they point to something that cannot be described in words. They are the best possible representation of something unknown. We must try to remain open to their possibilities, rather than discard them because they seem threatening.

Whitmont (1969) describes these two types of energy well. He notes that in Chinese philosophy the Yang principle is represented as the universal element, or archetype, that generates and creates. It is "initiating energy." This is energy in motion, energy empowering, energy that moves outward "assertively" or "aggressively." Customary representations of Yang are heat, light, stimulation, the sword and spear. It is "positive" energy that moves outward in a penetrating manner; sometimes it shatters. It is "heaven" and "spirit."

The Yin principle, on the other hand, is the "opposite," or, more accurately, the *complement*, of the Yin principle. It is receptiveness, the tendency and/or capacity to yield, the sense of withdrawing. Yin represents coolness, wetness, darkness. It is associated with the concrete world. It is "enclosing," "form-giving," "gestalting." Its movement is inward, not outward (introversive rather than extraversive). It corresponds not to spirit but nature. As with women, who are a concrete manifestation of the principle, the Yin concerns the world of creation, the "dark womb of nature." It is that which gives birth. It is symbolized by the earth and moon, darkness and space.

We need only point to ninjutsu's intimate involvement with Nature and darkness to indicate the importance of so-called "feminine" energy to the system as a whole. Indeed, if we think back to Chapter 4, Fujibayashi's *Bansenshukai*, three of the volumes are concerned with the *in* or dark side of the ninja's power.

We can differentiate the Yin and Yang principles in the psyche to gain a better understanding of what "archetypal powers" are associated with each. Beginning with the Yang principle we have four such archetypes, arranged in a quaternio. One pole may be described as the Father. Whitmont (1969) describes the Father ("Father" is, we must remember, symbolic of various energy forms and experiences) as "leadership," "authority," "rulership," "protection," and "legality."

Opposite the Father is the Son, Companion, or Brother. Whereas the Father does not see people, only "subjects," the Son interacts

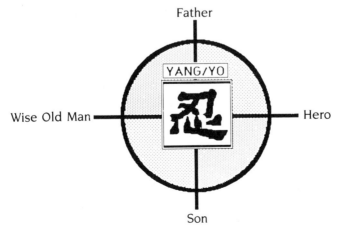

with people individually. The Son has personal concerns, regardless of what the social norms are. He is the eternal seeker.

Clearly this type of energy captures something of ninjutsu, but we must not be tempted into thinking this is an "all good" form of energy, and the Father "all bad." As always, a balance is needed. Both the Father and Son types of energy are needed. Wisdom determines which energy is appropriate when.

Another set of polarities, at right-angles, so to speak, from the Father-Son polarity, is that of the Hero and Wise Old Man. Whitmont (1969) describes the Hero as the soldier, that type of energy that represents "personal will" or "power effort." The complement of the Hero is the Wise Old Man. The Wise Old Man type of energy listens rather than fights. He is represented not by the warrior, but by such figures as philosophers, sages, mystics, teachers. Less Yang, and more Yin, but in a "male" way, the Wise Old Man is much concerned with receptiveness and perception.

Again, *both energy forms are needed.* In many ways the genin or ninja field agents embodied Hero (or warrior) energy, and the jonin warrior-philosopher heads of ryus the Wise Old Man energy.

The Yin principle also has four associated archetypes. Complementary to Father energy are Mother energies and forms. Here we find a sheltering attitude. This Great Mother energy which, symbolically, is at once "nourishing and protecting" and "destructively devouring," *regardless of the individual.* Her complementary energy is represented by the *Hetaira,* the Eternal Daughter, or Sister. Here we find an orientation toward love and personal interaction as an ultimate goal. Mother energy holds families together, *Hetaira* energy pays attention to individuals and cultivates personal love (Wolff, 1956).

The other set of polarities within the Yin principle is Amazon–Medium. The Amazon archetype is self-contained and independent, and interacts as "comrade" or "competitor." Fulfillment of individual development is intimately associated with this energy. The complement of the Amazon archetype is the Medium archetype. Here we find immersion in the "subjective experience of the psychic atmosphere." The archetypal world of the beyond is expressed in the energy and forms of this archetype (Wolff, 1956).

The important thing to remember about all of these types of energy is that *every man and woman has all four male and all four female energies and forms in some degree of development,* just as everyone has the four basic psychological functions of thinking, feeling, sensation, and intuition.

We are all variously composed of Yin and Yang energies, and in proportions that change moment by moment. We must not be fearful of our contrasexual energies, but be completed through them.

To attach psychological labels to these potentials within us, the *anima* is the feminine side of a man, the *animus* the masculine side of a woman. The anima, as an energy that shapes our character and behavior, is very similar to our conceptions of the Yin principle. It directs us toward life, especially toward that which is natural and spontaneous. Sadly, in the West, the anima is neglected and spurned by men. But herein is ninjutsu's intimate connection with Nature and Life.

Hayes speaks of "befriending the earth." In the realm of physical combat this means using the earth as part of your weaponry, not being afraid to get knocked down. (It is interesting that many self-defense teachers see the earth as an "enemy"—if you are knocked to the ground you are already defeated. What is also worthy of note is, as Jack Hoban has remarked, that nearly *all fights end up on the ground, so it only makes common sense to be comfortable fighting on the ground.*) But Hayes's comment also has tremendous meaning at the metaphorical level. If we fight our own earth, the very "ground" we stand on, our animas, we are—and there is no better word for it—foolish.

As Whitmont (1969) notes, if we can accept the anima within us, and acknowledge the energies encompassed here, we change what many people fight against (their "inner feminine side") *into an ally.* He adds that when this occurs "blind emotions," or what Hatsumi might call "useless emotions," are transformed into "genuine feelings"—feelings that might aid our feeling function, our judgment of the world. The anima, when accepted in the way that the Shadow is accepted, opens the door to the world of the soul. The anima enhances our spontaneity and our receptivity. Adaptability is contained in anima energy. The anima, when taken as a guide, aids in the integration of our undeveloped psychological functions. The anima also permits the constructive working with our aggressiveness, transforming it into available energy that can be put to constructive use.

It is interesting how many of the benefits resulting from an alliance with the anima sound like basic tenets of ninjutsu: sensitivity to the environment and others, adaptability, "mature emotions," the tempering of foolish aggressiveness, and receptivity. Again we see that acceptance of the inferior parts of ourselves leads to important gains. And again we find the ninja exemplifying this ability.

The animus when realized in women also results in increased personal power. If we bear in mind that the female ninja agents were not only important to the survival of the ninja families, but also crucial at times (because a woman could often go where a man could not, given the strict structure of Japanese social life) we see the importance of the animus in ninjutsu.

The animus is to women what the anima is to men. The animus is woman's "recessive maleness" or Yang energy. Successful integration of the animus results in self-assertion and individuality. It allows a woman to learn and use many of the very "masculine" aspects of ninjutsu—especially the "assertion/aggressiveness" evidenced in the ninja combat method. Completeness is strength.

Uniting Consciousness and Unconsciousness

When we look at the ninja through Western eyes, aided by a psychology that places a high premium on balance and wholeness, we see that much of what we have been referring to when we talk of bringing into harmony the four psychological functions, the two basic attitudes, or the self with the contrasexual side (anima/animus) is a working together of the conscious and unconscious levels of awareness.

When a function is regarded as inferior or an attitude is neglected, it is "discarded" in the unconscious. We are *un*conscious of it, and so no longer know that it even exists. So if we are thinking dominant, with our sensations side available to us, our feeling and intuition functions will be in the unconscious. If we are extraverts, our introverted tendencies will not have been eliminated from our psyches, simply discarded in the unconscious. But the unconscious should never be considered a quiet, deanimated waste bin. In fact the unconscious is very much alive.

The ninja developed a working relationship with their unconscious sides not just because it housed great potentials, but because when the unconscious is not given expression directly, it finds expression indirectly, outside of the control of the directing ego. Imagine the dangers inherent for a ninja infiltrator or mole who was unaware of his or her unconscious side. Much could be "given away" or communicated to the enemy by actions that are unconscious only to the person, not to onlookers. Hence "personal development" was not a luxury for the ninja which would bring a greater appreciation of life, but an urgent necessity.

The unity of consiousness and unconsciousness was crucial for the ninja. We could look at it solely in terms of the Shadow (with its great positive potential), the four psychological functions, two basic attitudes, and anima-animus, but there is another way we can look at it which will lead us into Chapter 7, which looks at the archetypes of ninjutsu, as well as into Chapter 8 which goes beyond psychology and looks at nin-po mikkyo, a part of the ninja's spiritual heritage.

We tend, in the West, to discuss "the unconscious" solely in terms of what is "rejected." This is the Freudian legacy in which the unconscious is seen as little more than a cauldron of seething sex and aggression. However, as we have noted, the unconscious possesses tremendous potential, if only we have the courage to look for the key to open it. And when we do we find not "one unconscious" but many! We also see why the East sees the psyche so differently from us in the West.

The Great Chain of Being

The ninja, as we have noted often, looked for every possible advantage to aid them in surviving against overwhelming odds. Put otherwise, *the search for wholeness was a necessity.* This included plumbing the depths of the unconscious. But the unconscious is more complex than it seems, certainly more complex than Freud ever knew. But the ninja were never interested in logical constructions of the mind—*only in fully developing it.* To understand what psychological structures they discovered in the unconscious *and superconscious* we must get a little technical for a moment, but this discussion into the various levels of awareness is worthwhile if we are fully to understand the ninja, especially their search for an overarching unity of consciousness.

In Chapter 5 we took a brief look at Wilber's (1981) "Great Chain of Being." This chain is the hierarchical layering of consciousness, which begins at the most unconscious levels of being and moves toward the highest spiritual realizations. In Chapter 5, we were interested in how the "Great Chain of Being" related to the collective Shadow of the ruling samurai elite being projected onto the ninja families. Here we are interested in understanding each of the levels of consciousness in relation to the ninja's search for wholeness. More correctly, we could say that through ascending the "Great Chain of Being" the ninja *realized wholeness.*

Realizing Wholeness

We have noted before, and we shall mention again, the Western world has tended to conceive of the spiritual quest as one in which the practitioner comes to establish a relationship with God, however "God" is conceived. But the godhead is *always separate from the self.* Hence, alienation is inherent—we are still separate from the Universe. How does one seek answers when such a basic assumption is felt to be inaccurate?

In the majority of Eastern spiritual traditions, and this includes the ninja's nin-po mikkyo, this intimate relationship with "God" is but a stage in the development of consciousness. The practioner *becomes one* with "God," or "Nature," or "the Cosmos." There is no alienation, no separateness. In essence, the infinite is not a big Daddy in the sky to whom you are inferior. Instead, the Infinite is seen as the Ground, the suchness, the "condition of all things." It is the "Nature of all Natures," the "Condition of all Conditions." The Infinite is not other, the Infinite is "sewn into the fabric of all that is.".

Hence the ninja were not seeking "salvation" from some greater Other, they were seeking, rather, to *discover* the essential wholeness of everything. Like a wave on the ocean "discovering" that it is of the same substance as the ocean, and therefore all other waves, so the ninja, through "transcendence," "enlightenment," "liberation," or whatever term you might wish to use, discovered through ascending the "Great Chain of Being" their oneness with the Wholeness that is. In a sentence, they became whole through realizing Wholeness.

Let us take some time, therefore, to flesh out the levels of consciousness realized, worked through, and transcended by the ninja. In this way we can arrive at an appreciation of what they attempted to unify both in terms of levels of consciousness, but also in terms of levels of unconsciousness/superconsciousness.

The Subconscious Realms

Very briefly, the subconscious realms involve the immersion of the self in matter. Consequently there is no consciousness. The *pleuromatic self* does not know "self" or "other." It has no concept of space. Here consciousness just floats in the oceanic feelings of timelessness. As Wilber emphasizes, we must not for a moment think that this is nirvana. This is complete unconsciousness. Certainly if one falls back to this level in psychosis one had "died," but not the constructive

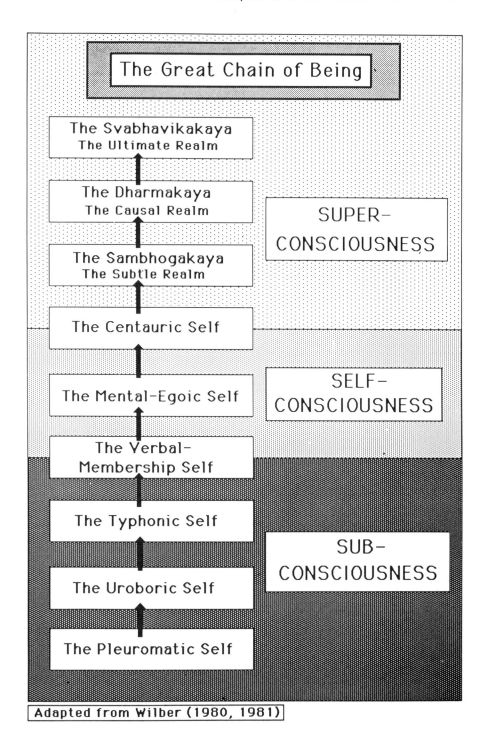

The Great Chain of Being

The Svabhavikakaya
The Ultimate Realm

The Dharmakaya
The Causal Realm

The Sambhogakaya
The Subtle Realm

SUPER-
CONSCIOUSNESS

The Centauric Self

The Mental-Egoic Self

SELF-
CONSCIOUSNESS

The Verbal-
Membership Self

The Typhonic Self

The Uroboric Self

SUB-
CONSCIOUSNESS

The Pleuromatic Self

Adapted from Wilber (1980, 1981)

death that marks the emergence into the next level of awareness; just the reverse.

The next level up is the *uroboric* self. Here the self begins to recognize that there is a world "out there." There begins the sense of needing to fight for survival. Hunger and fear emerge into awareness. But this is still a *very primitive* level of awareness.

The next level of consciousness is described as the *Typhon* by Wilber—half-man, half-reptile. At its lower level, the "pranic self" feelings begin, especially fear, greed, rage, and pleasure. Time exists only in the present, and the self is highly narcissistic, unable to "see" others. At the higher level, the "image-body self," emotions are not just experienced in bursts, but are sustained. Here the self is on the verge of recognizing that it is indeed separate from the world. Here we are verging on the human realm.

The Conscious Realms

At last we arrive at the "human realms," those realms that many have reached on the ladder of consciousness. With the "verbal-member-ship self" we find the beginnings of will power and the sense that one belongs to a group, that *one is related to other human beings*. With language there develops a past and a future. This is where "good" and "evil" distinctions can start to be made.

Moving up another link in the chain, we arrive at "advanced mind," or the *mental-egoic self*, the crowning achievement of modern times. Logical thinking arrives on the scene, as well as complex emotions. When this level has been well-realized will power and self-control are possible. There is a sense of history. It is worth noting that this is where the ruling samurai elite were, most likely, in terms of their level of consciousness.

It is worth stopping here for a moment. We in the West are heirs to a scientific legacy, and science, with its radical separation of self from world, logic, and will power well symbolizes this mental-egoic state. We believe in "reducing things to fundamentals." D. T. Suzuki (1960), the famous Zen scholar, noted that when a Westerner wishes to "know" a flower he pulls it out of the ground, dissects it, and runs a variety of tests on its elements. In short, he uses "science" to come to an understanding of the world. What he does not realize, of course, is that he has *destroyed the flower in the process*. The Easterner, on the other hand, does not pull the flower out of the ground and put it on the laboratory bench, killing it in the process. Instead, the Easterner seeks to "become one" with the flower, and so understand it "from the inside." These two approaches are *radically different*, and they lead to radically different ways of viewing the world.

If we stop in our building of consciousness at the "advanced mind" level then, as in Freud's psychology, we could say that all we "really" are, and all the unconscious "really" is, are all those stages we have been through. Hence the unconscious is little more than "animal instincts" and "early (immature) mind." We have tried to understand "advanced mind" by looking backward. We have "dissected it." We never consider looking at what is ahead, to put where we are in context.

"Advanced mind," for all its accomplishments (and there are indeed many), is rather "adolescent" in character. It is human, but far from fully human. Sadly, this is where the vast majority of people stop in their development. More dangerous is the fact that there is the tendency to "attack," physically and symbolically, those who move on.

The Superconscious Realms

As Wilber stresses, there are *many* realms above the "advanced mind" level of consciousness. These are the "Super-conscious" or "Trans-personal" realms. There are the "Psychic" (*Nirmankaya*), "Subtle" (*Sambhogakaya*), "Causal" (*Dharmakaya*), and "Ultimate" (*Svabhavikakaya*) realms of consciousness which lead from complete ego-body integration to complete "oneness with the universe"—not the oneness at the earliest stages (as the Freudians always think) but the oneness which lies at the end with the total development of consciousness.

With the realization of the *Centauric self* we find ourselves on familiar ground with respect to the ninja. Here we have what we in the West know as "self-realization." Here in the Centauric level there is "total body-mind being." This is where the genuine martial artist might begin to be placed. The self (*body and mind*) is integrated, not split up. Here time is experienced in the present, and all of time is seen, and *experienced*, as emanating from the present. This is not the present-orientation of the earlier stages, but a realization that comes only with the more advanced levels of awareness. It is only here that the person becomes truly autonomous. Here there is greater sensitivity and spontaneity. Here feelings are genuine and heart-felt. Here the person is no longer restricted to logical thinking, but to all the varieties of thinking available to the human organism. Here the heights of the superconscious realms are intuited.

In terms of Buddhism, the gross mind is let go and the subtle mind realized. In terms of the yogic chakras there is the integration of all of the six chakras already worked through. Clearly ninjutsu's working with feelings, as in the basic attitudinal kamae, the ninja's increased sensitivity, and the integrated and coordinated function of the mind and body, we find the foundation of the ninja way. This is our "best image of the ninja," but is it restricted by our inability to see further than this realm.

The Centauric self is at the border of, or may begin to straddle, the Nirmanakaya and Sambhogakaya realms. The Sambhogakaya, or subtle mind, realm involves two levels. With the realization of the "low-subtle self" there comes clairvoyant perception and cognition. Extrasensory awareness develops. Sensitivity is no longer restricted to oneself, but extends to others. This sensitivity is even more powerful than the sensitivity realized in the Centauric realm. The force behind one's life is no longer one's own, but comes from "beyond." Here, time is experienced in an entirely different way; it is "point time." There may even develop the capacity to actualize the astral self.

With the realization of the "high-subtle self" actual intuition comes into being. The practitioner is "outside of time." One is part of the archetypal divine. Here compassion dominates the feelings.

We have already established that the ninja were *at least* at the Centauric realm of consciousness. We should not find it difficult, therefore, to entertain the possibility that they penetrated beyond the gross mind levels through to the subtle mind levels. True, many tales and legends of the ninja were flights of fancy on the part of the samurai, but, as Hayes has noted, legends build up around kernels of truth. Clairvoyant perception and cognition, estrasensory awareness, transpersonal sensitivity, a drive that comes from the "void," the awareness of point-time (and the ability to "read the future in the present"), "actual-intuition," the actualization of the astral self, and the oneness with the "divine" were all definite possibilities for the ninja, given that they built upon the firm basis of the Centauric self and devoted their lives toward enlightenment. We do not mean to imply that all ninja at all times were at this level, but given the samurai's reactions (see Chapter 5), and the legends that grew up around the ninja, it should go without saying that a *significant percentage* of them did emerge into this realm.

It is not inconceivable, indeed it is entirely likely, that many ninja also penetrated into the *Dharmakaya*, the Causal realms. These realms are almost beyond words, but here, as Wilber puts it, the self is the "final-God," the "point source of all archetypal forms," "formless self-realization." Here there is the shin-shin shin-gan, the mind and eyes of God. Even beyond this there is the *Svabhavikakaya*, the final transformation. Here there is perfect integration of all of the preceding levels of awareness. Here there is "perfect wholeness."

The Wholeness Beyond Wholeness

Before we considered the ninja in relationship to the "Great Chain of Being," we saw many ways in which the ninja realized "wholeness" in their lives. We now see that there is, perhaps always is, a "wholeness beyond wholeness." "After the ten thousandth triumph, yet a beginner." We can stop at various realizations of totality, or we can push on ever further toward Totality. It goes without saying that nin-po, the higher order of ninjutsu, did just this.

Individuation and Our Attraction to the Ninja

It is no accident that the ninja phenomenon, or ninjamania, has emerged during a time in our culture where there is considerable interest in "self-realization" and "self-actualization." Indeed, as Morris (1986) has noted, there are striking parallels between "shinobi psychology" and the psychology of the humanistic psychologists such as Maslow and Rogers who are principal proponents of the Human Potential Movement. Ninjutsu, or nin-po as it is known in its higher order, exists not only as a *symbol* of wholeness, but also as a *process* toward wholeness. Jung refers to this process "by which every living thing becomes what it was destined to become from the beginning" as *individuation*.

The term "individuation" means a *becoming whole*. To do so it is necessary to reconcile, and bring into relationship, the conscious and unconscious aspects of the psyche. There are two aspects of the individuation process. The first is that of bringing together the "split off" aspects of the psyche. The second is that of amalgamating and coordinating them, especially the energies that these split-off portions of the psyche represent. What is sought is a *meaningful whole*, a "cosmos, not a chaos" (Harding, 1963/1973).

"Individuation" is a Western term that is paralleled by many Eastern concepts of personality development, concepts which are, in fact, centuries older. Many Jungian psychologists have drawn attention to the tantric levels of consciousness found in Tibetan Buddhism and elsewhere, levels which we have touched upon in the last section. Again it is not surprising to find ninjutsu generally, and nin-po mikkyo, in particular, having close ties to tantra. For us, the process of increasing awareness is identical with the process of individuation. What we refer to as the "Self" or "totality" is symbolized by the mandala. We shall have more to say about these ideas in Chapter 8, but it is important that we see them here as related to this process of personality development.

We all could be whole. This is part of what the ninja represents to many, including ninja enthusiasts and actual ninjutsu practitioners. Indeed, the pattern of wholeness is inherent within our psyches. The pattern is not just an image or ideal. It is dynamic, motivating energy. It is a driving force within us which, if we can learn to allow it, leads us to wholeness. Sadly, most of us choose to disregard this "instinct." How many of us read about the ninja, and about ninjutsu training, but fail to take the first step in following through with our intuitions that this is a promising path to be on? However, if we recall Wilber's hierarchy of consciousness it should be noted that each step "upward" into a new state of awareness involves a "death" to the previous level. Since we all fear death, we resist moving on and try to find some way of satisfying our desire for oneness. Unfortunately this turning away from wholeness results in a division. Division within us means sickness and misery, physically, mentally, and spiritually. Wholeness, on the other hand, means health, a health gained by healing ourselves, by uniting all of the split-off aspects of ourselves.

If a person can open himself to the process of growth he can avoid being a "house divided against itself." Fragmented people cling to the supports that a culture or philosophy might provide. "Total people" are self-reliant, not parasites. *Realizing wholeness brings a sense of standing on the solid ground inside within us, on a "patch of inner eternity which even physical death cannot touch"* (von Franz, 1975).

The ninja could not afford to be divided against themselves within themselves. Nor can we. Hence there is an attraction among many to the ninjutsu tradition, for it represents a way of healing ourselves. The tragedy is that the vast majority of this interest is superficial. There are many ninja movies, novels, magazines, and weapons, but there are a surprisingly small number of people who have the energy to actually begin training—not just the training at a festival or seminar, but the "twenty-four-hour training" Shidoshi Hayes talks about. All of this energy being generated by "the ninja" is certainly appropriate when we see that the ninja and their nin-po way offer us something we, in this culture, very badly need. But this energy is not being channeled effectively. In most cases it is insufficient to break through that fear of change.

Hence ninja books, magazines, uniforms, weapons, films, and paraphernalia all become *substitutes* for the wholeness for which the ninja stands. We identify with something that is whole and delude ourselves into thinking we are whole. But identification does not effect personality change. I may throw a football, and so does Joe Montana. That does not mean I am Joe Montana, nor a great quarterback, nor a professional football player, nor a fine sportsman. Although it may feel great to be tossing passes, and, although my imagination may put me in the Super Bowl, in *reality* I am simply throwing a football, nothing more.

And this is true for ninjutsu, too. I can dress up in a shinobi shozoku, slip nine shuriken into the hidden pocket, strap a ninja-to to my back, don tabi, loop a kusarifundo in my belt, and tuck a tanto someplace else, but I am not a ninja, regardless of what the magazine ads say. I may feel I am. I may even creep around for a few nights and evade

detection, and hit the bullseye on my target with my shuriken nine
times out of ten. But I *am still not a ninja.* I am not even a ninjutsu
practitioner. If I think I am, if I think that I now have all the powers of
a shinobi warrior, then I am substituting my fantasies for the reality.

It is true, everything valuable in life is costly. And as Jung (1978) has
said, the development of personality is one of the most costly of all
things. To achieve this we must take ourselves as the most "serious of
all tasks." We must be conscious of everything we do. Even those
aspects of ourselves that we despise within us, our Shadows, must be

looked at and worked with. It goes without saying that most people are unwilling to accept the cost of developing themselves. It requires too much energy, it is too frightening, it involves too many glimpses of our imperfections.

There is no substitute for ninjutsu but ninjutsu; there is no substitute for wholeness and totality but wholeness and totality. If we are to attain these goals we must energize our intentions and find the courage to move forward. If we wish to find that piece of eternity that even physical death cannot touch we must step onto the path and begin. And we are supremely fortunate in the West that legitimate *ninjutsu* training is possible. There are many ways to wholeness, but each way is right only for a certain type of individual. There are always doors open to totality, but we cannot open every door. If your door and path is the "warrior's path" then you will not reach your goal without opening that door and beginning the difficult journey. And Hayes, together with his senior instructors such as Jack Hoban and Bud Malmstrom, have now provided those doors in the West.

7

The Archetypes of Ninjutsu

"It is a great mistake in practice to treat an archetype as if it were a mere name, word, or concept. It is far more than that: it is a piece of life, an image connected with the living individual by the bridge of emotion."—**C. G. Jung** (1968)

"All ways of speaking of archetypes are translations from one metaphor to another."—**James Hillman** (1975)

"The origins of an archetype remain obscure, its nature unfathomable; for it dwells in that mysterious shadow realm, the collective unconscious, to which we shall never have direct access, and of whose existence and operation we can have only indirect knowledge . . ."—**Jolande Jacobi** (1959/1971)

"The archetype is manifested principally in the fact that it determines human behavior unconsciously but in accordance with laws and independently of the experience of the individual."—**Erich Neumann** (1955/1972)

HAVING LOOKED AT the ninja in relation to the Shadow, and at ninjutsu as a path toward wholeness, we now turn to the tremendous richness of the ninja image, especially the image that most closely corresponds to "reality." For us this translates into the image of the ninja as it is presented through the writings of Dr. Masaaki Hatsumi and Shidoshi Stephen K. Hayes, as well as in the workshops, lectures, seminars, and festivals arranged by The Shadows of Iga Ninja Society that are led by qualified instructors within the Bujinkan tradition. As we shall see, the image of the ninja is both a rich and complex one. We do well to catch a glimpse of what is beneath the surface. However, before we do that we must first dip into some psychological theory that will lay the groundwork for our discussion, and allow us to plumb the depths of the ninja image as best as we are able.

Archetypes and the Archetypal Power of Ninjutsu

The concept of the archetype is somewhat difficult to grasp. Therefore, as we make a quick departure into theory, it is worth remembering that archetypes are *pieces of life*, not abstract concepts. In order to discuss archetypes we are forced to use words, but our labels and concepts are there to point us toward parts of the human psyche, parts that are vital, powerful subpersonalities within us. Certainly what we refer to as archetypes were psychic energy manifestations that the ninja, referring to them by different names, were not only well aware of, but *cautious and respectful of.* It is only those who do not fully comprehend the power of the energies we are discussing who trivialize them and stir them unnecessarily. And they do so at their own physical, psychological, and spiritual peril.

Jung's most accessible description of the archetypes is one in which he sees them as riverbeds or watercourses within our psyches. Just like riverbeds in the external world, their purpose is to channel something; in the case of the real river that something is water, within the psyche it is "psychic energy," "life force," "ki," or whatever term we might use to indicate the empowering factor in our lives. These inner riverbeds are deep, fully capable of handling whatever energy may be generated, and shaping it in their own characteristic way. It may be, as in the desert, that there is no psychic "water" flowing in them at all times, but when energy is directed by external demands, *or by inner self-direction*, into the archetypal watercourses, then that psychic energy takes on a particular shape, quality, and form.

The archetypes tend to be designated by religious or mythological names. God, the Devil, the Shadow, the Hero (or Warrior), the Hermit (or Mystic), the Healer, the Wise Old Man (or Sage), Woman, Nature (or Universe, Cosmos), the Self are all ways of referring to the way psychic energy may be channeled in a person's life. They are labeled in this way because this is how they tend to appear in myth and art, a result of how this energy is realized and experienced *in life*. In addition to types of psychic energy, archetypes also represent energic *processes* such as Birth, Death, Rebirth, the Hero's Quest, Creativity, Destruction, and Individuation (the realization of your total being). Heaven, Earth, Yin, Yang, Nature, the Sun, the Moon, and more are also archetypes. In short these are all symbolic expressions indicating ways in which psychic energy might be channeled within us, just like the five elements are used symbolically in ninjutsu to refer to the variety of ways in which we might categorize a situation, respond to a threat, or verbalize our strengths and weaknesses. It is crucial we remember that these are *symbols* for something that is essentially unknown, and not signs, which indicate something we know well.

We must not underestimate the power of the archetype. Jung speaks of our personal psychology as almost *insignificant* in relationship to the archetypes within us. The archetypes, the various riverbeds and watercourses that exist in *all of our psyches* (no one "owns" an archetype), are vastly more powerful. They are the most powerful factors in our personal lives, in history, and in the world at large. They "decide the fate of man." The archetype of Wotan, the war god, possessed Germany and led to the horrors of World War II; in the West the Masculine (Yang) is far more important and influential than the Feminine (Yin) and has led to tremendous psychological imbalances and related problems; in our personal lives the Mother and Father affect our lives through the personal parents we have, through authoritative institutions, in the relationships we have with mates, etc.

In short, we are but driftwood in the riverbed when psychic energy turns the dry watercourse into powerful rivers. With this in mind we can immediately appreciate why the ninja wished to learn how to relate to and channel these forces. Through awareness they could see which archetypal powers were influencing which leaders or periods of

history. Through relating to, and channeling the archetypal energies within them they could best find ways to survive and bring about harmony in the nation.

Outside of our culture, there is another way we might look at the archetypes and archetypal energy. Consider the deities of Eastern religions such as Tibetan Buddhism. To the majority of people these divine beings are real. However, to the enlightened, the gods and goddesses are *manifestations of different qualities of energy* (archetypes). Advanced spiritual practitioners in the East do not pray to a deity, hoping to be saved by that god or goddess; rather, the practitioner attempts to become one with it. By becoming one with a deity the type of energy that deity symbolizes is realized within the practitioner.

Realizing the qualities represented by the archetypes leads us to a position in which we can work *with*, rather than *against*, archetypal energy. Clearly there are ways in Eastern spiritual traditions that open up this possibility. There are also ways in the West, particularly in the transpersonal psychologies such as Jungian psychology, to relate to the archetypal levels of the psyche. Within ninjutsu we see that a relationship with, and a channeling of, this archetypal energy is possible. And when we recall how powerful this energy that we are dealing with is, we realize something of the background of the ninja's force in the world.

Certainly part of the ninja's power derives from their ability to channel psychic energy consciously. Another aspect of that power is the fact that the "richness of ninjutsu," and by that we mean the variety of archetypes the ninja had to draw from, is enormous. Indeed, in this chapter we will only be able to look at a few of the more predominant ones. In other words, the nin-po tradition encompasses the means for actualizing and channeling many of the psychic watercourses within us. Hence, there was tremendous *flexibility* available to the ninja due to the wealth of energies with which the ninja could work.

Three final points. The first is this: archetypes span our existence, *from basest physicality to highest spirituality.* They are rooted in instinct but are the reflection of that instinct in consciousness. And from this ground they stretch toward the heavens. Second, archetypes are bipolar— they have both a positive (Yang) and negative (Yin) dimension. To be fully worked with, the archetype must be accepted *totally*, and transcended. To reject the dark half is to be one-sided and to allow that Shadow aspect to act out behind your back.

Finally, archetypes are like gods and goddesses. They are of a realm very different from that of normal consciousness, and they follow *very different laws*. To properly relate to an archetype we must first make efforts to understand, as best we can, those laws. We must then "personalize" the archetype, bring the powerful "cosmic" energy that it represents into a *constructive relationship* with us. If we are not up to this task, we may become possessed or inflated by the archetype.

As we shall see in the discussions that follow, all too often those who claim to be ninja masters are, in actuality, possessed by the various archetypal powers inherent in ninjutsu. Certainly the energy is flowing down an old riverbed, but they have failed to personalize it. Hence, they *confuse themselves with the river*. Through this confusion they feel they possess the power of the river, but in actuality *the power of the river possesses them*. They are, however, profoundly unaware of this. Their "light of conscious awareness" has been swamped by the ancient psychic energies from the collective unconscious.

"Negative" Archetypes of Ninjutsu

With the public, the media, and even many so-called practitioners and teachers of ninjutsu, generating rather "stereotypical" images of the ninja (and selling them), it would seem the logical place to start would be with the archetypes behind these images. The Shadow, the Enemy, the Devil, Death, and Destruction are all archetypal powers that are closely associated with the ninja as the ninja are presented in the West. All these archetypal powers are "negative" to our usual way of thinking. However, as we noted earlier, archetypes have two poles, a positive aspect and a negative aspect. If we are seeing only negativity in these qualities of energy, then we know only half of the story. Energy is energy. If we are to understand it we must understand it *in its totality*.

The Ninja as Shadow and Enemy

In Chapter 5 we looked at the ninja's relationship to the Shadow. The Shadow is itself an archetype, a way in which energy flows in us, and in the world at large. How many wars have been fought because the Shadow was not owned, but projected instead on another group of people who became the Enemy, and had to be destroyed? This is the power of the archetypes to effect changes in our world, this is the kind

of archetypal power, as manifested through the ruling samurai elite, which the ninja families of ancient Japan had to fight.

The Shadow, as we noted earlier, contains what has been rejected within the psyche. It thus contains all the negativity associated with the ninja—or more accurately, all of our negativity that *we project onto the ninja*. Herein lies Death, the Devil, Destruction. But the ninja themselves have done something very different with these energies. They have not "given them away"—they have *owned them, accepted them, and worked with them*. As we look at each of the so-called negative archetypes we shall see the hidden reserves of energy and possibility to which the ninja had access, but was unavailable to the ruling samurai elite.

The Ninja as Lucifer, the Devil

In *Shogun*, the ninja were regarded as "devils." Indeed, as both Dr. Hatsumi and Stephen K. Hayes have noted, for centuries the ninja have been regarded as "demonic." As we have seen they often used this to their own advantage since their opposition was, in essence, giving them power, but this did not alter the fact that the ninja were seen in such a negative manner. And today the ninja are seen as "devils" also, although we now use different terms. Editors of ninja magazines, genuine ninjutsu teachers, writers, and practitioners of ninjutsu have all had the experience of speaking with others who are absolutely convinced that the ninja are metaphorical, even actual, "agents of the Devil himself." Regardless of which way you turn, the shadow warriors represent the Devil incarnate.

We need not dwell on all the highly negative aspects of the Devil. The archetype of the Devil has existed in all cultures from antiquity, and within the Judeo-Christian culture he has held a powerful, albeit negative, place in our "mythology." What may come as a great surprise to many, and a shock to others, is that the Devil also has many *positive attributes*. And, in actuality, this is as it should be, for the Devil, *as archetype* (we are not discussing theology here) is a channel for our energy. And our energy is neither good nor bad, it simply is. Hence, the Devil is merely a channeling of energy of which we do not approve, but as we shall see, "approval" may not aid us in growth, or guide us toward enlightenment. It may, in fact, do just the opposite.

It is noteworthy that one painting of the Devil by William Blake portrays him as a *warrior*! One commentator noted that the Devil thus portrayed is not just a warrior, but an *experienced warrior*. He is equipped with a lance and shield, and carries both with great authority. This clear parallel with the ninja as warriors is both fascinating and meaningful.

Most fascinating, and quite unbelievable to many, is the fact that Lucifer means "light bringer!" Like Prometheus, the hero of ancient Greek mythology who stole the fire of the gods such that man might have light on Earth, Lucifer also brings something of the heavens to Earth. (The Gods represent "authority," and fire represents "insight," the potential for growth. If we remain forever chained and subservient to authority we can *never grow*.) Lucifer is, in fact, *an angel*, and although fallen, still a creation and messenger of "God." Without the Devil in the Garden of Eden there would be *no awareness, no consciousness*. Adam and Eve were not living in the "human realm" at all, but in the pre-human realm. Hence the Devil, Lucifer the light-bringer, created the human realm of good and evil.

We must bear in mind, as Wilber stressed, that there is the Eden of unconscious childhood, and the Eden or nirvana of complete aware-ness. But the two are *not the same*. To attain the higher and more refined levels of enlightenment we must first fight, as *warriors*, out of our "animal unconscious" and develop our own egos. We must fulfill our *human destiny*. As Nichols (1980) has put it, it is thanks to the Devil that we are no longer like obedient little children following a rigid ethical code. It is incredible that this should come from the Devil. Hence, we see the tremendous value of realizing the Devil in our lives, to aid us in leaving our various infantile "Edens" and to embark on the human path.

It is a sad reflection of our current society that so many are not free. They remain fettered to cultural norms, unable to take an individual stance, to make an individual decision. If our obedience to a moral code is blind and automatic, *we cannot be free*. If we refuse to confront our own dark side, however dark it may be, we cannot be fully human (Nichols, 1980). On the other hand, ninjutsu, as a tradition that extends over 900 years, has *always accepted the responsibility for moral choice*—the choice that is *free* from what everybody else says is right, the choice that is truly *individual*. And this could only have arisen with the ninja's courage to look the Devil straight in the face.

The Devil, then, when *positively realized* within us, daily wrenches us out of our safe Edens of unconsciousness, into the harsh "cold" world of humanity, into *the only world that can lead toward enlightenment*. Psycho-

logical children do not change the world, nor do they make the difficult decisions that affect many people's lives, nor are they particularly aware, especially of the spiritual dimensions available to us. Only fully realized humans have this power in the world, people who leave comfort and safety behind, and allow themselves to suffer the pain of growth. And this is the "gift" of the Devil—the opportunity to realize ourselves in the world. Hence, the accusation that the ninja are like the Devil might almost be seen as a compliment!

Just as the ninja could take on many personalities through their art of hensojutsu, so the Devil takes many forms within us. In addition to being a force that cracks our rigidity and opens us, sometimes painfully, to reality, the Devil can also represent a variety of psychic contents. Most important is the fact that when we are not whole, when we are not integrated, those parts of us that act autonomously are devilish. It is perhaps not surprising, therefore, to find that when we are out of harmony with ourselves we are "in sin" (Nichols, 1980). So the more we neglect and push away, the more our rigid concepts of good and evil cause us to divorce ourselves from much that we are, the more the Devil acts within us. We do indeed become devilish, but only because we refuse to open ourselves to the reality of total being.

In many ways the Devil as "light bringer" and the Devil as split-off parts of ourselves are one and the same thing. The autonomous parts of ourselves get us into difficulties. But if we face our difficulties, consider our weaknesses, then we *create the possibility of seeing and then integrating those split-off parts of ourselves.* We have the possibility of taking one step closer to wholeness. In fact, the Devil laughs at the widespread belief that all the positive human qualities are available only from Heaven, from God's good graces (Nichols, 1980). The reality is that the Devil is capable of giving us remarkable gifts.

There is another interesting perspective that relates the Devil to ninjutsu. As Nichol (1980) says, the Devil is not chasing us; instead he is *building a trap for us.* We step into that trap when *we allow ourselves to be victims.* If this can be positively realized then the Devil is what shows us our own victimization of ourselves.

Compare this to what is taught in the sanmitsu, the "thought, word, deed" of the ninja. Jack Hoban has addressed our self-victimization tendency, and notes that to prevail in a situation you must have a clear grasp of the situation, knowledge of certain self-protection techniques, and *a firm belief in your personal right to live life unmolested.* Most people have great difficulty with the latter precept. Intellectually we may think that no one has the right to do us harm, but in the face of an impending attack this firm emotional stance may well give way. How many of us actually believe in the *sacredness of our own being*? How many of us can open ourselves to an enemy, during an attack, such that our right to live unmolested, our sacredness, our very being "neutralizes" the enemy's onslaught?

The self-protection philosophy of sanmitsu beautifully reveals the Devil at work, *showing us our own self-destructive attitudes and behaviors.* Thus, if we listen to the Devil rather than reject him out of hand, he can become Lucifer the light bringer. Light is symbolic of consciousness, and it is indeed a greater self-awareness that he can bring to our lives. Not coincidentally, this is also one of the things that the ninja bring to our lives.

Death (and Rebirth)

Given that the ninja are so often portrayed as Devils, and always negatively (without any deeper understanding of the archetype), it is only natural that the ninja should also be strongly associated with Death. Indeed, as has been said in many ninja films, the ninja were masters of "a thousand ways of death." On the screen the ninja have a multitude of weapons to maim, injure, and kill others; in many martial arts publications the ability to take the life of an opponent is lauded, often at length; and in most fiction the predominant ability of the ninja is to assassinate and murder. Regardless of the accuracy of these various portrayals of the ninja, at least in the West, the link between the ninja and Death has been powerfully forged.

We in the West have a very negative view of Death. We see it as the antithesis of life. It is something that we must fight and hope to conquer. We do not accept it as part of life, but, like the Devil and other seemingly negative aspects of reality, we reject it, and force it out of our awareness. But this view of Death is one-sided. Certainly we fear death, but if we can pass through our fears we find that all is not as it seems.

Throughout the ancient world, including Japan, Death was never seen in isolation. Death was always seen *together with rebirth*. The sun left the skies each night, but each morning it rose again. The Sun God dies, but he is *always reborn*. And when the Sun God was reborn, he was born anew, revitalized and strong. Hence Death was simply part of life; it prefaced rebirth.

The Eastern way of thinking does not deny the pain and the sense of loss that accompanies the death of a loved one. From the material realm this is right and proper. But it acknowledges that there is *also another perspective*, the eternal perspective. And when Death is viewed from this vantage point it appears very differently. What we tend to lack, very often, is that second way of perceiving Death. Hence we can only fear it, we can never see it as parallel to going to sleep unhappy one night.

What the image of the ninja does, then, is to bring us into connection with the whole of life's cycle—*Death and Rebirth*. Through the more sophisticated images available to us, those from the writings of Hayes and Hatsumi in particular, this is clearly delineated. But even in the more primitive portrayals of the ninja, where rebirth is but a shadow, the Death archetype has been activated. Indeed, why are so many so fascinated by the ninja as a bringer of Death? Why the glorification, dramatization, and ritualization of the ninja's "thousand ways of death," if behind it there were not also that sense that Death is not the end, but simply one night in the course of our lives.

Naturally there is another way of looking at Death alongside the Western images of the ninja. Freudian psychology would see the rampant killing associated with the ninja as simply an expression of "the aggressive drive" in all of us. This has some validity to it, particularly with regard to the unsophisticated forms of ninjutsu propagated on the screen, in the martial arts world, and in most fiction. But, ultimately, this really does not get us very far, especially when considering the image created in the historical tradition. When we look at the ninja, and realize what they faced in ancient Japan, we realize that ignoring the political and military reality of the ninja strips the development of ninjustsu of all genuine meaning.

For ourselves, we are not only responding to the superficial images of the ninja, we are also, hopefully, responding to the image that is deepest, and closer to reality. It is, therefore, not helpful for us to see our attraction to the ninja's "thousand ways of death" as simply "aggression." Our way through this quagmire is twofold. First, in understanding Death in relation to the ninja we must place it within their historical context and in relation to their spiritual tradition. Second, for ourselves, we must understand Death at a deeper level of meaning. But first some general comments about Death.

As Wilber (1980, 1981) so astutely points out, we are very much involved in denying Death. One way in which immortality is grasped is by killing others—"they" are dead and "I" am *alive*. The fantasy is that this will go on forever. So by watching, and revelling in the murderous ninja on the screen or in fiction—or in our own personal fantasies—we are also denying Death. *We are aggressing against the fearful need to die to who we are*, the Death that would be required if we are to move upward on the Great Chain of Being. With each step upward in awareness we must "die" to the level that we have been living on. And this is not a simple intellectual death, but an *experiential one*. So in refusing to "die" we refuse to move toward the more refined states of enlightenment. And this has an ironic twist to it. We refuse to "die," only to maintain ourselves in a deadened state of awareness.

As we have already established, the ninja were very much concerned with an active, "living" relationship with the universe. Ascending the Great Chain of Being was not only the original empowering force behind the ninja, but it also became a necessity to survive against the ruling samurai elite. Hence, the "ninja as Death" represents for us the courage to awaken from our deadened existence, *to die to it*, and so become more fully alive. The way to wholeness involves dying to our attraction to "the ten thousand things." Indeed, wholeness, by virtue of uniting and containing the opposites, included Life *and* Death.

There is another important way of looking at Death that is of great relevance to the ninja. When we deny Death what we are really doing, as Wilber says, is *refusing to live without a future*. Put otherwise, we *refuse to live "timelessly."* Hence, when we deny the possibility of living a "no-future" life (which we, from our limited perspective, think of as Death) *we deny eternity*, for *eternity is timeless*. This brings us to a stultifying, stagnating, and lifeless "death," a condition of living permanently split off from "eternity."

The goal of the yamabushi and sennin was the realization of Eternity. They sought the "immortality of the present moment." Since they realized, and not just intellectualized, that "all is one," including past, present, and future, they gave up the notion of having to live with a future. Hence the eternity of the present moment opened itself to them. And the legacy of the warrior-mystics of Japan's remote wilderness regions had a powerful influence upon the ninja.

Chogyam Trungpa (1984), a *tulku* himself, wrote that to live our lives as though there were no death is an *act of cowardice*. Bearing in mind what we have said, it is cowardice on two counts: we refuse to move upward on the Great Chain of Being, and we refuse to live in touch with Eternity. Hence, if we truly realize the type of energy that the ninja image represents for us, we must face death, face the fears that we have of death, and then, as Trungpa notes, go beyond those fears.

There is yet another fundamental fear of Death that frightens us, a fear that the ninja most certainly overcame, and continue to overcome. Consider our usual representations of Death. Not infrequently a skeleton is a symbol for Death, and in the course of the year, winter is most often associated with Death. What the skeleton and winter share is a sense of the *true essence of the body and of Nature, stripped of the veneer*.

The sense of stripping away the unessentials mirrors other conceptions of Death in which Death is seen as a long journey. The best way to prepare for a lengthy, difficult journey is to get rid of things you do not really need. This is equivalent to the Buddhist teachings of "letting go of attachments." Indeed, Zen practice is sometimes described as "learning to die," and the spiritual teacher Krishnamurti,

when asked how he was preparing for Death, said, "Each day I die a little."

Death, then, takes a variety of forms. Death in the context of Death-and-Rebirth, is simply a part of life. We are fearful of it when we cannot place it in context, or see it from the eternal perspective (the ninja's kongokai realm), but if we can overcome our own fears, and press on beyond them, then Death takes on a new meaning. It is that which precedes birth. Death also appears when moving on toward higher levels of awareness. We must die to the stage of consciousness we are at to realize the next stage up. Then there is the Death that allows us to see who we really are, the Death which, when accepted, allows us to touch eternity and timelessness. But there is also the "death" of unconsciousness, of the lack of awareness, of ignorance. This is the "death" of cowardice. And it is precisely this "death" that nin-po shatters through the realization of the Death archetype. We are therefore drawn to the ninja for they represent the way out of our "death" lives. But all too often we are lacking in the spiritual courage to follow the path they point out to us.

How many times have we heard, "Unless you accept death fully you cannot live fully?" From our consideration of Death it should be clear that this statement carries much weight, and much wisdom behind it. *Death did not frighten the ninja, and it is their courage in the face of one of our worst fears that so attracts us to them.* Ninjutsu is not a cult of Death without Rebirth, it is a tradition of *Death-and-Rebirth*, a tradition of *life in its totality.* Only our fears and cultural blinders prevent us from seeing this.

The "Positive" Archetypes of Ninjutsu

Having looked at the "negative" archetypes of ninjutsu, all of which had "hidden" positive energy, we can now turn to those energies that many regard as "positive." Among others we find the Warrior (or Hero as he is known in mythology) and the Warrior's Quest (or Hero Cycle). We also find the Healer, the archetype that energizes the healing of self and others along a variety of dimensions. Clearly we see these energies as entirely creative, but we must not forget the fact that the archetypes are bipolar. We must never forget that there is always darkness where there is light. The Warrior is, in essence, a way in which energy is channeled. Consciously attended to and nurtured this may indeed be positive. But how many "warriors" are bold on the battle front, but utterly incapable of looking at themselves and accepting their Shadows, of being open to the world, of making the Warrior's Quest? The archetypal energy that does not find a vessel sufficiently large enough and flexible enough in which to flow will break it—and others may feel the power of this, too. The Healer is also capable of destruction through lack of awareness, lack of insight, lack of compassion, etc. Again the ideal is to see both the negative and the positive, to realize both, and to transcend both.

The Warrior and the Warrior's Quest

The warrior is an archetype fundamental to ninjutsu. Hayes addresses warriorship in virtually all of his books and discusses it at almost every seminar and festival he leads. The ninja's life is the life of the warrior. We shall therefore look at this particular manifestation of archetypal energy in some depth, especially the warrior's dynamic aspects—the Warrior's Quest.

Although speaking of warriorship in a different context than Hayes, Chogyam Trungpa (1984) notes that within the Tibetan "Sacred Path of the Warrior," the Warrior is "one who is brave." Warriorship in this context is a "tradition of fearlessness"—a tradition not of reducing fear, but of going beyond it, transcending it. Fundamentally this means *not being afraid of who you are*. To be a warrior is to be *fully* yourself—and this includes Shadow (negative *and* positive). The warrior's life is one of synchronizing mind and body, of awakening to higher levels of awareness, of relaxing within yourself and within the world, of "letting go," of facing darkness, of taking a deep and spontaneous interest in all of existence, of being "all-victorious" at all times (without fighting) and realizing "unconditional confidence," of being sensitive and receptive to the world, of dissolving barriers between self and other, of being daring and taking a jump into the unknown, of letting go of deception and illusion, of living fully.

The warrior realizes these potentials in the course of his life, as he embarks upon the Warrior's Quest. Too often we see the warrior as an image etched in stone. Our image of the warrior is usually composed of a fearless man trained in the ways of combat, and emanating a certain personal power. Almost always he carries a sword, perhaps two. However, few stop to look at this image and realize something that is at once all too obvious, but also too often overlooked. Our image of the warrior tends to be *static*, or, if in motion, that motion is

restricted to the battlefield. What we fail to see is the warrior ideal set against a person's life development and growth.

Ninjutsu, or ninpo as it is known in its higher order, is the "way of the warrior"—and "way" here signifies more than the successful application of combat techniques in a confrontation. Among other things it refers to a path or life course. And that path extends from the moment a person realizes his or her destiny until that person dies. Put otherwise, the way of the warrior has a history, the history of a person's life.

Fundamental to the warrior's path in ninpo is the musha shugyo. Sometimes translated simply as "training in warriorship," Shidoshi Hayes notes that it also carries the connotation of the "Warrior's Quest." In other words, the musha shugyo embodies not only apprenticeship in the various disciplines within ninjutsu, but also the leaving behind of all that is known and journeying into the unknown. Even a highly trained fighter can be mentally and spiritually lacking in awareness simply because he or she has never taken an objective look at his or her basic assumptions. This objectivity is gained only through the deep awareness of a fundamentally different way of life. Gaining this appreciation gives the warrior something to compare the familiar with, thus giving the old new meaning, since it can be looked at from a new perspective.

Leaving the known and entering the unknown also involves leaving the comfort of the ego and our fabricated constructions of ourselves, and walking to face the Shadow and all that the Shadow represents. There, in that psychic land of darkness lie the qualities we do not know how to relate to and, therefore, push away, as well as qualities we have no inkling of whatsoever, jewels within us that need only courage to be discovered.

Historical Perspective on Musha Shugyo

The musha shugyo has great meaning from a psychological perspective, a meaning we will explore after a brief look at the most important musha shugyo in the history of ninjutsu. We will also make use of this perspective in looking at two contemporary ninja musha shugyos, that of Toshitsugu Takamatsu, the 33rd Grandmaster of Togakure-ryu ninjutsu, and that of Shidoshi Stephen K. Hayes.

It is interesting to note that the very foundation of ninjutsu rests upon the musha shugyo of Daisuke Nishina of Togakure. As we noted in Chapter 4, Daisuke was originally trained in the ways of the Togakure Mountain tradition of warrior asceticism which, as Hayes has noted, emphasized "power development in which attunement with and direction of the natural elements is gained." But the Togakure shugenja practitioners were politically unpopular, and in 1181, Heike troops moved against them.

Although Daisuke fought for the way of life he had found great meaning in, after three years the Heike troops met with success. Daisuke was forced to flee, and escaped from Nagano (his birthplace) to the remote region of Iga. Although he escaped with his life he lost everything, including his samurai status. In feudal Japan, where status and family carried great weight, this was the equivalent of losing his identity. Put otherwise, Daisuke's musha shugyo involved dropping from the elite of society to the lowly position of a homeless wanderer.

But it was in the mountainous regions of Iga that Daisuke met the warrior-priest Kain Doshi, who had left China to come to Japan. Kain Doshi was a mystic priest, a Taoist sage who propounded a system of "integrated mind-body awareness" founded on a *personal understanding* of the universe. Hence, as Hayes has written, Daisuke learned the outer and inner aspects of reality, aspects that complemented his knowledge gained from the yamabushi shugendo practices of Togakure mountain.

It is here, in the remote forests of Iga, that Daisuke took the name Togakure to symbolize both his origins with the yamabushi and his rebirth upon a new plane of awareness taught to him by Kain Doshi. And it was the bringing together of these two traditions that marked the beginning of Togakure-ryu ninjutsu.

With this image of Daisuke we gain an important insight into the nature of the ninja way, for a cultural institution is given its character and direction by its founder. And it is Daisuke's musha shugyo that provides the key to understanding this influence.

From a psychological perspective, the musha shugyo symbolizes a crucial, always frightening, step in personality development—perhaps one of the most important steps that an individual takes in his or her life. Often seen as "the hero's cycle," a rubric taken from studies in mythology, this step is characterized by well-established phases. As we examine the hero cycle, and plumb its psychological depth, we will see that the events of Daisuke's musha shugyo follow the phases precisely.

The hero's cycle expresses that movement in the personality when an individual enters the unknown regions of his or her psyche and begins to explore, usually in search of an answer, or greater knowledge. If we remember that this region includes things that we do not want to know (usually because they are frightening), as well as powerful parts of ourselves that we have never met before, it is not difficult to realize that this is an inner journey experienced as dangerous. In myth and legend this movement is symbolized by the main character making the decision, or being forced to make the decision, to leave his or her home and begin a long journey to a distant land.

This journey always involves leaving everything that is known and entering the unknown. And it is at the border between two regions that an important event occurs. The main character is crushed, defeated, or badly wounded by a powerful opponent, animal, or spirit known as a "threshold guardian." Almost always the hero is made unconscious. In many stories it seems as if the end is here and that the story is oddly tragic.

What is expressed psychologically is that the person is leaving the known regions of the psyche, the "ego"—that part of us that is conscious and filled with light—and coming to the border with the "unconscious"—that part of us full of mystery and darkness. What happens at this point is that the ego is "extinguished" by the vastly more powerful forces of the unconscious. As important and as powerful as we all feel we are, we are nothing compared to the strength and potential of the unconscious within us.

Before moving to the next phase, the parallels with Daisuke's life will be examined. Daisuke was living in a place he knew well near Togakure Mountain. This was his "region of the known." But he was driven from his home and defeated. Hence, we see Daisuke was forced to leave the comfort of "the light" and forced to begin a journey to parts of Japan—and parts of himself—which he had never experienced before. What he knew no longer helped him. He had to learn an entirely new way of relating to himself and others. Having lost his "identity" as a samurai, he also had to rebuild his sense of self worth and personal power from nothing.

In myth and legend it is at the point of unconsciousness and defeat that there is a supernatural intervention. Magical animals, spirits, or a "Wise Old Man" (or "Wise Old Woman") are among the characters

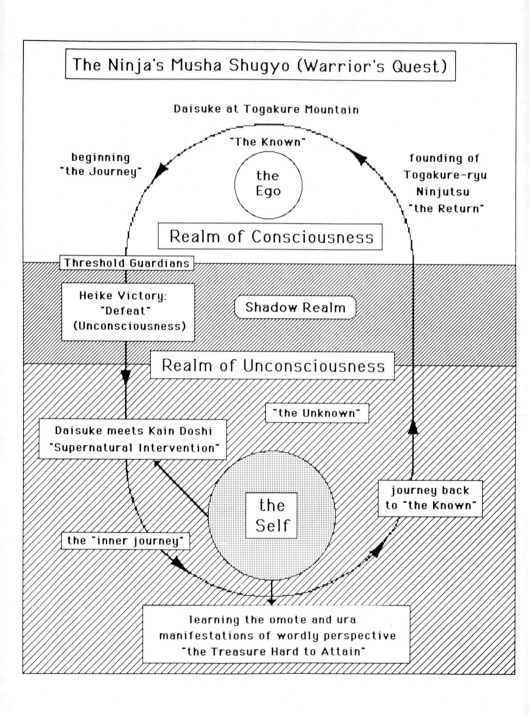

The Ninja's Musha Shugyo (Warrior's Quest)

Daisuke at Togakure Mountain

"The Known"

the Ego

beginning "the Journey"

founding of Togakure-ryu Ninjutsu "the Return"

Realm of Consciousness

Threshold Guardians

Heike Victory: "Defeat" (Unconsciousness)

Shadow Realm

Realm of Unconsciousness

"the Unknown"

Daisuke meets Kain Doshi "Supernatural Intervention"

the Self

journey back to "the Known"

the "inner journey"

learning the omote and ura manifestations of wordly perspective "the Treasure Hard to Attain" used to express this. Whichever type of intervention there is, the new character aids the hero on his or her journey to the distant lands, or across the sea.

Psychological interpretation sees this moment as the person's coming into connection with his or her deeper self. This deeper, or "total" self, is symbolized in a supernatural way since it is subjectively experienced as something "beyond the human realm." What is happening is that the ego—usually seen as "young" (since it is but a small part of the whole person but thinks that it is the whole), is encountering the unconscious (usually symbolized as "old"). And with this connection comes a working together of the conscious and unconscious regions of the psyche, a true wholeness.

Defeated and stripped of his worth within feudal Japanese society, Daisuke wandered the remote regions of Iga. In addition to the defeats at Togakure Mountain he also, no doubt, suffered the fear of discovery or pursuit, the hardships of little food and living off the land, and the terrible self doubts and inner torment commonly experienced by persons who are living under conditions of terrible stress.

But in the midst of his defeat he made a connection with a man who represented a new way of viewing the world. Kain Doshi was, in many ways, that "supernatural force" that came to the aid of the defeated ego. He is the archetypal "Wise Old Man," and he gave to Daisuke something more precious, and more powerful, than he ever would have received had he stayed in Nagano and lived the life of a samurai. And we know of the power of what he received since the ninja families, and the system of ninjutsu, has survived some 900 years throughout the ups and downs of Japan's checkered history.

Daisuke's newly acquired knowledge is equivalent to what is gained at the end of the hero's journey: "the treasure hard to attain." Sometimes symbolized by gold, sometimes represented by a beautiful princess, each stood for something of tremendous worth, something that would complete and deepen the life of the seeker. The hero can then return to the land of the known, and his or her "treasure" makes him or her stand out as a person with knowledge and power from the beyond.

Daisuke's musha shugyo has been mirrored by many ninja. With the limited available information about ninjutsu we can speak of only two journeys in any detail. This first is that of Toshitsugu Takamatsu, the 33rd Grandmaster of Togakure-ryu ninjutsu. After his training with Shinryuken Masamitsu Toda, the 32nd Grandmaster of Togakure-ryu ninjutsu, and Takakage Matsutaro Ishinitani, 26th Grandmaster of the Kuki Shinden-ryu happo hiken (secret weapons art) of ninjutsu, Toshitsugu Takamatsu journeyed throughout China, studying with the best of the boxing masters. It was here that he earned the name "Mongolian Tiger." He returned to Japan and lived for some years in the mountain wilderness. In 1919 he returned home and studied the teachings of the Buddhist tantric sect of mikkyo. He was later ordained as a mikkyo priest of the Tendai-shu.

Again we see the journey from the known into the unknown, and the development of spiritual power. There can be little doubt that despite the fact he was a Grandmaster of Togakure-ryu ninjutsu before he eventually prevailed in new combat systems there were defeats at the hands of the Chinese boxing masters—defeats that probably were considerably harder for a Grandmaster to take than for a novice— hence, they were psychologically more powerful. Defeats of an entirely different order were also experienced, no doubt, during his years as a recluse in the wilderness. And yet, after these defeats, we see the eventual development of personal power, drawn from the unknown regions of the mind: the tantric lore of mikkyo.

It is interesting to note that the introduction of ninjutsu to the Western world was also the result of a musha shugyo. Stephen K. Hayes was already an established instructor within a martial arts tradition before he made his first trip to Japan. He had his own school and had attained a high ranking. However, like Toshitsugu Takamatsu, he had the sense that greater knowledge lay in the realm of the unknown, in some form or another. Hayes then journeyed to Japan to begin an apprenticeship in a system so alien to his previous ways of thinking and training that he had to give these up to devote himself to attaining the knowledge contained within Togakure-ryu ninjutsu.

Hayes's musha shugyo is beautifully chronicled in *The Ninja and Their Secret Fighting Art*. But the essential parallels to the hero's cycle should not go unnoted. Indeed, Hayes's Warrior's Quest was almost more pronounced than that of either Daisuke or Toshitsugu Takamatsu. Whereas both of these men journeyed in unknown lands, they were still Asian lands; Hayes left the U.S., which epitomizes the scientific West, and journeyed to the East with its very different, very intuitive ways of thinking. And Hayes had gone to Japan not to visit, but to live and train. Consequently he became immersed in a culture fundamentally different from his own.

The "defeats" Hayes received at the hands of Tanemura, one of Dr.

Hatsumi's assistants, are well noted. Hayes received almost humiliating demonstrations of dakentaijutsu and jutaijutsu for which his previous training, even with his high ranking, was useless. Tanemura also demonstrated the use of the "dynamic force of the universe" within ninjutsu, again "defeating" Hayes, but this time with a "force"

unheard of in the West. Hayes felt he had been hit by a cannonball. He was thrown to the ground and found himself unable to breathe. He felt dizzy, and completely drained. For a man well-trained in the fighting arts, a more humiliating defeat would be hard to imagine.

And after this "demonstration" of ninjutsu, Dr. Hatsumi told Hayes that he did not have time for the "idly curious," the "emotionally unstable," or those who were on an ego-trip. It seemed like a dismissal. But then the Grandmaster added that in the "broader sense of reality," Hayes had been on his way to train in the ninjutsu combat method for longer than he realized. He was then accepted for training.

With Hayes currently the only American holding the rank of Shido-shi, or "teacher of the warrior ways of enlightenment," we see that although his musha shugyo incorporated defeat, it also involved the intervention of a "supernatural force" in his life: Dr. Hatsumi with his view of the "broader reality." Now recognized by the Grandmaster as the foremost authority of Togakure-ryu ninjustsu in the West, it is clear that Hayes returned from his journey with "the treasure hard to attain."

Ninjutsu is a system of life that was founded on the musha shugyo, or Warrior's Quest. Ninja warriors throughout the ages have chosen, or been forced, to set out on this journey. But of far greater significance than the physical journey is the inner transformation of which the musha shugyo is but an outer manifestation. The journey into the depths of our own being is a frightening venture, one which the vast majority or us refuse to begin. But if it is our calling to be a warrior, the rewards from such defeats as humiliating as losing your identity, or suddenly discovering that all your knowledge is pale in comparison to a deeper and wider realm of knowledge, is "the treasure hard to attain"—an awareness of the world, and of yourself, on a different plane and from a different perspective.

This is the essence of ninjutsu, and what it is to be a ninja warrior. You must leave the known, and enter the unknown. You must have the strength to survive defeat, and the ability to see the higher order of things when they are there for you to gain knowledge from. To be a ninja is to have the courage to look at, and learn from, yourself, a task easier said than done. But true knowledge comes from within. But that knowledge lies in our darkness, and we must gather the courage to enter it.

It goes without saying that the Hero/Warrior archetype, as well as the archetype of the Hero Cycle/Musha Shugyo, are fundamental to ninjutsu. Warrior energy, as Hayes has noted, is perhaps at the very basis of the nin-po approach to living. Considering how often we discussed the need for "courage" in our examinations of the Great Chain of Being and so-called "negative" archetypes associated with ninjutsu, we gain an appreciation of the centrality of the Warrior archetype. Indeed, each step forward is a step into the unknown, yet another musha shugyo. It should therefore not be surprising that one of the energy constellations that most attracts us to the ninja is the warrior.

The Ninja as Healer or Shaman

It should not be surprising to find the archetype of the Healer active in the ninja tradition. If we consider the fact that the ninja were outcasts from society at large, it should be clear that they could not call upon the traditional healers of the time to aid them when there was sickness or injury, *they had to heal themselves.* On the individual level, the genin ninja operative while on a mission also could not call upon anyone else in times of trouble, *he had to heal himself.* Hence, we find that the Healer is an important archetype within ninjutsu.

In addition to healing physical damage to the body the ninja had to be able to heal their own psychic wounds and weaknesses. This leads us directly to something that Hayes emphasizes again and again: the ninjutsu practitioner must begin training with an acknowledgment of his weaknesses. To ignore our wounds is sheer foolishness, although we all do it. Should you have to enter a fight or a difficult confrontation, far better to know the weak links in your chain, and proceed with this in mind, rather than charge in convinced that the stongest link is what you really are, only to find your opponent attacking your weak spot.

Many would consider having wounds, or realizing you are weak in certain areas, to be a terrible personality flaw. This is not necessarily so. First, as Hayes notes, we turn to our weaknesses and *through them* find opportunities to succeed. Second, *the Healer within us is not activated unless there is something to heal.* If you never recognize your own wounds, you attempt to navigate life's difficult waters without the assistance of an inner Healer. Bearing in mind the idea that the ninja sought to use everything possible at hand to their advantage, it should be clear that they would not "leave behind" the type of archetypal energy that the Healer represents. Nor would they venture forth in blindness, thinking they were without wounds.

The first step in the activation of the Healer archetype within is to recognize the need for healing. The second stage is to do everything in our power to correct these areas. In many ways this corresponds to doing everything we can with our egos in "the land of the known." When we have extinguished these possibilities we open ourselves up to allowing the Self to act. This is the third stage, and like the Hero who fails in his confrontation with the Threshold Guardians, our failures to completely heal ourselves in consciousness leads to the intervention of the Self. Finally, we must be open to the power of the Self to heal us, to both know and follow the healing direction the Self offers us (Harding, 1973). It is the allowing of the archetypal powers within us to work according to their laws which heals and transforms us (Perry, 1976).

Another way of looking at the Healer archetype is as the Shaman. Just as we have already noted many of the similarities between the Warrior's Quest and the process of healing, so, too, we should mention that the Shaman's journeys into the unknown were similar in many ways to the inner paths followed by the yamabushi and sennin, the forefathers of the ninja. What is fascinating about the Shaman is that he does not heal. Rather he mediates between the wounded and the divine powers (archetypal energies) to bring about the healing process (von Franz, 1975). Indeed, many ancient cultures believed that illness was the result of divine intervention, and therefore required divine (archetypal) intervention to correct (Adler, 1961).

So what the ninja image calls forth, in addition to the many other archetypes we have already looked at, is the Healer. Like the Warrior, this archetype brings us face to face with the Self, our own inner divinity, our own numinosity. In a world where so many are wounded, it is perhaps not surprising to find the ninja such a powerful image. Fearless in their capacity to enter the darkness, they are therefore granted the capacity to heal themselves. Such is what all persons wish for themselves. Such is part of our attraction to the ninja.

The Ninja as Magician and Alchemist

One of the most familiar images of the ninja is the magician. From the mists of legend wherein the ninja were conceived of as sorcerers and wizards, to today's films where the ninja perform all manner of tricks and illusions, the ninja as trickster and magician looms before us. It is one of the perennial fascinations we have of the ninja that they are "quick of hand" and in touch with powers that we can only call "magic."

There is something oddly appealing about the "magic" of the ninja, both in its demonic form, as expressed in Saigo's (*The Ninja*) fascination with the Kobudera or in the sanmitsu, the unification of "thought, word, and deed" to realize intentions in the physical world. The reason for this is that the Magician points to certain potentialities within us.

The Magician has many qualities. He symbolizes, among other things, the ability to harness the powers of nature consciously, and to put those energies to creative use. The Magician is also fully capable of fooling us with deception and illusion. But at the same time, and more positively, he is capable of showing us that what we so often take as "reality" is but "appearance." He is, therefore, able to take us through the illusory surface of things to the fundamental oneness beneath reality as we normally see it. As Nichols (1980) and others have noted, magic is often referred to as the "science of hidden relationships." And through the Magician's power we may begin to see that these hidden relationships bring about a unity of all phenomena. Most important, the Magician enables us to realize that what we see around us is *not* the result of an external and supraordinate energy acting on matter. Such a viewpoint is dualistic; energy and matter are seen as being separate. Instead, the phenomenal world results from the life force acting *upon itself*, that is, energy and matter are essentially one. From itself, from the energy/matter universe, all that we know arises. Hence, the Magician shows us the Void, the "seamless" nature of the universe.

When we consider that the archetype Magician is a "piece of life," rather than an abstraction, we begin to understand something of the ninja's inner power. To realize that all is one, and to realize that each person is part of the life force acting upon itself, is to open up the possibilities of channeling that energy, or directing it, of guiding it toward aspects of the current situation that, in the scheme of totality, appear out of balance.

The Magician ordinarily carries a "wand," an instrument whereby he can concentrate and direct energy. As Nichols (1980) notes, energy is in need of direction. Only man's consciousness and awareness can shape and channel archetypal energy, taking it from the realms of the gods and goddesses and actualizing it in the human realm. Immediately the final scenes of *Tulku: A Tale of Modern Ninja* come to mind:

Kozo, armed solely with a Tibetan vajra thunderbolt (which Hayes actually calls a "wand"), "directs" the lightning bolt, that quintessential symbol of the forces of Nature, toward the Korean assassin. Clearly this primordial force has been "shaped to human use."

The ninja's mystic finger entwining is another means of channeling energy, of coordinating and modulating elemental forces. It is important to realize that this power is not intellectual, rather, it is a "natural, unconscious gift." It is through participation in Nature, rather than opposition to Nature, that allows the ninja access to power of this kind. Intellectual activity, on the whole, is divisive and separating, not

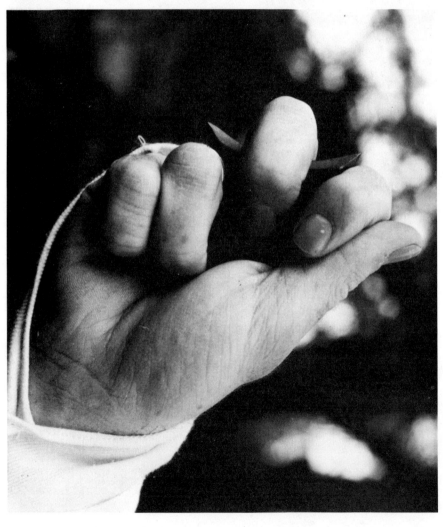

synthesizing or unifying—especially as it has been utilized in the West. Hence, we see that the Magician is "in touch" with the cosmos, at once a part of it and a force able to redirect it.

For us, the Magician archetype, as constellated by the image of the ninja, brings about psychological and spiritual "revelation." The Magician archetype is a channeling of psychic energy which, when activated and fully realized, is capable of allowing us to experience that "the wave is one with the ocean—both are made of the same substance." This is the potential flow of energy within us that this aspect of the ninja captures. The ninja, therefore, hold up to us the possibility of realizing our oneness both within ourselves, and with the universe around us.

One of the Magician's unique abilities is to open us up to our Shadows, and, more importantly, to the acceptance and integration of our dark sides. What is "black magic" if not the involvement with this aspect of the psyche. But "black magic" must be handled consciously, and in the context of the scheme of totality. The genuine Magician realizes his oneness with the universe, it is not "he" that is "great," but the universe itself. The "psychopathic black magician" misuses the inner experience "for personal power aims." He claims collective power with his ego (not with the sense of oneness) and is therefore physically ill (von Franz, 1975).

When an individual is *genuinely* on the path toward wholeness, "social power claims" are incompatible with this movement. Hence, we see that the true essence of *nin-po* was not toward personal gains, but a working in harmony with the universe. It goes without saying that there were doubtless some "ninja magicians" who used their powers for the glorification of their own egos. Indeed, we need simply look at the many bogus ninja masters today. Clearly these are persons drawn toward the "magic" of ninjutsu, but who approach the art egotistically rather than from a perspective of openness.

Of Synchronicity

In Chapter 8 we shall look more closely at the sanmitsu, the ninja's empowering of "thought, word, and deed" to effect the realization of intentions in the world. However, we should note here the close affinity between the Magician and Jung's concept of synchronicity. "Synchronistic phenomena" refer to the seeming coincidence between internal states and external events. It is a *co*-incidence, the simultaneous occurrence of two things: one, a psychic event; the other, a physical event, which are separated in space or time and, therefore, not to be related causally. As Jaffe (1967) puts it, these *apparent* coincidences, and they are only apparent, stem from the fact that space, time, and causality are not, in actuality, separate. It is only our conscious minds that see reality in this way. Our usual way of perceiving reality struggles to relate space, time, and causality, but synchronistic events are not just "meaningful coincidences," they are revelations of "acausal orderedness."

As we shall see in the next chapter, Hayes makes clear that there are "no coincidences" in the universe. In part, he is referring to synchronicity. The ability of the ninja to realize their intentions might be looked at from the perspective of synchronicity. They were able to bring together the "thought" and "word" of the psyche with the "deed" or "action" of the physical world. They were able to "break through" the surface of the many "differences" we see between things to the oneness of all things, including psyche and matter. Their ability to make their "thoughts" become "actions" can be frightening— because it shatters accustomed ways of seeing reality. The relationship between synchronicity and the sanmitsu will be looked at more closely in Chapter 8.

One last point: since synchronistic events tend to occur most frequently when an archetype is activated, we may assume that the ninja were capable of activating the archetypal levels of consciousness at will, or lived lives that continuously caused archetypes to be activated. Certainly their mystical heritage put the ninja in touch with the archetypes, and certainly living at the "border between life and death" activated the most powerful archetypes in the psyche, so it should not come to us as too great a surprise to find the ninja quite adept at "facilitating synchronistic events."

The Ninja as Alchemists

Another way of approaching the energies of ninja which seem somewhat magical is to see the archetype of the Alchemist. Certainly there is overlap with the Magician, but the differences are great enough to allow us to look at the ninja from a slightly different perspective.

When most people think of alchemy they tend to think that this was merely a somewhat off-course precursor to chemistry. This is, in many ways, a half-truth, but a half-truth that the alchemists, like the ninja, allowed to stand. In actuality, far more important than the "chemical experiments" was the spiritual development and search for knowledge that these persons engaged in. But as with shugendo or nin-po, this search challenged the prevailing views of the time, and so there was the need for secrecy. To many, alchemy was a form of black magic.

The basic idea behind alchemy, and the channeling of energy that the Alchemist captures, is to free a "divine" or "greater man" from imprisonment within matter and darkness. The alchemists used "matter," as in lead, for their symbol with which to work. In the East, Taoist alchemy took the body as the "matter" with which to work. Like the sennin forerunners of the ninja there was a search for "immortality," but an immortality that was "within the present" rather than one that had reference to "living forever." All of this was symbolically expressed as "turning lead into gold." Note that the lead was not destroyed or rejected, *its basic nature was transformed.*

In ninjutsu the "matter" to be worked with is symbolized by the body. Dr. Hatsumi speaks of the nine levels of power in the nin-po tradition, but he emphasizes that one begins to ascend the steps of the ladder at the physical level. It is through the body, through the development of ninjutsu skills that the higher, more refined levels of awareness are made possible. This is the alchemy of ninjutsu: realization of your total entity through the transformation of who you are in the present at the physical, mental, and spiritual levels.

To the archetypal Alchemist, matter is not dead. Matter is something that we need to establish a good relationship with. Consider the ninja's use of Nature, especially for escape and concealment. Here there was an intimate association between the ninja and the cosmos. No *artificial barrier such as man versus matter separated the two.* The alchemists, like the many mystic forerunners of the ninja, used meditation techniques to realize "the god (archetype) of revelation."

The archetype that the Alchemist leads us to is Mercurius who carries the light of Nature, the heavenly spirit. He contains all opposites—he is a "stone uplifted by the wind," he is "heavier than metal and lighter than air," he is the Old King and the Eternal Child at the same time (von Franz, 1975). Since the alchemists were searching for many of the same things as the shugenia, sennin, and yamabushi, it is not surprising to find these paradoxical descriptions of the "essence" of the cosmos.

There is another interesting parallel here. As in nin-po there is a certain "light" that is sought and perceived in alchemy. This light, though, shows up the darkness in which others live. But since others do not want to undergo the spiritual training and suffering required to view the world with "the eyes and mind of god," they attack those who have found the light. Hence, this light was often regarded by others as a manifestation of Lucifer! To most, as we have already discussed, Lucifer is the personification of all Evil, he is the Devil. But Lucifer is also the light bringer. In essence what this symbolizes is that if we are not mindful of the "light," this "light" becomes dangerous.

Realizing the spirit in matter, progressing through the ninja's nine realms of power is the path of individuation, the path toward wholeness and totality, and ultimately, oneness with the universe. The Alchemist leads us through the blackness. Here is our confrontation with our dark sides, a task the ninja certainly did not shy away from. They followed the albedo in which *yin/in* and *yang/yo* are brought together within us. Finally comes the *unification of all opposites*—the realization of the Self.

Hence we may look at the ninja's working with the body as the manifestation of the Alchemist archetype. We seek, *through the body*, the liberation of a greater man within, the union of all opposites, the "immortality of the present moment," the "light" which will allow us to see with "the mind and eyes of god."

The Ninja as Actor

Very often the "acting," or impersonation abilities of the ninja are emphasized. In many movies ninja disguise themselves. In *Tulku: A Tale of Modern Ninja* the ninja infiltrate a warehouse pretending to be guards. Even in the historical sources the ninja regarded disguise as important. Hayes (1981a) notes that the seven most common disguises were the mountain warrior-mystic (yamabushi), Buddhist monk (shukke), traveling priest (komuso), actor (sarugaku), musician (hoka-shi), merchant (akindo), and "free" samurai (ronin). Indeed, when Hayes was speaking with the Grandmaster for the first time he was asked what his previous line of study had been. Hayes replied that he had been trained as an actor. Dr. Hatsumi had nodded with approval, noting that the ability to disguise one's true intent, and to be sensitive to the hidden motives of others, approached the true skills of the ninja. Again it is not surprising to find the "wearing of masks" an important psychological aspect of our make-up.

The archetype we are dealing with here is the persona (*persona* in Latin refers to an actor's mask). This is the "face we show the world." Now, although this is useful to us there are dangers to avoid. The most serious of these involves identifying with your persona, confusing yourself with your social role. This usually leads to arrogance. Consider the many bogus ninja masters around who have marketed themselves as "ninja masters" and now indentify with that persona completely.

Thinking that "you are your mask" opens you up for archetypal possession. Hence, many of the self-proclaimed ninja masters believe themselves to be spiritual guides, mystics, people with powerful intuitive insight, and possessors of great knowledge. In reality they have become actors without personality. Between the mask and the possessing archetype there is little left. The personality that could relate to and personalize the archetypal energy, the personality that could freely change masks depending on the situation, has been squeezed out. Only the archetype and the mask remain.

Clearly the ninja could not afford to become overidentified with one mask. To survive they needed the flexibility to change masks as quickly and as expediently as possible. Neither could they afford to be arrogant, for such people rapidly attract attention, usually of a negative variety. Instead the ninja had to forge a healthy relationship between themselves and their Persona. This was accomplished in the first place simply through their tradition of total personality development. If you have a strong sense of who you are there is no need to "become your mask"—you are something considerably more substantial inside. Second, the ninja were also taught various forms of acting skills, which would loosen up the identification with any one mask, and facilitate the flexible interchange of life roles required for survival. Hence a firm personality base and a tendency toward flexibility led the ninja to a healthy relationship to this aspect of themselves.

Archetypes of the Spirit

So far the most central forms of archetypal energy that relate to the ninja might appear to be the Hero/Warrior and the Hero Cycle/musha shugyo. However, if we pause for a moment and recognize what the "goal" of the Hero/Warrior and Hero's Cycle/musha shugyo is, we shift perspective. We realize that the ninja were focused upon realizing increasingly higher states of awareness. In archetypal terms, we could say that the ninja were approaching the archetype of Spirit. And the

Spirit archetype takes forms with which we should be familiar now, especially the Hermit (mystic), Wise Old Man (sage), and the Self (the center of our being, the center of the cosmos).

The Hermit

From the historical tradition it is clear that the Hermit is one of the more crucial archetypes activated in nin-po. The yamabushi and sennin ascetic mystic-warriors were the forerunners of those who would later be referred to as ninja. Hence understanding the Hermit archetype is fundamental to understanding both the power of the historical tradition and our current fascination with the ancient art of ninjutsu.

Perhaps the most common association to the yamabushi and sennin mountain mystics is solitude. The Hermit, by nature, chooses to live alone, far from the hustle and bustle of everyday life. He forgoes the comforts of the world to seek something deeper, something more meaningful. He may live in a distant cave, or on top of a mountain, but always far from the beaten track.

In our extroverted and group-oriented society, it is not surprising to find many viewing the Hermit as a pathological introvert, or a recluse unable to face reality. It may therefore come as a shock to realize that the Greek word *monachoi*, which is usually translated as "single ones" or "solitaries" could also be translated as the "unified ones" (Edinger, 1972). Hence we see that the Hermit, far from cutting off and divorcing himself from reality, in fact sees through the "ten thousand things" to the oneness of the universe. He is not divided against himself, as are so many in our schizophrenic culture, but "unified" and "whole."

One way of looking at this relationship between the Hermit and unity is to think of what happens in most of our lives. Few of us, even those of us most dedicated to doing so, manage to find time alone for ourselves each day for a walk, for meditation, or for quiet reflection. We are caught up in the stimulation that bombards us from the outside: work, family, television, politics, national disasters, personal tragedies, etc. Clearly when we are dealing with these things we cannot pay much attention to what goes on inside. Put otherwise, we cut ourselves off from much of who we are. Now what the Hermit does is to withdraw from that outer stimulation. When this occurs, not only is he able to pay greater attention to what is occurring inside him but his inner world comes to life. He is, therefore, in a position to integrate the outer and the inner to become unified.

Nichols (1980) puts it beautifully. She likens the rhythm of life to our breathing, to our cyclic inhalation and exhalation. She notes that just as both are needed in order to breathe, so introversion and extroversion are needed for a healthy perspective on life. We cannot live by only inhaling, nor only exhaling, and it is the Hermit who helps us find our own rhythm. He frees us to breathe fully and deeply, to balance extroversion with introversion. And this is accomplished through being "solitary"—not constantly solitary, but appropriately so, in balance with our lives and our needs.

Not only is the essence of the Hermit's life unity, but so is the process. When we think of the yamabushi and sennin we tend to think that they are poorly equipped to deal with other people. But this is a prejudice we have on this side of the experience that the Hermit undergoes. In actuality, through differentiating himself from the masses, through becoming his own person, the hermit is *better* able to relate to those still "trapped" in the collective. Only by truly seeing something can we understand it and fully related to it. If we are part of "it" we simply do not have the objectivity necessary; we need to separate ourselves, to become ourselves, to relate better to others.

As we shall explore more in detail later on, the path of individuation, the process of becoming all that we are predestined to be, is both an intensely *personal* experience and a lonely one (Nichols, 1980). We must "disentangle" ourselves from others to become ourselves. We must "withdraw our projections," take back the energy that we unconsciously give to others, and fully realize our own energic capacity.

Not surprisingly others do not always like this. They dislike the fact that you no longer give them power to take some control over you, and they dislike being shown by you that they are not unified, but divided. And just as the ninja of ancient Japan were hunted down and killed for following a mystic path, so the person who decides to become an individual is often misunderstood and rejected by those around him or her.

The Hermit must carry his own light amid the darkness. Immediately we hearken back to Dr. Hatsumi's comments about the ninja being able to call upon their own inner light when in utter darkness and confusion to guide them into making the correct choices, and to walk *freely* where others would lose their footing due to their lack of understanding. The Hermit's light, therefore, dispells spiritual chaos and darkness.

The Hermit then, among other things, is that riverbed within us that carries the potential of directing our chi in the directions we have discussed. In many ways the Hermit is one of the founding fathers of the ninjutsu tradition—psychologically speaking, of course. And it is the ability of the Hermit archetype to open us up to our individuality and oneness that is particularly appealing to us in our age of disarray. The Hermit is, indeed, an expression of the Self, our total being.

The Wise Old Man

In addition to the Hermit, who well corresponds to the origins of the ninja tradition, there is also the Wise Old Man, who corresponds to the warrior-philosopher jonin who headed the various ninjutsu ryu throughout Japan's history. The mark of these men was a wisdom based upon a philosophical view of reality. They ultimately made the difficult decisions of how best to employ the limited resources of the ninja families to bring about maximum effect. They were the ones who decided to whom the ninja would lend their services, for what purpose, and for how long. Without this wisdom the ninja families would never have survived.

As we saw in our discussion of the Hero Cycle, the Wise Old Man, or simply Sage, appears in a situation when the Hero/Warrior's insight and understanding have reached their limit, and he can proceed no further under his own steam (Jung, 1972). Like the Hermit, the Sage is a manifestation of the Self. It is useful, however, to look at this representation separately because, among other things, his appearance in our lives emphasizes our *moving through life*, not just our status in the present.

The Wise Old Man forces us to face the issues at hand in our lives. Indeed, the Wise Old Man is himself the "purposeful reflection and concentration" of archetypal energies. The Wise Old Man appears outside of consciousness, especially when consciously directed thought is no longer possible" (Jung, 1972). He asks those difficult questions of life that force us in upon ourselves to find an answer. In essence, he *mobilizes* us toward wholeness.

The Wise Old Man gives to us something "magical" with which we can achieve the goal of our lives. Put otherwise he gives us the *power to succeed*. Immediately we see a connection with a fundamental aspect of ninjutsu, the "art of winning." The ninja's "realization of intentions" is the ability to bring about the effect one wishes—the power to succeed. Archetypally we can say that the Wise Old Man has been activated. As Jung (1972) notes, the activation of the Wise Old Man archetype is often *crucial*. Jung stresses that simple will-power is rarely able to unite the personality to such a degree that it manifests the "extraordinary power to succeed."

This is where we most clearly see the involvement of something "beyond the human realm." As Jung said, we are usually unable to unite ourselves. To do so entails realizing the totality of our being, *including those parts of ourselves that we do not want to face*. That is why "trying" to become whole, or "trying to realize intentions" is counterproductive. Instead we must "put ourselves aside." Then the power of the Self can touch us, then there is unity, and through unity power. This is where the activation of the Wise Old Man archetype is so important.

The Wise Old Man brings about this effect by aiding us on our travels of self discovery. He knows which roads lead to our goal, and he points them out to us. He knows of the dangers upon the path, and he knows ways of overcoming those dangers. In short, he is a spiritual guide.

In sum, then, the Wise Old Man represents "superior insight," true knowledge, reflection, and wisdom. He also represents the desire to help those on the Path, hence his spiritual dimension (Jung, 1972). When this archetype is activated within us we are opened to the possibilities of realizing these qualities in our lives. As with the Hermit, the Wise Old Man leads us to the Self, along the path of self-discovery.

The Self and Individuation

Throughout the second half of this book we have been referring to the Self, the totality of our beings, a goal to which ninjustu directs us. The archetype of the Self is the most important to us. Not only are all other archetypes ultimately manifestations of the Self, but, as we shall see, *the ninja image itself is a symbol for the Self*. More precisely, then, what is the Self?

There are a variety of ways of conceptualizing the Self. Although these conceptualizations will help us understand the essence of the Self, and through it the ninja, *they are only intellectual abstractions*. To "know" the Self is to have experienced the Self. There is no other way. However, if the image of the ninja is very powerful for you in an emotional and motivating way, then chances are in some manner the Self has been constellated. Here would be a glimpse of the Self through the image of the ninja. It would then be necessary to "follow" the ninja symbol to your own totality.

One way in which Jung described the relationship between the ego and the Self was to relate it to the solar system. The ego would be the earth, the Self the sun. Others described the ego–Self relationship as equivalent to moved–mover (Whitmont, 1969). Indeed, if the ego is the mayor, the authority in a large town, the Self encompasses the authorities that govern that town, adjacent towns, the capital, the country, and includes authorities in other countries, even other worlds. In short, the ego, your conception of who you are, is minuscule in comparison to what lies buried beneath the thin surface of your ego personality. Indeed, as Jung has said, we do not create ourselves, *we happen to ourselves.*

Often the Self is regarded as the "god within us." If we consider the ninja's goal of seeing "with the mind and eyes of god" we capture some of the meaning in this phrase. Realizing the Self is not setting up a confrontation between man and god (ego and totality), but realizing that you are *one with the Self, one with god.* When you fully realize the Self, there are no seams, no artificial joinings of one thing to another. You are continuous with the Self, just as a wave is continuous with the entire ocean.

Many of the ways in which the Self is described parallel ways in which totality is expressed in nin-po. Indeed, the Self has been described as an *indestructable totality.* The Self is, at once, and paradoxically, the Center and the Totality. It is the Whole, but also the guidance system that leads us toward wholeness. Drawing upon the language of physics, the Self is the "unitary field." To our intellects these paradoxes seem irreconcilable, but that is because we do not comprehend the oneness of the cosmos. The Self can be, simultaneously, the Center of our personalities and the Totality of our personalities because the Center and the Whole are not different. They only appear different. This parallels the Buddha's teaching that we are already enlightened—we just do not know it, and so we go "searching" for something "we already have."

The Self appears at its most mystical when we realize that it governs not only the conscious and unconscious aspects of our being, but also the *outer and the inner.* We balk at the thought that the Self could govern that which occurs outside our personalities, but again this is due to our very limited perspective. As in the ninja's sanmitsu, which will be looked at more closely in Chapter 8, where "thought, word, and deed" are brought together to realize intentions in the world, the Self, although it manifests itself through our egos, does not belong to us, but to all of humanity—*it is inside us and outside us.* It can "govern" what occurs within our individual psychologies and the events that occur around us. This is the concept of synchronicity resting upon the notion that all divisions of person and world, spirit and matter, past, present, and future, space and time are simply divisions our minds have created—the ten thousand things. When we realize the unity of the universe this concept no longer seems strange.

As we have already noted, the Self not only "is," it also "acts"—it leads us toward the realization of oneness. If we look upon the Self as

a form of energy rather than as something solid we see that it is the center of our energy field. Its purpose is change, for only in change is there growth. It, therefore, runs up against the ego that desires the status quo. Another way of putting this is that the Self is fluid, flowing, and flexible, and the ego is rigid. And here we come to another fundamental aspect of ninjutsu—*flexibility*.

Abandoning our attachment to our egos means abandoning rigidity. But this is far easier said than done. The confrontation with the Self that changes all is experienced as terrifying within consciousness, we fear the "loss of ourselves." This also leads us directly to a change in the way we see good and evil. The Self is intent upon the realization of wholeness. It may, at times, employ means that seem "evil" from the perspective of the ego to break up the rigidity. If we can accept our Shadows, messengers from the Self, then, as we have seen, we can grow and change. If we retreat into our ego's fixed definition of good, then we bolster our rigidity and find that we have permanently cut ourselves off from the movement of the cosmos.

In Conclusion

The purpose for this excursion into the various archetypal energies at work in ninjutsu was to demonstrate the tremendous physical, psychological, and spiritual richness of the tradition. Indeed, ninjutsu captures many of the most powerful archetypes, thus captivating us and drawing us to them. Most important, of course, is the capacity of the ninja to face these various energies, to bring them into relation with the human realm, and then to channel them. In this capacity they were unequaled.

Ultimately, then, it is the courage of the ninja to realize the Self which is at work in ninjutsu. Indeed, we could day that the ninja image as presented in the historical tradition is a symbol for the Self. This only makes sense since the ninja were often seen as supernatural ("beyond human") in ancient Japan and have been granted "godhood" in our popular culture. With this in mind we now turn to the numinous, spiritual heritage of nin-po mikkyo.

8

Beyond Psychology: Nin-Po Mikkyo

"From the mystic teachings of *mikkyo* came the ninja's insight into the workings of the universe, and from the application of this understanding came the ninja's personal power."—**Stephen K. Hayes** (1981b)

"Once the *kuji* technique is mastered, the ninja then has the power to create physical reality by means of his intention alone. Focused intention becomes completed action itself; cause blends with effect until the distinction fades."—**Dr. Masaaki Hatsumi** (1981)

"Attaining the core essence of the ninja art begins with the paring away of unessentials to reach a base state of personal spiritual purity, and culminates in the ability to move freely without defilement between the polar realms of brightness and darkness as necessitated by the scheme of totality."—**Yasuyoshi Fujibayashi**

"Before the bar of nature and fate, unconsciousness is never accepted as an excuse; on the contrary, there are very severe penalties for it."—**C.G. Jung** (1969)

MOST MARTIAL ARTS books present techniques to readers. If the tradition being written about has a spiritual side this is usually given only lip service. Then the book gets back to its original goal of presenting stances, punches, kicks, or holds. The same is also true in a great many dojos, especially in the U.S., where any hint of something beyond the physical is carefully avoided. The martial arts are a means of *self-defense*, a good way to get *exercise* or *recreation*, an almost psychotherapeutic approach to *building character and confidence*. Just as our culture has lost much of its connection with "the mysteries," so has most teaching in the martial arts.

The books and teaching of Stephen K. Hayes stand in stark contrast to this overall situation. In each of his seven technical books special attention is given to spiritual training. His book of poetry, *Wisdom from the Ninja Village of the Cold Moon*, and his novel, *Tulku: A Tale of Modern Ninja*, also focus on the spiritual/philosophical aspects of ninjutsu. Whereas most writers and teachers consider the body only, Hayes approaches the person as *mind-body-spirit*. In the way he presents ninjutsu the *whole person* is actively and intimately involved in growth from the very beginning, not an isolated and alienated part.

It is not surprising, therefore, to find Stephen K. Hayes and his senior instructors referring to *nin-po* not as a "martial art" but as a "way of life," or a "total way of living." Indeed, it is frequently said at Shadows of Iga Ninja Society seminars and festivals that training in ninjutsu occurs *twenty-four hours a day*, not just during training sessions. Nin-po certainly includes the most highly developed combat system in the world today. But *it is neither confined nor limited by this*. Indeed, nin-po, at a deeper level, is concerned with attuning yourself with the universe, becoming increasingly sensitive to what is around and inside of you, expanding awareness of mind-body-spirit.

In the first four chapters of this book, we looked at the image of the ninja as it is presented in the West. In the next three chapters we looked at the psychology behind the image, looking particularly at why we are so attracted to the ninja of ancient Japan. To conclude we will take a brief look at nin-po-mikkyo as Hayes has presented it in his books. Although this will not be an exhaustive examination by any means, it is hoped this will give the reader a sense of the depth and richness of the ninja way.

The Origins and Evolution of Nin-po Mikkyo

As we noted in Chapter 4, the early ninja were greatly influenced by many of the scholars and monks who arrived in Japan after the fall of the T'ang Dynasty in China. They brought with them teachings from Tibet and India, especially tantra and the mikkyo teachings. This knowledge was integrated with the traditions surrounding the yama-bushi, sennin, and gyoja mountain warrior ascetics, and eventually became the spitiual heritage of the ninja families.

The mikkyo teachings are still transmitted in Japan, although through the centuries they have evolved and, as Hayes has noted, are now somewhat different than the original form introduced into Japan. Hence modern mikkyo does not correspond exactly to the mikkyo teachings found in nin-po. Perhaps the most striking difference is simply the fact that the mikkyo teachings as they are transmitted in the Tendai sect of Buddhism, and in Shingon Buddhism, are part of an "elaborate religion" with "ornate trappings" and "complex rituals." The ninja, on the other hand, were, and continue to be, more concerned with a "working set of principles or laws," "the original universal principles of causation." More important to us than an understanding of the intricacies of mikkyo is, perhaps, a general understanding of tantra.

Tantra

As expressed in Tibetan Buddhism, tantra is connected with working with energy. However, the ability to work with tantra comes only after considerable spiritual work. The entrance into tantra is *samadhi*, enlightenment. It is that point where we are no longer in a state of *knowing* wisdom, but have entered into a stage of *being* wisdom (Trungpa, 1973).

As Chogyam Trungpa (1973) has written, in the *Vajrayana* or tantric teachings understanding deeply the *principles of energy* is crucial. He stresses that tantra does not advocate the suppression or destruction of energy, but its *transformation* or *transmutation*. Trungpa expresses this more straightforwardly as "going with the pattern of energy." If you can allow yourself to go with the pattern of energy then "experience becomes very creative." The world takes on a different quality. Peace, compassion, and wisdom become such that they cannot be influenced by the "frivolity of ego."

The practitioner of tantra sees things *as they are*. There is no longer any dualism, no divisions, no splitting of the "one" into the "ten thousand things." The practitioner sees through the complex veneer of reality to the "*stoneness* of stones and the *waterness* of water"

(Trungpa, 1973). There is a vast understanding of symbolism and energy. The practitioner no longer has to force results but allows life to flow around him.

Already we should be understanding the tantric influence within ninjutsu. There is the working with energy, the philosophy that life energy should not be rejected, destroyed, or suppressed because we may not like the form it takes, but alchemically transmuted. There is also the position that energy should not be "fought" but "followed." And most important, there is the seeing of reality *as it is*, not as we want it to be.

Very briefly there are five basic categories of energy within tantra. Each is associated with a particular aspect of the awakened mind, colors, elements, landscapes, directions, and seasons. The first is vajra. It is associated with anger and is transmuted into "Mirror like Wisdom." It is associated with water, the color white, the East, dawn, winter. Trungpa (1973) describes vajra intelligence as "leaving no stone unturned" (the ninja's "good intelligence gathering"). He likens it to water flowing over a smooth surface. The water completely covers the surface, but the surface can still be seen clearly due to the water's transparency.

The second basic category of energy is ratna. It is associated with pride and is transmuted into the "Wisdom of Equanimity." It is associated with earth, the colors gold, amber, and saffron; the South; mid-morning; and autumn. Trungpa (1973) notes that with ratna energy there is an awareness of "the solidity and stability of earth" (chi awareness). This awareness or, rather, this connection is so strong that there is no fear of losing it. In short, it brings fearlessness. Immediately we should be reminded of Jack Hoban's comments with regard to the sanmitsu in which knowing "solidly" our own rightness, such that we *do not lose touch with it in an attack*, allows us to "open ourselves" to an attacker, and neutralize his negative energy.

The third category is padma. It is associated with passion, or a "desire to possess," and is transmuted into "Discriminating Awareness." It is associated with fire, the color red, the West, early spring. Here, Trungpa (1973) warns, there is the danger of becoming such a slave to your desires that an "automatic" stupidity and ignorance results. As we shall see in the next section, Dr. Hatsumi addressed the question of desire during Stephen K. Hayes's long training with him. Dropping desire is fundamental to the ninja's lifestyle. Realizing the inherent dangers in this type of desire allows the transformation of passion into Discriminating Awareness Wisdom.

Karma is the fourth category of energy. It is associated with jealousy and envy and is transmuted into the "Wisdom of All-Accomplishing Action." It is associated with wind, the color green, the North, dusk, summer. Karma energy views a situation, immediately sees what may result in the future because of the present, and guides appropriate action. It bears striking parallels to the intuitive function we have looked at, and certainly corresponds to the ninja's phenomenal intuitive powers, especially when it came to "predicting the future." Trungpa (1973) notes simply that it "fulfills the purpose"; ninjutsu is often described as the "art of winning."

The fifth, and final, category of energy is buddha. It is associated with dullness and is transmuted into "All-Encompassing Space." It is associated with the "foundation" or "basic ground" (Void), the color blue, the spacious quality of the sky. Trungpa (1973) makes clear that buddha wisdom contains *tremendous energy and intelligence*. This energy and wisdom is the "elusive element" that gives rise to the other "elements." It is the ocean that exists in all waves. Buddha energy activates the other forms of energy. This is the creative Void of which Stephen K. Hayes speaks, the element at work in the Earth, Water, Fire, and Wind techniques, but which cannot be taught separately because it is already present in the other four.

Put simply *tantra* is concerned with taking facts of everyday life, such as anger or jealousy, and releasing the inherent energy in them. Rather than becoming wrapped up in the emotion or quality under consideration or repressing it (and making it part of the Shadow), the practitioner of tantra learns to transmute it.

Among the many themes in tantra, two are particularly important for us to realize. The first is that tantra involves the transmutation of energy. The ninja were oppressed by the various daiymos and shoguns of ancient Japan. To gain the upper hand they took their "lead," which we all have, and through spiritual alchemy turned it into "gold." This gave them the upper hand against the "leaden" samurai. Second, tantra involves a *direct experience of reality*. As we shall see, the ninja were able to use their direct experience of reality to defeat the samurai, who looked such immediate sensitivity. This crucial difference gave the ninja the edge, for they could see more clearly, and take the appropriate action to prevent disaster. As we look more deeply into nin-po mikkyo, many of these tantric elements will be readily seen.

Enlightenment

We have mentioned the fact that the ninja strove for enlightenment throughout the preceding chapters. Before moving on, it would be beneficial to còme to some understanding of how this is presented in nin-po.

Hayes frequently notes that moving toward the enlightened state involves giving up "desire." He recounts how he struggled with this somewhat elusive concept when training in Japan under Dr. Hatsumi. The Grandmaster had noted that the first step in the development of spiritual power was to rid oneself of "desire." After Hayes had made an effort to understand the meaning of this, Hatsumi rephrased it. It is necessary to abandon one's "preconceived impressions of the way things are." He stressed that there is very often a great gulf between what we *want* to believe and what is "real" (Hayes, 1981).

The "desires" to be given up, then, are not so much the desires for material belongings and power, although these are also important things to look at in yourself, but the desires to see reality as *we want to see it*, rather than *as it is*. These are the desires that "cloud the mind" and make us lose touch with the world. These are our self-deceptions. And these are "luxuries" the ninja could not afford—not if they wished to survive. They had to see reality in all its harsh grimness, or the warlords would have taken advantage of their "desire" for peaceful coexistence.

Hence, one of the most important goals of a ninjutsu practitioner is the development of the strength and knowledge to experience life, and to react to situations in life, with "natural knowing." Hayes (1980) notes that the way we penetrate through to this natural knowing is to "remove" the various barriers that have been erected around us both by our own actions and by the culture around us. Hayes (1983) puts it even more powerfully elsewhere, stating that for the *mystic warrior* realizing the potential within to see beyond the "ten thousand things," the "clouds of deception," or "the illusory surface of things" is itself enlightenment.

Naturally there are many other meanings and descriptions of enlightenment, but the way Hayes has presented the concept is perhaps the most useful to us as we consider nin-po mikkyo. However, it might be useful to mention one other way of looking at enlighten- ment since it is somewhat similar to the way Hayes describes it, and thus grants us a second glance at a human state of awareness which is difficult to comprehend.

From a psychological perspective, enlightenment may be defined as "removing our projections from the world." It is absolutely normal for us to experience parts of ourselves we do not know yet as "out here"—especially Shadow aspects of ourselves. Although this is natural, it both interferes with our view of reality and it results in giving away our energy and power. As we come to learn more of ourselves, and take back our projections, we see the world for what it is, not clouded by our expectations and convictions of how it should be. We also take back the energy that is ours. The samurai who allowed his Shadow fears to be projected onto the ninja gave away power to his own detriment. The ninja who worked with their Shadow qualities, who integrated all aspects of themselves and withdrew their projections, increased their energy. Hence we see that "enlightenment" brings with it tremendous power.

The Doctrine of In and Yo

Perhaps the most accessible aspect of the nin-po mikkyo to Westerners is the fundamental classification of phenomena into *in* and *yo* (or *yin* and *yang* as they are pronounced in Chinese). However, although this means of viewing reality is widespread in the East, and familiar to us in the West, the doctrine of *in* and *yo* is frequently misunderstood. We in the West tend to divide and separate things, and so we see *in* and *yo* as *opposites* instead of *complements* of one another. We also fail to understand why Eastern philosophies and spiritual traditions adhere to what appears to be a somewhat simplistic dualism.

To gain some insight into the complementarity of *in* and *yo* we need only to look at the origins of the concepts in Taoist China. As Wilhelm (1967) has noted in this introduction to the I *Ching* (or *Book of Changes*), the primary meaning of *yin* is the "cloudy," "the overcast." The primary meaning of *yang* is actually "banners waving in the sun," or, more correctly, something "shone upon," or "bright." Eventually these two concepts were used in regard to the light and dark sides of a mountain or river. When considering a mountain it is the south side that is bright (*yang*), and the north side that is dark (*yin*). When considering a river from above, it is the north side that is bright (*yang*), because it reflects the light, and the south side that is in shadow (*yin*).

Just like a coin that cannot have only one side, so there cannot be a north side to a mountain without there also being a south side, nor a south side of a river without a north side. Although there are two aspects to the coin, mountain, or river they are all fundamentally *one thing*. The southern side of a mountain is not the "opposite" of the northern side, but the "complement"—it makes the mountain complete, whole.

To introduce a modern "*in* and *yo*" view of the human we need only look at current theories about the two hemispheres of the brain. The left hemisphere (which controls the right side of the body) handles information in a linear, sequential manner. It makes sense of the world in an intellectual or scientific way. The right side of the brain (which controls the left side of the body) processes information simultaneously. It sees the world in a more spatial or intuitive way. Hence we have polarities such as analytic-intuitive, verbal-nonverbal, sequential-simultaneous, etc. Clearly the left side of the brain corresponds to *yo*, while the right side corresponds to *in*.

This analogy is helpful in two ways. First, it allows us to see that both *in* and *yo* are needed. Were we to have a left hemisphere, or just a right side, we would be intellectual and emotional cripples. Second, it allows us to take the next step in understanding the importance of *in* and *yo*: they are *always in motion*, always changing from one to the other. Just like the flow of information back and forth between the two sides of the brain, so *in* and *yo* alternate.

Wilhelm (1967) stresses that "the world of being" arises from the interplay of *in* and *yo*, and this world of being is seen as constantly in flux, constantly changing. We see this change in two ways. First, as the endless transformation of one form of energy into another (*in* into *yo*, and *yo* into *in*). Second, we see the "cycles of phenomena," such as day turning into night, summer into winter, etc.

Both aspects of the *in* and *yo* doctrine—their complementarity and their endless changing one into the other—are visually captured in the familiar yin-yang symbol. Here we see that only together do the darkness and light create a whole. We also see that the two primal forces are in motion. As *yin* declines in strength, *yang* increases, and vice versa. And each possesses the seed of the other within itself.

The Ninja's Use of In and Yo

As we noted in Chapter 6, ninjutsu can be viewed as a "path toward wholeness." We saw that the ninja did not reject the "dark," or *in*, aspects of being, but, rather, cultivated them and completed themselves through them. They did not run in fear from shadows, but befriended the shadows and thus survived against overwhelming odds. Hence we see that while many of the world's cultures rejected the *in* in favor of the *yo* (and so became unbalanced because of it), the ninja strove for balance: they sought to have *in* and *yo* in harmony.

But there is more to the ninja's use of the *in* and *yo* doctrine than that. Stephen K. Hayes addresses two crucial areas. First, Hayes (1981a) notes that the universe is too large and too overwhelming for anyone to comprehend. However, through a deep understanding of the concepts of *in* and *yo*, the ninja can recapture an overview of the workings of the cosmos. An essential key to this is seeing the universe as *one process.* The first, powerful result of realizing this in our lives is the dissolving of our feelings of isolation, alienation, and separateness. The second effect of actually *living* within this framework is freedom from beliefs that paint us victims of life, forever blown about as feathers in the wind or as corks in a stormy ocean.

The ninja did not decide to incorporate the philosophy of *in* and *yo* into their lives for any intellectual or aesthetic reasons, but solely for pragmatic reasons. When fully actualized it permitted the ninja to gain a deep understanding into the workings of the universe. As Hayes (1980) has stressed, the ninja's outlook on his purpose in life rests primarily upon the total picture, the "larger scheme of things." At the same time working with the concepts of *in* and *yo* is a means of personal empowerment. As Hayes notes, many societies, religions, and cultures create a negative mindset of "me-against-the-world." This can be dissolved by the realization that we are not at war with the universe, but an integral part of its process; we are not pawns, but an intimate part of the kingdom. Failure to realize this results in enslavement at your own hands. And this the ninja could not afford, for their enemies were powerful.

In addition to allowing the ninja to grasp the workings of the universe and to advance their own personal development, the "doctrine" of *in* and *yo* allowed the ninja to free themselves from the time-worn, and usually arbitrary, understanding of "good," "right," and "fair," and their opposites, "evil," "wrong," and "unfair." All of existence is in movement. What is right today may be wrong tomorrow, what appears to be right may, in actuality, be wrong. To be rigid and inflexible about what is, and what is not, "good" or "evil" is to stand in opposition to the natural process of change in the cosmos. Realizing this gave, and continues to give, the ninja a larger perspective and freedom within which to judge what was "appropriate" and what was "inappropriate" at any particular time.

To us in the West this sounds as if the ninja were amoral, unable to distinguish between good and bad. And here we run into a huge cultural obstacle that often stands in the way of West understanding East. The best way to state this simply is to say that like *in* and *yo*, "good" and "evil" are complementary—you *cannot have one without the other*. And what is considered good and what evil is *always changing*. The only way to have freedom of action is to transcend the polarities. This way there is the realization of both occurring together, set against an understanding of the scheme of totality.

A final note on the *in* and *yo* classification. When the world is divided up into opposites—"good" and "evil," sacred and profane, etc.—you are "cut off" from much of the universe. What you may, and may not do, consider, think, feel, experience, understand is *greatly restricted*. But from our look at the Shadow in Chapter 5, it should be clear that great power and opportunity for growth lies in the darkness. And the ninja did not reject this, but embraced it. As Hayes (1981a) has noted, what may be regarded as sin in one cultural tradition might be the key to enlightenment in another. One man's Shadow is another (wiser) man's light.

Five Element Theory

The *yin/in* and *yang/yo* classification originated in Taoist China, at least in its formal philosophical presentation. Even older, however, was a scheme of classification found in Tibetan tantric lore, the idea that the physical aspects of what we know as the universe originate from the same source. At their most fundamental level, these aspects may be broken down into five "elemental manifestations" (Hayes, 1980). The resulting "Five Element Theory" is another of the mikkyo teachings that are highlighted in the writings of Stephen K. Hayes.

As with *in* and *yo*, the Five Element Theory is a means of gaining access to the workings of the universe. It only makes sense that if the ninja were operating in a world they understood, fighting against stronger forces that refused to comprehend the "Totality," they were at an advantage. They "knew the land" (and "all land was theirs" because of their "oneness with the universe") whereas the samurai were strangers (even in their own territories).

The five elements that Hayes usually refers to are *Chi* (the earth), *Sui* (the water), *Ka* (the fire), *Fu* (the wind), and *Ku* (the emptiness or the Void). Since the ninja were not rigidly wedded to any doctrine they also employed another five element classification schema commonly found in Eastern medical practices. Hence, the other five elements

Hayes refers to in his works are Earth, Water, Wood, Fire, and Metal. Both systems, however, serve similar functions and allow the Totality to be grasped.

The five elements, among other things, refer both to "states" and "processes." Once concrete example of the classification system is in its application to the human body. Chi corresponds to the bones, teeth, muscles, and other solid body parts. As Hayes noted once at the 1985 Bujinkan Dojo Training Camp, Chi may also refer to the food we take into our bodies. Sui corresponds to bodily fluids, as well as those parts of the body that enhance flexibility. Sui may also represent the fluids we drink. Ka is represented by our metabolism, the transformation of elements into an "energy-releasing" state. Our bodily warmth results from this, and we can increase it further through exercise. Fu refers to our breathing, and Ku to our ability to communicate (Hayes, 1980).

The Five Element Theory also involves processes. Two of the processes Hayes (1980) refers to are superordinate, and actually encompass all of the others. In the first, the universe may be seen as created through the progression Ku→Fu→Ka→Sui→Chi, from the "nothingness" (Ku) before the "Big Bang" to the physical reality we see around us today (Chi). This process is an example of the creative

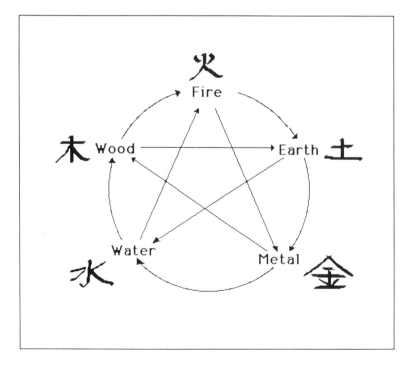

aspect of the universe. In the second process, as exemplified by death, the reverse process is initiated, with Ku (consciousness) disappearing first, then Fu (breathing), and so on down to Chi (the decomposition of our solid bodily tissues). This second example is representative of the destructive aspect of reality.

The creative process of the Five Element Theory finds expression in its close correspondence with the chakras of yoga. Kundalini Yoga describes the evolution of consciousness in terms of passing through various "energy points" in the body, beginning at the base of the spine and culminating at the crown of the head. In terms of the five elements, Chi has its center at the base of the spine, Sui in the lower abdomen, Ka at the lower tip of the breastbone, Fu in the center of the chest, and Ku in the center of the throat. We should not be too worried because of the lack of "exact correspondence" between the five elements and the chakras since both the elements, in this context, and the chakras, actually represent *states of consciousness* rather than physical points on the body. Only five chakras are usually spoken about since it is a great rarity that a person passes beyond the fifth chakra. The important point here is that nin-po mikkyo is intimately involved with the evolution of consciousness, and at times uses the Five Element Theory to communicate this.

Whereas many of the processes described by the five-elements grouping are linear (having a "beginning" and an "end"), the Earth, Metal, Water, Wood, Fire five-elements grouping tends to describe cyclical processes. Hayes refers to this second classification as *gogyo*, or "five element transformation." It goes without saying that each element is a metaphorical or symbolic representation of an aspect, or set of aspects, of the universe.

The two basic "cycles" are as follows. First the creative (*yo*) or productive cycle. Water represents sinking energy and gives rise to Wood, or upward growth energy (think of water sinking into the earth and permitting trees to grow). This upward moving energy gives rise to free dissipated energy represented by Fire (burning wood). Eventually dissipation comes together into solidifying energy, or Earth (the ashes and earth of the wood return to the earth). Solidifying energy gives rise to hardness, as symbolized by Metal (the ashes and earth are compressed and become rock). Eventually the hardness cracks and becomes sinking energy; Water (erosion breaks up the hardest of rocks) (Hayes, 1985a). And we have come full circle.

The destructive (*in*) cycle touches upon ways in which energy can be overcome, rather than created. Fire can melt Metal, thus rendering hard energies ineffective. Metal, as in an ax or saw, can destroy Wood, thus stopping growing energy. Wood, as in sprouting seedlings and tenacious roots, can break up Earth, gathering, stabilizing, and condensing energies. Earth, as in a dam, can stop Water, the sinking down energies. Water can put out Fire, evasive free-moving energy (Hayes, 1985a). And again we have come full circle.

The Ninja's Use of the Five Element Theory

The Five Element Theory is used by the ninja in a variety of ways. One of the most striking uses is in *gotonpo* ("five elements concealing and escaping methods"). Both Hatsumi and Hayes write at length about this usage. A lengthy discourse on *onshinjutsu*, the art of making oneself invisible, is not in order here (the interested reader is referred to Hayes, 1985a, and Hatsumi, 1981). However, a brief illustration of each element as it might be employed to escape or conceal oneself will give an adequate sense of the Five Element Theory in action.

Since, as Hayes stresses, a rigid and literal adherence to each element is erroneous, each element will be characterized by a

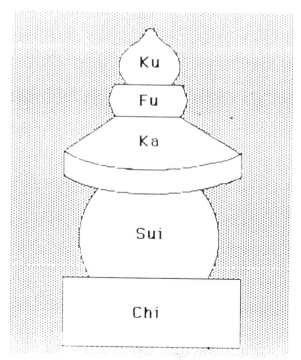

Symbolic representation of the five manifestations. (Adapted from Hayes, 1981a)

somewhat abstract and metaphorical statement. For example, *moku-tonjutsu*, the wood escape arts, might be strategically described as follows: "My forces marshal more troops and move against you with growing intensity as your forces attempt to hold onto your own territory" (Hayes, 1985a, p. 115). Clearly Wood, "rising, growing, swelling energy" is most effective against Earth, "gathering, condensing, stabilizing energy."

Along the same lines *katonjutsu*, the fire escape arts may be characterized strategically as: "My forces scatter and evade to frustrate and dissipate the power of your forces as they attempt to launch a piercing attack." *Dotonjutsu*, the earth escape arts, is described by a statement such as: "My forces draw together and intensify their hold on the territory as your forces attempt to slip in easily and surreptitiously." *Kintonjutsu*, the metal escape arts, may be expressed as: "My forces launch an immediate and decisive attack against your forces as they attempt to build strength and move into an advantageous position." Finally, *suitonjutsu*, the water escape arts, may be characterized by the following statement: "My forces quickly melt into your territory as your forces scatter and thin out in an attempt to cover even more territory" (Hayes, 1985a, pp. 115–116).

One final point needs to be made in this area. Just as the doctrine of *in* and *yo* could be used as a vehicle for removing separateness from the universe, so, too, with the Five Elements Theory. What is important to realize here, for an appreciation of how mikkyo interfaced with ninjutsu, is that the shinobi warrior who was "at one" with his surroundings, with Nature, will always be in "familiar territory," whether at home or deep inside enemy territory. If he is forced to escape and conceal himself in order to survive, he has intimate, intuitive knowledge of the workings of the universe as expressed in the Five Elements Theory. Hence, the shinobi warrior is able to move through his surroundings with a sensitivity that the rigid samurai did not have.

It should go without saying that the Five Element Theory has limitless other physical, mental, and spiritual applications. It is a model of the workings of the universe, and where it is useful the ninja uses it, where it is not he approaches reality in a different way. The ninja never makes the mistake of "confusing the map for the territory." A model is a map, a representation of reality, a set of signposts. But reality is of a different order, and we are wise to follow Hayes's advice not to take *in* and *yo*, or any of the five elements too literally. They are there to help us in whatever physical, mental, or spiritual situation we might find ourselves in. It is our responsibility not to become enslaved to these "doctrines," "classifications," and "schemas."

Sanmitsu: Thought, Word, Deed

As we saw in the above discussion of *in* and *yo* and the Five Element Theory, the ninja were able to take philosophical and spiritual ways of viewing the world and, in addition to furthering their own spiritual development, were able to put these concepts to use in the battle-field. Part of the way the ninja achieved their ends so effectively was because they deeply understood the workings of the universe and put it to practical use.

But there is more to the ninja's ability to realize their intentions in the world than these methods. Remember, despite the remarkable effectiveness of the ninjutsu combat system and way of life, the ninja were still outnumbered by very powerful and antagonistic political, economic, and military forces. Hence they needed something more than combat techniques and insight. They needed a way of *actually transforming intentions into reality*. And this brings us to sanmitsu.

Hayes (1981b) notes that the basis for working one's will in the world of reality, "realizing intentions," is the bringing together of "thought, word, and deed" such that each of these qualities is in harmony with the other two. The power which results from this "balancing" is known as the sanmitsu, or the "three secrets of mikkyo spiritual power." In essence, and in *greatly oversimplified terms*, sanmitsu is a means of channeling thoughts into physical reality. It is based on the notion that thought, word, and deed are, at the root, one. We see them as separate because we have been trained to see reality in that way. But the original unity can be experienced with dedicated study, and when achieved, the powers evoked are, as Hayes describes them, "dynamic," even "dramatic."

At the Shadows of Iga Ninja Society Bujinkan Dojo Training Camp in 1985, Hayes presented the participants with a basic exercise in sanmitsu. He encouraged each person to establish for himself a "goal," or "intention"—something that he wished to realize in his life. Within the "thought" realm of the sanmitsu he suggested that the goal be *visualized*, and that each person should produce a clear and precise *symbol* of his intentions.

The next stage was to *verbalize* that goal. Here, in the "word" realm of the sanmitsu, the intention should be translated into language. In addition, language and communication were to be engaged to secure the necessary information and contacts for the realization of the intention. This aspect of this stage might be referred to as "intelligence gathering."

Hayes noted that even in this simple example of sanmitsu, most people never get past the first two stages. They visualize their goal, and they can verbalize it. But this is not enough. The "deed" realm must also be activated, and this requires *energy*. The intention must be *vitalized*, brought to life. From deep within, the necessary energy for realizing any goal must be discovered, nurtured, and appropriately channeled. At this level a lack of personal power results in a pipe dream rather than reality.

As with many of the aspects of ninjutsu discussed in this book there are many dimensions. The above example of sanmitsu is a simple one that we can actually use in our lives. However, to advanced practitioners of nin-po there is much more. We are very fortunate in the West to have been granted a glimpse of the higher forms of sanmitsu through Hayes's writings. But it must be emphasized that it is just that: *a glimpse*. If you feel drawn to these realms of knowledge there is only one path for you: the study of ninjutsu from a *genuine, certified instructor*. No book could ever give you such knowledge—not even a book by Dr. Masaaki Hatsumi or Shidoshi Stephen K. Hayes that had been written with the expressed intention of transmitting such knowledge. Knowledge of this kind is transmitted from teacher to student. This is not to prevent anyone from knowing it. It is, quite simply, *the only way*.

Synchronicity: A *Western Bridge to Glimpsing the Sanmitsu*

As we mentioned earlier, Jung's concept of synchronicity bears many similarities to the sanmitsu. It may therefore serve as a "bridge," so to speak, between our Western ways of thinking and the Eastern mind which has traditionally dealt with such realities as the sanmitsu. At root, then, Jung felt that there is an "equivalence of psychic and physical processes." The result of this is an "acausal orderedness"— the *co*-incidental occurrence of a mental focus ("thought" and "word") and an action ("deed") in the physical world that cannot be explained in ordinary "cause-and-effect" terms. Not surprisingly he was *exceedingly cautious* about mentioning this in the West since our usual ways of conceiving of reality cannot comprehend these types of apparently "magical" or "mystical" thoughts.

It is no coincidence that synchronicity is closely related to Jung's positioning of man between the two "eternities" of *microcosm* (the "lesser" or "inner" world, the "lower sphere of personal experience) and *macrocosm* (the "greater" or "outer" world, "the world of transcendental being"). Man is seen as a "portal" between these two realms, a portal through which they are *connected* (Hoeller, 1982). Hence, man sits at the pivot point, at the "joining surface" where the "two become one." It is but one small jump to see that man, as manifested by the ninja, could therefore learn to make use of the "oneness" of these two realms through the sanmitsu's "realization of intentions."

Synchronicity, then, is seen by Jung as a "coincidence in time of two or more causally unrelated events that have the same or similar meaning." Hoeller (1982) is quick to point out that this "coincidence in time" is a *subjective* judgment. He adds that this is, in actuality, more powerful, and ultimately more real, since "space" and "time" are not as separate as we are usually inclined to think. In fact, the "two spaces" (where the "thought" occurred and where the "action" took place) and the "two times" (when the "thought" occurred and when the "action" took place) *become one.*

One way of looking at synchronicity that certainly helps our understanding of the sanmitsu is the notion that synchronistic phenomena are "acts of creation in time" (von Franz, 1975). When viewed this way, as creative, as "bringing something forth or into being," we see the potential behind this joining of the "two spaces" and the "two places."

Now it would seem, as Hoeller (1982) notes, that one would have to be an advanced student of yoga or a "natural psychic" for synchronicity to occur in his life. Not so. The only prerequisite for the "activation of synchronicity" is the appearance of an archetype. And this is where the concept of the archetype does indeed verge on the mystical, for Jung did not regard the archetypes as entirely psychic. Rather, he saw them as "psychoid," *only partly psychic.* They are, he notes, *psychophysical,* to put it cryptically, at once psychological and simultaneously physical. Von Franz (1975) notes that when a synchronistic event occurs the duality between mind and matter is *eliminated.* Hence, as Hoeller concludes, the archetype can manifest itself either psychologically (in "thought" and "word") or physically (in "action"), *or both.*

At times synchronistic events can be "awesome" and "miraculous." To paraphrase Hayes, and make cryptic this already difficult subject, we might say that, "There are no coincidences in life because there are coincidences." Clearly what we mean here is that what appears to be coincidental, seemingly "chance occurrences" (to use that sense of the word) are not "chance events" at all, but the *co*-incidence of the psychological and physical worlds.

Synchronicity, then, transcends the "forces of dispersion and fragmentation" that are at work in our "lower aeon" (Hoeller, 1982). It is concerned with the "interdependence" of all things, including the psychological realm and the material realm (Jung, 1950/1967). Von Franz (1975) notes the parallels between vision of the *unus mundus* which synchronicity provides and enlightened view of creation as a whole. Synchronicity, in a word, unites the "ten thousand things." Most powerfully it brings together the seemingly irreconcilable realms of thought and matter. As Jung has put it, psyche and matter are simply *two different aspects of the same thing.*

Jung (1963) makes a number of interesting remarks concerning our inability to accept synchronicity, and, by logical extension, the power of the sanmitsu. He notes that it is only our "ingrained beliefs" in causality that makes these things believable. They are "unthinkable" only because our *intellects* refuse to grapple with them. Put otherwise, we have to drop "desire" as Hatsumi described it, the desire to see the world only in causal terms. Then, and only then can we begin to see through to the world of synchronistic phenomena and the "magic" of the sanmitsu.

It is interesting to note that synchronicity (in a different guise) has been known for centuries in Taoist China. In fact, as Jung (1950/1967) has demonstrated, synchronicity is the working principle behind the I *Ching Book of Changes.* It is even more interesting to note that the "new physics" in its explorations of the universe at large, and the infinitesimally small regions of the atom, are discovering much the same thing—there are not hard-and-fast divisions between "thought" and "matter." So from ancient China to the modern day, the basis of synchronicity and the sanmitsu has been established. It is simply for us to open our minds to these concepts.

Esoteric Sanmitsu

Having looked at sanmitsu at a fairly simplistic level we now move on to a brief look at its more esoteric aspects. Since the film industry is quite taken with the power words and finger entwining of the ninja—representing them in rather shallow, usually inaccurate ways—it would serve us well to establish some basis of fact in this area. Again, we are indebted to Hayes for granting those of us in the West a glimpse of this side of nin-po.

In essence, the practice of power generation in nin-po mikkyo is comprised of three interrelated aspects that are used in combination. They are: 1) *mantra* ("sacred" or "charged" words), 2) *mandala* (pictoral representations of the structure of the universe, used in meditation for directing and concentrating the mind), and 3) *mudra* (the "energy-channeling" hand posturings) that coordinate all the energies of the personality (Hayes, 1981b). This power generation is closely allied with the "realization of intentions." It also involves the three aspects of the sanmitsu: thought, word, and deed.

Mandala (Nenriki)

We have already encountered the mandala in our discussion of the Self, or totality of the psyche (see Chapters 6 and 7). Here the mandala was a symbol for our total being, a symbol of wholeness. This same completeness is expressed through the idea of the mandala as a "map of the universe." However, in addition to serving as a symbolic expression of totality, the mandala also served as an aid to concentrated intention. Put otherwise, it was a meditation device. Mandala (*nenriki* in Japanese) essentially symbolizes the will, and corresponds to the "thought" aspect of the *sanmitsu*.

Hayes emphasizes two important mandalas in nin-po: the kongokai mandala and the taizokai mandala. "The *kongokai mandala* is the so-called right-hand view of the structure of the universe and represents the natural laws as they are reflected in the spiritual or 'ultimate truth' realm" (Hayes, 1984b, p. 153). Hayes stresses that his is one way of viewing the universe, as though we could see it in its totality. This is how the universe would appear were we "god."

At this point we should note something important. In Western religions there is usually a radical separation between "man" and "god," although this is not always the case in esoteric forms of Judaism and Christianity. In essence, "man" and "god" can never be the same. And so Westerners are separated from the universe ("god"), and thus alienated. But in the East there is the appreciation that once "god" has been experienced, the next step in the evolution of consciousness is to realize that the barrier between man and god is an *artificial one created by our own minds*. Man and god become one.

Thus when Hayes talks about the kongokai realm he is not referring to a perspective that we can never appreciate, but one that is accessible given thorough training in nin-po. It is by transcending the material world, through what Hayes (1981b) describes as "the mystic's process," that it is possible to experience the "universal law itself."

"The *taizokai mandala* is the so-called left-hand view of the structure of the universe and represents the natural laws as they are manifested in the physical or 'material reality' realm" (Hayes, 1984b, pp. 153-154). Here we have a more familiar image of the universe—the universe as it appears from our perspective as parts of a great integrated whole.

It would appear that the kongokai realm is somehow superior to the taizokai realm. Not so. Although the taizokai realm is our "natural" perspective, most people have forgotten what is natural.

> The *Taizokai* matrix realm
> is the immediate moment's realization
> of the temporal manifestation of truth—
> this second, this second, this second—
> the glimpse of our own interaction
> with all other aspects of the universe
> right here in this very fleeting instant,
> the being's eye view of reality
> **(Hayes, 1984c).**

Many of the great Eastern spiritual traditions speak of living in the present, but the majority of people dwell on a past that has gone and anxiously anticipate a future that does not exist—instead of being totally in the moment at hand. Hence, not only did the ninja seek a view of reality in its totality, the kongokai realm, but they also sought complete awareness in the eternal present, the taizokai realm.

> The present is our only opportunity for power.
> The passage of time controls
> and bends all things
> only when we believe
> in the passage of time.
> The future lived
> is merely yet another
> Now.
> **(Hayes, 1984c)**

Like *in* and *yo* the kongokai "diamond spiritual realm" and taisokai "material womb realm" complement one another. In fact, they are *one and the same thing*. It is only from our limited perspective that they seem like two distinct entities. We fail to see the whole mountain—instead we see a "north side" and a "south side," and sometimes go so far as to think one is separate from the other. And if we should emphasize one realm more than the other, the result would be warped and unbalanced personality development.

There is a parallel with the Buddhist tantric teaching that "samsara is nirvana, and nirvana is samsara." *Samsara* refers to the world of suffering, *nirvana* to the ultimate and final liberation from suffering. It would seem that the two states of being are radical opposites. But, again, this is only how we see them from our perspective of limited awareness. What the enlightened sages teach is that they are, "in reality," the same.

What this ultimately leads back to is the tendency for us to divide the universe up into the "ten thousand things" rather than seeing it in its fundamental "oneness." We see the individual "parts" of the cosmos, not "the system." And it is this tendency that the ninja sought to overcome through *nin-po mikkyo*.

Mantra (Jumon) and Mudra (Ketsu-in)

The power words of nin-po mikkyo are known as mantra, or *jumon* in Japanese. They symbolize the "intellect" and correspond to the "word" aspect of sanmitsu. As Hayes (1981b) notes, it is the jumon mantras ("charged words of power") within nin-po mikkyo that give a "vibrant, verbal reality" to the ninja's intentions.

The "hand-posturings" of nin-po mikkyo are known as mudra, or *ketsu-in* in Japanese. Sometimes referred to as hand "seals," the kuji-in mudra of nin-po evolved from the mudra hand postures of esoteric Indian, Tibetan, and Chinese spiritual traditions (Hayes, 1981b). They represent the "channeling of subtle energies." In addition, wisdom teachings are "contained" within each mudra, and psychic protection may be generated for oneself and for others. Ketsu-in symbolizes "physical action" and is associated with "deed" in the sanmitsu.

One set of mantras, or "jumon vow," which Hayes discusses is "*rin, pyo, toh, sha, kai, jin, retsu, sai, zen*," the *jumon* vow that accompanies the nine finger weavings symbolizing the nine levels of power. Because Hayes has written about it, it is not surprising to find this jumon vow appearing in films of the ninja. Unfortunately this has resulted in a distorted sense of what the mantra·and mudra are all about. Let us, therefore, take a brief look at this vow and sketch something of its reality.

Rin, Pyo, Toh, Sha, Kai, Jin, Retsu, Sai, Zen

There is tremendous symbolism associated with the hands. This should not be surprising since it is the hands that have given man the ability to use tools and build the world we have. What is more, from a psychological perspective, the hands are representative of our capacity to reach out, interact, and connect with the world. They represent the active part of our involvement with others, and our ability to relate. Next to language it is our hands that make us human.

As a background to our consideration of the jumon vow in question, it is important to first understand the energies represented by each of the hands, as well as the fingers of each hand. To begin with, the left hand is representative of the taizokai (material) realm, and the right hand representative of the kongokai (cosmic) realm. Therefore, with the bringing together of the hands in each mudra we see a symbolic joining, or unification of the two basic aspects of reality. Other complementary pairings are similarly brought together, the left hand representing the first of each pair, the right hand the second: in-yo, negative-positive, inner-outer, Moon-Sun, temporal reality-ultimate reality, sentient beings-gods/goddesses, healing-power, "arresting the active mind"-"realization of pure knowledge," and "receiving-coming forth" (Hayes, 1983; Saunders, 1960/1985). In short, the clasping of the hands is a symbol of unification, of wholeness and Totality.

With respect to each of the fingers we must recognize that although the same finger on each hand represents the same overarching quality, the finger of the left hand represents the inner manifestation of the quality, and the finger of the right hand the outer manifestation of the quality in question. With that in mind, the little finger symbolizes Chi, the earth; its quality is stability; it is represented by such forms as the (physical) body and by rocks. The ring finger symbolizes Sui, the water element; its quality is adaptability; it is represented by such forms as the emotions and plants. The middle finger symbolizes Ka, fire; its quality is aggression (or assertion); it is represented by such forms as the intellect and animals. The pointer symbolizes Fu, the wind; its quality is benevolence; it is represented by such forms as Wisdom and mankind. Finally there is the thumb which symbolizes Ku, the Void or the seamless; its quality is creativity;

it is represented by such forms as communication and the fundamental building blocks of the universe (Hayes, 1983; Saunders, 1960/1985). Therefore, with the joining of the hands each of the five elements, in both of their primary manifestations (*in* and *yo*) are brought together and made one.

There is one final point we need to make about the hands, one that goes beyond the symbolic channeling of energy. Those familiar with Chinese and Japanese traditional medicine will know that the twelve meridians, or "energy channels" in the body all run through the hands, and, in fact, have "turn-around points" in the fingers. Therefore, the mudra, in addition to evoking powerful mental energies (and we must *never* underestimate the power of this) *also physically effect the energy balance and flow within the body.* Hence, the mudra are capable of altering the physical, psychological, and spiritual positioning of a person.

We now turn to a brief look at the *jumon* vow we have chosen to illustrate this aspect of nin-po mikkyo. Hayes notes that each of the mudra has its own mantra sequence, mind-setting procedure, and breathing pattern. He has purposefully not included these in written form since these are aspects of the tradition which, for reasons we have often alluded to, *cannot* be passed on in an impersonal, textbook way, but *must be transmitted by a legitimate and competent teacher of ninjutsu.*

Rin. Here we have the hand-form that represents the vajra thunderbolt of Tibetan Buddhism. Along the same lines as we have noted earlier, the vajra thunderbolt is concerned with destroying ignorance and creating an inner environment into which the "awesome power of wisdom and pure knowledge," the Primordial intelligence, can enter (Hayes, 1983). Hayes notes that the ninja used this mudra when facing threatening and potentially overpowering forces to inspire strength, and evoke the energy required for success.

Pyo. Here we have the hand-form that represents the "great diamond" (*daikongo-in*). The diamond, the most precious of (spiritual) jewels, symbolizes that knowledge that reaches far beyond the human realm. It was used by the ninja, therefore, to evoke personal power by energizing the appropriate level of consciousness required to permit them to succeed (Hayes, 1983).

Toh. Hayes (1983) describes the mudra accompanying this mantra as the "sign of the outer lion" (*sotojishi-in*). In essence, the complex symbolism behind this hand-form evokes the capacity for connecting with and following the "patterns of the universe." This is intimately associated with the ninja's knowledge of the "scheme of totality," and it is for this reason that the lion, the "king of animals" is represented here.

Sha. *Uchijishi-in* is the "sign of the inner lion" (Hayes, 1983). The "inner lion" is associated with our bodies, especially the various chemical, electromagnetic, and physical processes. Just as the "outer lion" brings the ninja into a creative and constructive relationship with the pattern of the universe, so the "inner lion" brings the ninja into a positive relationship with the physical body. This results in the enormous potential inherent in the body being actualized. Hence, the energy associated with the uchijishi-in is concerned with healing.

Kai. Passions bind us. They are, symbolically, aspects of ourselves that "bind" (as well as "blind") us. The *gebakuken-in*, or "sign of the outer bonds fist," is the mudra that symbolizes the breaking of these bonds. As Hayes (1983) notes, this produces a heightened awareness. Most important for the ninja was the ability of this mantra/mudra to sensitize the ninja to the presence, or approach, of danger.

Jin. Passions limit us in one way, our refusal to believe in, or be sensitive to anything beyond the physical realm does so in another way. The "sign of the inner bonds fist" (*naibakuken-in*) is the mudra that symbolizes the shattering of this bond that "binds" and "blinds." Hayes (1983) speaks of the energy thus constellated aiding in the realization of cosmic consciousness and of the power of intuition. For the ninja this translates into knowing, intuitively and with *shin-shin shin-gan* ("the mind and eyes of god"), what others, especially adversaries, are thinking. It also opens the psyche to "thought projection."

Retsu. In this mudra the index finger of the left hand is held. If we recall the symbolism of the pointer finger we recognize that mankind, wisdom, the wind, and benevolence are being highlighted here. These qualities are enveloped, and thereby protected, by the right hand, especially by "ultimate actuality" and "pure knowledge" (Hayes, 1983). Although all of the mudra bring together the *in* and the *yo*, the material realm and the cosmic realm, this mudra emphasizes this in a direct energy channeling way. The way Hayes writes about this it would appear to stress *man's* (the index finger) oneness with the spiritual realm. Hence, man rises from the world of duality, of split time and space, to the essential unity of reality. Pragmatically, this energy channeling (*chiken-in*, "sign of the wisdom fist") allowed the ninja to draw upon knowledge from distant places and times to aid in the present. Given the realization of the Great Chain of Being (see Chapter 6) it may not be inconceivable that the ninja made use of what many call "projection of the astral body," although Hayes does not mention this in any of his books.

Zai. This mantra, together with the nichirin-in mudra, would appear to be the ultimate state of this jumon vow. If the vow is seen as a progression this would make sense: "desire" is dropped, (*rin*), knowledge is evoked and properly channeled (*pyo*), there is attunement with the universal pattern (*toh*) as well as inner alignment (*sha*), followed by the inspiration of a heightened conscious state (*kai*) and the mobilization of intuition (*jin*), finally leading to the coming together of man's realm with the spiritual realm (*retsu*). What *zai* appears to symbolize is the final oneness with the universe. The mind *fully realizes* the taizokai and kongokai realms *as one.* Hayes (1983) notes that here, with the energy channeled by "sign of the ring of the sun," the ninja is able to control and alter matter through intentions ("the power of the will"). Clearly this is a very powerful statement about the essence of the sanmitsu.

Zen. With this progressive channeling of energy resulting in the powerful ability to realize intentions in the world, guided by *shin-shin shin-gan* there would remain but one final stage in the sequence: protection of that which has been constellated from those who are of lesser mind and who might be moved to attack those with such knowledge and ability. And this is precisely what zen symbolizes. This is where, Hayes (1983) notes, the ninja desired to become "invisible," to not be seen as bearers of knowledge in order to maintain and transmit that knowledge unhampered by the "unenlightened."

As Hayes stated clearly at the Bujinkan Dojo Training Camp in 1985, esoteric religious objects, such as the kongo diamond thunderbolt, secret mantras, and intricate mudra finger entwinings mean nothing, and therefore do nothing, for a person who has not been initiated into these mysteries. Again, he states this is not to exclude people, but because it is a simple fact. The type of knowledge that nin-po mikkyo contains is of such a nature that *it can only be passed on through a personal transmission from teacher to student.* Just as a child cannot learn to ride a bicycle from a book, nor an adult learn to perform surgery unguided by a senior surgeon, so, too, with those wishing to learn the secrets of the sanmitsu. As Hayes notes, if it is our destiny to know of these things, we will seek a teacher as guide.

We have included a discussion of this jumon vow for the same reason Hayes presents it in his books: to demonstrate the richness of the nin-po tradition, and to indicate to those who have been drawn to this Path what lies ahead.

Kuji-Kiri: Directing the Power of the Surroundings

Kuji-kiri has been romanticized in both fiction and film, usually as something evil. In actuality it is merely a part of the ninja's realization of intentions in the world, the sanmitsu. Hayes discusses the *kuji goshin ho*, or "nine-syllable method of protection" of nin-po mikkyo. This method contains each of the sanmitsu elements: nine jumon, nine ketsu-in (*kuji-in*, or "nine syllable seals"), and nine ways of concentrated intention.

Within nin-po mikkyo the number nine is representative of comple-

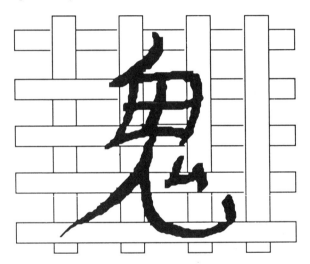

tion. It is therefore a symbol of ultimate power. Should the need arise to carry the power needed for a certain situation to "symbolic extremes" it is possible to go beyond completion. Hence, in addition to the *kuji-goshin ho* there is nin-po's *juji no ho* (tenth syllable method, also known as ju-jutsu). Ten is seen as the place to which one returns once one has passed through all phases of development in one's life. In addition to the *kuji no ho* power methods, in the *juji no ho* a *juji* a letter or graphic symbol is affixed to the thought/word/deed (Hayes, 1983).

Another means of combining thought/word/deed to realize intentions in the world is the kuji-kiri, or "nine-syllable grid of slashes." The *kuji goshin ho kuji kiri* is portrayed in myth as having been handed down from Marishi-ten, one of Japan's divine warrior guardians (Hayes, 1983). The "esoteric power formula" of the *kuji goshin ho kuji kiri* was employed, primarily, to overcome so-called "evil," the tendency to be deceived by the surface manifestations of things, lack of awareness or insight, and weakness. At the same time it also served as a means of protection for the ninja in "any environment." It is simply worth noting here that this impression of the kuji-kiri is radically different from that which Lustbader portrays in his novels, and others portray on the screen.

In Conclusion

Our glimpse of the ninja's nin-po mikkyo is small at best. For starters it is simply not possible to present an entire spiritual tradition in a few short chapters as Hayes has done in his various books on ninjutsu. What is more, as we have noted several times, the nature of these secret teachings is such that, even if someone wanted to, it would be *impossible* to pass them on solely in written form. If you feel drawn to these teachings the only way to further your knowledge is to find a teacher who can pass his or her knowledge on to you.

A word of warning is important here. As Hayes has stressed, fooling around with the kuji and juji power techniques can be dangerous. According to the *Kuiji Denjyu no Makimono* scroll, which Stephen K. Hayes was presented at the Zenkoji Temple near Togakure Mountain, it is possible to harm oneself by attempting to invoke the power of the kuji-kiri, especially if the person attempting to do so lacks "total commitment and faith" (Hayes, 1983). Without a firm sense of self and a thorough training in the power generation methods, "confusion, hesitancy, and scattered energies" will result, leaving the person more vulnerable than before. It is for this reason that Hayes has presented only a small glimpse of this aspect of *ninjutsu*, "for information purposes only."

It follows that were you to begin training under a teacher who himself or herself lacked the necessary faith and commitment, you would be endangering yourself. We in the West are not accustomed to spiritual practices of this kind. We would do well to approach such things with caution, and be convinced that the person we are learning from is indeed what he claims to be.

At the same time that we realize that our understanding of *nin-po mikkyo* is limited at best, it is extremely important that we do not lose sight of what this glimpse means positively. As we noted earlier, Stephen K. Hayes is one of a very few "martial arts" writers who *explicitly* includes a spiritual side to the physical manifestation of his tradition. Hence we are afforded a look at a tradition that is not one-dimensional—techniques only—but three-dimensional: *mind, body, and spirit.*

Should you decide to follow the warrior path of enlightenment when you move beyond the books by legitimate ninjutsu authors, and actually begin training, you will discover that all aspects of your being are important in the study of the art. As Hayes (1983) puts it, unlike most of the martial arts, ninjutsu is a path that moves the practitioner toward a balance of the physical, intellectual, and spiritual realms *from the very first lesson.*

Books are useful, entertaining, and inspiring. But ultimately you must move beyond thought to action. If you visualize yourself as a warrior, and you have begun empowering the verbal realm through information gathering and speaking with others about your interests, you must vitalize your intentions and begin training. The ninja of ancient Japan did not survive against the vastly more powerful samurai by reading books on ninjutsu. They got down to the nuts and bolts and learned the art with the body, the mind, and the spirit.

Afterword

I T IS NO secret that the abilities of martial arts teachers vary widely, something I learned from personal experience. Years ago, when I studied karate-do, I made a terrible mistake. Unaware that a "second *dan* blackbelt" did not *necessarily mean* that the instructor was good, I began my martial arts training under an immature and unethical kenpo karate teacher, a disgrace to that tradition. Keen to learn I found my enthusiasm taken advantage of and my time and money wasted. After much search I eventually found a very fine and eminently qualified Japanese *shotokan karate sensei—and I had to relearn everything because my body had not been taught to move correctly.* Not knowing I had been studying under an incompetent teacher I had no way to protect myself from his influence.

Immature, unethical, incompetent, and egotistical instructors can do *tremendous damage* to their students on all three levels of being: physical (ripped muscles, broken bones), mental (getting "ripped off"), and spiritual (thinking your body is beginning to become sensitive to the universe, when in fact it is getting more rigid). The reader interested in studying ninjutsu is therefore cautioned to

scrutinize any teacher *very carefully*. Again from experience, I can vouch for the fact that it is better to train less and travel more in order to study with a qualified instructor, than to study with a third- or fourth-rate instructor because you have a dojo just around the corner. Since there were *no authentic ninjutsu instructors* teaching in the U.S. prior to Hayes's return, it is *highly suspect* that the ·many "authentic ninja teachers" out there have *any credible licensing whatsoever*. And there are many bogus teachers doing tremendous damage to unsuspecting students.

Having seen the best that the karate world had to offer I was *very wary* when I became involved in ninjutsu training. I saw numerous advertisements for "ninja camps," but quickly discovered *no one had any idea who these people were*. A variety of "ninja masters" toured my part of the country—*every one of them fakes*. I read articles and books by so-called ninjutsu instructors, only to be profoundly affected by the amount of psychological and spiritual *pathology* in the writers. I finally stumbled upon The Shadows of Iga Ninja Society and went to Ohio for a "festival," worried lest my money simply go out of my bank account into someone else's with nothing gained, but willing to take a chance. I was pleasantly surprised.

I have since attended festivals and seminars run by the Shadows of Iga Ninja Society in both the U.S. and the U.K. The organization is run

ethically, and there are few who would say they had not gotten more than their money's worth at festivals and seminars. The instruction I have received from Shidoshi Stephen K. Hayes, Jack E. Hoban, and Bud Malmstrom has been of the highest order. All three of them are personal students of Dr. Masaaki Hatsumi, the 34th Grandmaster of Togakure-ryu Ninjutsu. At the time of printing, Hayes has been studying the art for well over a decade, Hoban and Malmstrom almost as long. The black belts under them are the best black belts I have worked with. In short, the Shadows of Iga Ninja Society is an excellent organization, run with integrity, with an eye to quality.

Just as I refer people asking for therapy to the very best therapists I know, so I refer the reader to the very best ninja organization there is. As Hayes notes, "There is a grandmaster of the art in Japan, who is the recognized source of knowledge for those who pursue the training path of the ninja in today's world." Dr. Hatsumi oversees the training in the dojo network bearing his name. If this is the level of quality and authenticity you want, you can write to the Shadows of Iga Ninja Society for information on training seminars throughout the world.

The Shadows of Iga Ninja Society
P.O. Box 1947
Kettering, OH 45429-0947

Bibliography

Adams, A. (1970). *Ninja: The Invisible Assassins*. Burbank, CA: Ohara Publications, Inc.

Baldwin, J. (1972). "Mass culture and the creative artist." In: W. Hammell (ed.). *The Popular Arts in America (2nd edition)*. New York: Harcourt Brace Jovanovich, Inc.

Barker, W. (1985a). *Dragon Rising*. New York: Warner Books, Inc.

——— (1985b). *Lion's Fire*. New York: Warner Books, Inc.

——— (forthcoming). *Serpent's Eye*. New York: Warner Books, Inc.

——— (forthcoming). *Phoenix Sword*. New York: Warner Books, Inc.

Barlow, D. (1985). "The 'phantom major' would have made a great ninja." *Ninja Realm, 9* (2), 14–15, 24.

Bateson, G. (1972). *Steps to an Ecology of Mind*. New York: Ballantine Books.

Brooks, K. (1985). "The *ichimonji no kamae*." *Ninja Realm, 9* (3), 18–21.

Castaneda, C. (1974a). *The Teachings of Don Juan: A Yaquai Way of Knowledge*. New York: Pocket Books.

——— (1974b). *Journey to Ixtlan: The Lessons of Don Juan*. New York: Pocket Books.

Cater, D. (1984). "Ninjamania: America Goes Wild Over Art of Invisibility." *Black Belt, 22* (12), 20–26, 112.

Chagrin, C. (1984). "Shidoshi Stephen Hayes: America's number one ninja on the meanings—and myths—of modern ninja training." *Inside Kung Fu Presents The Master Ninja: Warrior of the Night,* (September).

Chuang Tzu (1964). *Basic Writings.* New York: Columbia University Press.

Clavell, J. (1976). *Shogun.* New York: Dell Publishing Co., Inc.

Coburn, J. (1985). "Interview: Stephen K. Hayes, chief instructor and founder of the Shadows of Iga Ninja Society," *Ninja Realm,* 9 (3), 14–17.

Dalai Lama, The Fourteenth (1984). *The Buddhism of Tibet and the Key to the Middle Way.* New York: Harper & Row, Publishers.

——— (1984). *Kindness, Clarity, and Insight.* Ithaca, NY: Snow Lion Publications.

de Moville, B. (1985). "Networking." *Ninja Realm,* 9 (4), 7.

Edinger, E. F. (1972). *Ego and Archetype: Individuation and the Religious Function of the Psyche.* Baltimore, MD: Penguin Books, Inc.

Endo, S. (1969/1980). *Silence.* New York: Taplinger Publishing Co.

——— (1980/1984). *The Samurai.* New York: Aventura (Vintage Books).

Evans-Wentz, W. Y. (ed.) (1927/1960). *The Tibetan Book of the Dead.* London: Oxford University Press.

Flemming, I. (1964). *You Only Live Twice* New York: New American Library.

Fremantle, F., and **Trungpa, C.** (trans.) (1975). *The Tibetan Book of the Dead.* Boulder, CO: Shambala.

Gort, K. (1985). "Sho Kosugi: The Ninja as Martial Arts Superstar." *Inside Kung Fu, 12* (2), 36–41.

Govinda, L. A. (1966/1970). *The Way of the White Clouds: A Buddhist Pilgrim in Tibet.* Boulder, CO: Shambala.

Guenther, H. V., and **Trungpa, C.** (1975). *The Dawn of Tantra.* Boulder, CO: Shambala.

Harding, M. E. (1963/1973). *Psychic Energy: Its Source and Transformation.* Princeton, NJ: Princeton University Press.

Hatsumi, M. (1964). *Ninja/Ninpo Gaho (Ninja and Ninpo Illustrated).* Tokyo: Akita Shoten Publishers.

——— (1981). *Ninjutsu History and Tradition.* Hollywood: Unique Publications.

——— (1984). "The Realm of the Ninja." *Inside Kung Fu Presents The*

Master Ninja: Warrior of the Night, (September).

Hayes, S. K. (1980). *Ninja: Spirit of the Shadow Warrior.* Burbank, CA: Ohara Publications, Inc.

——— (1981a). *The Ninja and Their Secret Fighting Art.* Rutland, VT: Charles E. Tuttle Co.

——— (1981b). *Ninja Vol. II: Warrior Ways of Enlightenment.* Burbank, CA: Ohara Publications, Inc.

——— (1983). *Ninja Vol. III: Warrior Path of Togakure.* Burbank, CA: Ohara Publications, Inc.

——— (1984a). *Ninja Vol. IV: Legacy of the Night Warrior.* Burbank, CA: Ohara Publications, Inc.

——— (1984b). *Ninjutsu: The Art of the Invisible Warrior.* Chicago: Contemporary Books, Inc.

——— (1984c). *Wisdom from the Ninja Village of the Cold Moon.* Chicago: Contemporary Books, Inc.

——— (1985a). *The Mystic Arts of the Ninja: Hypnotism, Invisibility, and Weaponry.* Chicago: Contemporary Books, Inc.

——— (1985b). *Tulku: A Tale of Modern Ninja.* Chicago: Contemporary Books, Inc.

——— (1985c). "The deadly shuriken." *Ninja,* (winter—special issue).

——— (1985d). "Roots of the tradition," *Ninja Realm,* 9 (4), 1–4

——— (1985e). "Winter training advantages." *Ninja Realm,* 9 (4), 5.

——— (1985f). "Training clubs." *Ninja Realm,* 9 (4), 6.

——— (1985g). "Ninjutsu illegal again?" *Ninja Realm,* 9 (4), 8–9.

——— (1985h). "Going to the source." *Fighting Stars* 12 (6), 8–9.

——— (1986). "Back to the Source." *Ninja Realm, 10* (1), 1–3.

Hillman, J. (1975). *Re-Visioning Psychology.* New York: Harper & Row, Publishers.

Hoeller, S. A. (1982). *The Gnostic Jung and the Seven Sermons to the Dead.* Wheaton, IL: The Theosophical Publishing House.

Homans, P. (1972). "Puritanism revisited: an analysis of the contemporary screen-image western." In: W. Hammell (ed.). *The Popular Arts in America (2nd edition).* New York: Harcourt Brace Jovanovich, Inc.

Huss, R., and **Silverstein, N.** (1972). "The film experience." In: W. Hammell (ed.). *The Popular Arts in America (2nd edition).* New York: Harcourt Brace Jovanovich, Inc.

Jacobi, J. (1959). *Complex, Archetype, and Symbol in the Psychology of C. G. Jung.* Princeton, NJ: Princeton University Press.

Jacobi, J., and **Hull, R.F.C.** (eds.) (1953/1973). *C. J. Jung: Psychological*

Reflections—A New Anthology of His Writings 1905–1961. Princeton, NJ: Princeton University Press.

Jaffe, A. (1967). "The influence of alchemy on the work of C. J. Jung." In: *Spring, 1967.* Irving, TX: Spring Publications.

Jung, C. G. (1950/1967). Forward. In: R. Wilhelm. *I Ching or Book of Changes.* Princeton, NJ: Princeton University Press.

———— (1954/1981). *The Development of Personality (Volume XVII of the Collected Works).* Princeton, NJ: Princeton University Press.

———— (1958/1969). *Psychology and Religion: West and East (Volume XI of the Collected Works).* Princeton, NJ: Princeton University Press.

———— (1967). *Memories, Dreams, Reflections.* London: Fontana.

———— (ed.) (1969). *Man and His Symbols.* New York: Dell Publishing Co., Inc.

———— (1970). *Civilization in Transition (2nd ed.) (Volume X of the Collected Works).* Princeton, NJ: Princeton University Press.

———— (1971). *Psychological Types (Volume VI of the Collected Works).* Princeton, NJ: Princeton University Press.

———— (1972). *Four Archetypes.* London: Routledge, Kegan, and Paul.

Lustbader, E. Van (1980). *The Ninja.* New York: Fawcett Crest.

———— (1984). *The Miko.* New York: Fawcett Crest.

Malmstrom, B. (1985). "Just ordinary people." *Fighting Stars, 12* (6), 14.

Neumann, E. (1972). *The Great Mother: An Analysis of the Archetype.* Princeton, NJ: Princeton University Press.

Merton, T. (1965). *The Way of Chuang Tzu.* New York: New Directions.

Morris, G. J. (1986). "The *shinobi* psychology." *Ninja Realm, 10* (1) 4–7.

Musashi, M. (1982). *A Book of Five Rings.* Woodstock, NY: The Overlook Press.

Navon, D. [as told to Gattegno, I.] (1985). "My six years with Hatsumi: a personal look at the man behind the myth." *Ninja, #9,* 31–38.

Nichols, S. (1980). *Jung and Tarot: An Archetypal Journey.* New York: Samuel Weiser, Inc.

Pearson, M. (1985). "Stephen K. Hayes returns to the source." *Ninja Realm, 9* (3), 6–8.

Perry, J. W. (1976). *Roots g Renewal in Myth & Madness.* San Francisco: Jossey-Bass Publishers.

Peterson, K. C. (1986a). "The Western world and the ninja brain." *Fighting Stars, 13* (1), 26–29.

———— (1986b). "Thinking and living like a warrior: highlights of the

Bujinkan Dojo *Ninpo* training camp." *Ninja Magazine #12* (April), 48–54.

———— (1986c). "Ninja Dreams." *Fighting Stars Ninja, 13* (2), 35–38.

Rinbochay, K. S. (1982). *Tantric Practice in Nying-ma.* Ithaca, NY: Gabriel/Snow Lion.

Salome, L. (1984). "Sho Kosugi in *Revenge of the Ninja." Inside Kung Fu Presents The Master Ninja: Warrior of the Night,* (September).

Saunders, E. D. (1960/1985). *Mudra: A Study of Symbolic Gestures in Japanese Buddhist Sculpture.* Princeton: Princeton University Press.

Salmonson, J. A. (1984a). "Challenge of the ninja films: Which Japanese studio was best?" *Inside Kung Fu Presents The Master Ninja: Warrior of the Night,* (September).

———— (1984b). "In pursuit of the ninja film." *Inside Kung Fu Presents The Master Ninja: Warrior of the Night,* (September).

Smith, M., and **Thomson, J.** (1985a). *Avenger!* Sevenoaks, U.K.: Knight Books.

———— (1985b). *Assassin!* Sevenoaks, U.K.: Knight Books.

———— (forthcoming). *Usurper!* Sevenoaks, U.K.: Knight Books.

Stanich, F. (1985). "Fifth Annual Shadows of Iga Ninja Festival." *Ninja Realm, 9* (3), 10–13.

Suzuki, D. T. (1959) *Zenand Japanese Culture.* Princeton, NJ: Princeton University Press.

———— (1960). "Lecture on Zen Buddhism." In: Fromm, E., Suzuki, D. T., and De Martino, R. *Zen Buddhism and Psychoanalysis.* New York: Harper Colophon Books.

Tajiri, L. (1984). "The ninja: America's sinister new hero." *Inside Kung Fu Presents The Master Ninja: Warrior of the Night,* (September).

Toda, K. (1982). *Shadow of the Ninja.* Thousand Oaks, CA: Dragon Books.

———— (1984a). *Revenge of the Shogun's Ninja.* Thousand Oaks, CA: Dragon Books.

———— (1984b). *The Ninja Star: Art of Shuriken Jutsu.* Thousand Oaks, CA: Dragon Books.

Trungpa, C. (1966/1971). *Born in Tibet.* Baltimore, MD: Penguin Books.

———— (1973). *Cutting Through Spiritual Materialism.* Boulder, CO: Shambala.

———— (1976). *The Myth of Freedom and the Way of Meditation.* Boulder, CO: Shambala.

———— (1974). *Shambala: The Sacred Path of the Warrior.* Boulder, CO:

Shambala.

Urata, R. (1985). "Names of the Ninja." *Ninja Realm* 9 (1), 7–11.

von Franz, M. L. (1975). *C. G. Jung: His Myth in Our Time*. New York: C. G. Jung Foundation for Analytical Psychology.

Whitmont, E. C. (1969). *The Symbolic Quest: Basic Concepts of Analytical Psychology*. Princeton, NJ: Princeton University Press.

Wilber, K. (1980). *The Atman Project: A Transpersonal View of Human Development*. Wheaton, IL: The Theosophical Publishing House.

———— (1980). *Up from Eden: A Transpersonal View of Human Evolution*. Boulder, CO: Shambala.

Wilhelm, R. (1950/1967). *The I Ching or Book of Changes*. Princeton, NJ: Princeton University Press.

Wolff, T. (1956). *Structural of the Feminine Psyche*. Zurich: privately printed. (See also Whitmont, 1969).

Index